CASEBOOK SERIES

Dickens

Hard Times
Great Expectations
and *Our Mutual Friend*

A CASEBOOK

EDITED BY

NORMAN PAGE

M

First edition 1979
Reprinted 1982, 1983

First published by
THE MACMILLAN PRESS LTD
London and Basingstoke
Companies and representatives
throughout the world

ISBN 0 333 24037 5

Printed in Hong Kong

CONTENTS

Part Three: *Our Mutual Friend*

ACKNOWLEDGEMENTS

The editor and publishers wish to thank the following, who have kindly given permission for the use of copyright material:
John Butt and Kathleen Tillotson, 'Hard Times: The Problems of a Weekly Serial', from Dickens at Work (1957) by permission of Methuen & Co. Ltd.; G. K. Chesterton, extract from Charles Dickens (1906) by permission of A. P. Watt & Son on behalf of the Estate of G. K. Chesterton; Philip Collins, extract from Dickens and Education (1963); Barbara Hardy, article 'Great Expectations' from Essays in Criticism later included in The Moral Art of Dickens (1970) published by The Athlone Press; Humphry House, extract from The Dickens World (1941) by permission of Oxford University Press; Arnold Kettle, extract from 'Our Mutual Friend' in Dickens and the Twentieth Century (1962) ed J. Gross and G. Pearson, by permission of Routledge & Kegan Paul Ltd.; Jack Lindsay, extract from Charles Dickens (1950) by permission of the author; David Lodge, extract from 'The Rhetoric of Hard Times' in Language of Fiction (1966) by permission of Routledge & Kegan Paul Ltd.; Martin Meisel, extract from 'The Ending of Great Expectations' in Essays in Criticism (1965) by permission of the editors; Julian Moynahan, essay 'The Hero's Guilt: The Case of Great Expectations' from Essays in Criticism (1960) by permission of the author and editors; Kenneth Muir, essay 'Image and Structure in Our Mutual Friend' from Essays and Studies (1966) by permission of the author and The English Association; Robert B. Partlow, extract from 'The Moving I: A Study of the Point of View in Great Expectations' in College English, 23 (1961–62), by permission of the author and the National Council of Teachers of English, © 1961 by the publishers; Bernard Shaw, Introduction to Hard Times, 1912, by permission of The Society of Authors on behalf of the Bernard Shaw Estate.

GENERAL EDITOR'S PREFACE

The Casebook series, launched in 1968, has become a well-regarded library of critical studies. The central concern of the series remains the 'single-author' volume, but suggestions from the academic community have led to an extension of the original plan, to include occasional volumes on such general themes as literary 'schools' and genres.

Each volume in the central category deals either with the one well-known and influential work by an individual author, or with closely related works by one writer. The main section consists of critical readings, mostly modern, collected from books and journals. A selection of reviews and comments by the author's contemporaries is also included, and sometimes comment from the author himself. The Editor's Introduction charts the reputation of the work or works from the first appearance to the present time.

Volumes in the 'general themes' category are variable in structure but follow the basic purpose of the series in presenting an integrated selection of readings, with an Introduction which explores the theme and discusses the literary and critical issues involved.

A single volume can represent no more than a small selection of critical opinions. Some critics are excluded for reasons of space, and it is hoped that readers will pursue the suggestions for further reading in the Select Bibliography. Other contributions are severed from their original context, to which some readers may wish to turn. Indeed, if they take a hint from the critics represented here, they certainly will.

A. E. DYSON

INTRODUCTION

Dickens's career as a novelist extends for some three and a half decades, from *Pickwick Papers* (serialised in 1836–37) to the unfinished *Mystery of Edwin Drood* (serialised in 1870, the year of his death). Chronologically speaking, therefore, its mid-point occurs about 1852–53; and as it happens there are good grounds for regarding *Bleak House*, the novel which appeared during precisely those years, as inaugurating the author's later period. (It is itself the subject of a Casebook, edited by A. E. Dyson.) Barbara Hardy has argued that *Bleak House* initiates a series of 'novels of the sociological imagination':

> While no one would deny the social concern and analysis of the earlier novels, there are some, like *Martin Chuzzlewit* and *David Copperfield*, which deal only loosely or obliquely with contemporary England, but all the novels I am calling 'late', with the exception of *A Tale of Two Cities*, set out a full map and large-scale criticism, in the expressive form of art, of Dickens's England.[1]

Professor Hardy rightly reminds us that the transition was not sudden, and one would perhaps want to make a further exception to her categorisation in regard to *Edwin Drood*, an exercise in a specialised genre. Still, it seems clear that to speak of 'the later Dickens' is meaningful in more than a merely chronological sense. To ask why his art should have developed in that particular direction at that time is to pose a question that is not susceptible of an easy answer. Like any major artist, he was not content to repeat past successes (though many of his readers and critics would have been only too delighted for him to do so), but struggled towards—and triumphantly achieved—the realisation of a new kind of fiction.

Our Mutual Friend is as different from *Pickwick* as *Antony and Cleopatra* is from *Two Gentlemen of Verona*—and the Shakespearean comparison is not an idle one: see the comments by Jack Lindsay on *Our Mutual Friend* in his study of Dickens (1950) [*], and by F. R. Leavis on *Hard Times*, quoted later in this Introduction. Biographical factors cannot be ignored. The author of *Great Expectations* was twice the age of the author

---

* Here and elsewhere in the Introduction, an asterisk within square brackets indicates reference to material included in the relevant part of this Casebook.

of *Pickwick*, and personal distresses—notably the breakdown of his marriage—had taken toll of his youthful optimism, confidence and energy. England had changed too: the society, and even the landscape and air, of the 1850s and 1860s were not those of Dickens's youth. Humphry House has said that Dickens 'lived through the years which saw the making of modern England', and adds:

Some measure of the changes can be made if we compare *Pickwick* with *Our Mutual Friend*. The books are plainly by the same author; but when all allowances have been made . . . it still remains clear that the two books are the produce of different climates. . . . [By the 1860s] the very air seems to have changed in quality, and to tax the powers of Sanitary Reform to the uttermost. In *Pickwick* a bad smell was a bad smell; in *Our Mutual Friend* it is a problem.[2]

Not surprisingly, Dickens's contemporaries were fully conscious of the differences between his earlier and later work. Many regretted the change, though their motives seem often to have been mixed, with political and doctrinal objections colouring their aesthetic response. His increasingly comprehensive and uncompromising diagnosis of the ills of society brought him into conflict with the prevailing faith in progress. A dozen years after Dickens's death, Frederic Harrison could still write, with Positivist enthusiasm:

The cause of progress is bound up with every principle worth having; and material progress is an indispensable step in general progress. . . . We all feel a-tiptoe with hope and confidence . . . . It is the age of great expectation and unwearied striving after better things.[3]

Long before this date, more radically and farsightedly, Dickens had questioned the ideal of progress, including material progress. It is curiously ironic that Harrison's panegyric of his own times should have echoed (surely unconsciously?) a phrase made famous by the title of one of Dickens's late novels.

George Ford has said that Dickens's 'wide-sweeping criticism of society . . . alienated conservative and liberal alike' and led 'hitherto faithful admirers . . . to abandon him after reading *Bleak House*'.[4] Certainly a harsh note creeps into criticism of his work in the 1860s. Philip Collins has shown that '*Bleak House* is a crucial item in the history of Dickens's reputation' and that 'for many critics in the 1850s, '60s and '70s, it began the drear decline of "the author of *Pickwick, Chuzzlewit* and *Copperfield*"'. Later in the fifties the reviewer who pronounced *Little Dorrit* 'decidedly the worst' of the novelist's works was not alone. Another reviewer spoke for many in lamenting the 'wilderness' of that novel: 'for in that wilderness we sit down and weep when we remember thee, O *Pickwick!*'.[5]

The process was a slow one by which these and some of the other later novels came to be generally recognised as constituting the peaks rather than troughs of Dickens's achievement. G. Bernard Shaw was one of the earliest to insist on the significance of the later work. His introduction to a new edition of *Hard Times* was published in 1912 [*], and two years later he declared: 'I regard the books of Dickens's second period, from *Hard Times* to *Our Mutual Friend*, as of much greater importance than those of his first period. They can be read by thoughtful and cultivated adults as serious social history.'[6] There is genuine originality and penetration in this comment; as the second sentence quoted here shows, however, Shaw was more impressed by their propagandist power and informative quality than by their merits as works of literary art, and the revolution in taste and esteem was still some way ahead.

The inter-war period, which saw a proliferation of books with titles like *The Inns and Taverns of Pickwick* (1921) and *Mr Pickwick's Pilgrimages* (1926), witnessed little evidence of serious attention to the later novels. The traditional association of Dickens with good cheer and good fellowship, the notion of him (not false, but not the whole truth either) as a purveyor of comedy and pathos—the 'Mr Popular Sentiment' of Trollope's satire—went largely unquestioned.

In so far as the revolution in attitudes was engineered by a single critic, it is to Edmund Wilson of America that we must look. His essay 'Dickens: The Two Scrooges', in *The Wound and the Bow* (1941), lays emphasis on the 'dark' aspects of Dickens's work which find their fullest expression in the later novels. Wilson subsequently conceded (in 1952) that his account of the novelist had incorporated a deliberate bias. Since he 'did not feel there was anything fresh to say about . . . the humour of *Pickwick*', he had taken for granted the familiar aspects of Dickens and had stressed a 'neglected aspect of his work'.[7] Biassed or not, his essay was influential in drawing attention to the masterpieces of the 1850s–60s; and thereafter important studies were produced on both sides of the Atlantic. (One may cite as examples, in the mid-1950s alone, the essays by Lionel Trilling on *Little Dorrit*, Dorothy Van Ghent on *Great Expectations*, and Sylvère Monod on *Our Mutual Friend*.) Even so, it had taken nearly a hundred years to achieve a just estimate of the later Dickens.

The present collection assembles Victorian and modern materials as an aid to the understanding of three of these later novels and as a stimulus to critical discussion. For each novel three kinds of material are offered.

1. Background documentation recounts important aspects of the novel's genesis and composition and cites relevant sources and contemporary parallels. Often the progress of a book can be traced in

Dickens's surviving letters, or the preoccupations expressed in his fiction can be located also in his public speeches and journalistic work.

2. Samples are given of reactions from his contemporaries, especially the reviewers in influential periodicals and newspapers. This material is of double interest: it is an indication of those aspects of his work which were most significant and striking to his first readers (to find *Great Expectations* hailed as a comic novel, for instance, or observe Betty Higden's looming so large in discussions of *Our Mutual Friend*, may force us to re-examine our own orthodoxies); and, more often than one might suppose, it affords critical comment that is still valid.

3. A selection of modern discussion is offered, chosen to exemplify a wide variety of critical and scholarly approaches as well as to represent critics of different generations.

In what follows we summarise the circumstances in which each of the three novels was written and published, and the development of its reputation over the last hundred years or so.

Hard Times

Towards the end of 1853, the publishers of the weekly magazine *Household Words*, edited by Dickens, concerned at its falling sales, proposed to him that he should bring his reputation to its rescue by contributing a novel, to be serialised over a period of several months. In spite of well-founded misgivings about the straitjacket of weekly instalments, he agreed.[*] He quickly warmed to his task. Later he wrote to a friend that the idea for the novel had 'laid hold of me by the throat in a very violent manner', but precisely what 'idea' he had in mind is open to speculation. By the end of January 1854 he had begun writing, and at about the same time he paid a brief visit to Preston in Lancashire, where a prolonged strike of the workers in the cotton mills was in progress. An immediate outcome of the visit was an article in *Household Words*, 'On Strike' (11 February). Although it would be rash to make too much of the parallel between Preston and Coketown, *Hard Times* obviously owes something to his Lancashire experiences. An earlier article, 'Frauds on the Fairies' (1 October 1853), shows that the antithesis of fact and fancy, utilitarianism and the nourishing of the imaginative faculty, as educational principles was already at work in Dickens's mind. [*]

As he had already foreseen, the compression demanded by short instalments—a compression running very much against the grain of his exuberantly inventive genius—proved very irksome. 'The difficulty of the space', he remarked in a letter, 'is CRUSHING.' The novel is in fact Dickens's shortest (only about one-third of the length of his previous novel, *Bleak House*, for instance), though its brevity is arguably a source of strength as well as limitations. It was published as a weekly serial from 1 April to 12 August 1854 and was a considerable success in this form, the sales of the magazine doubling and then doubling again as serialisation proceeded. In the same year it appeared in volume form, with no significant alterations to the text but with titles added to the books and chapters, and with a dedication to Carlyle. Unlike most of Dickens's novels, it carried neither preface nor illustrations. There were at least two dramatic adaptations: *Hard Times: A Domestic Drama* was produced in August 1854, to coincide with the conclusion of the serial, and *Under the Earth: or, The Sons of Toil* in 1867.

Few contemporary reviewers took *Hard Times* very seriously. Richard Simpson, the Shakespearean scholar, applied to it Hamlet's phrase 'stale, flat, and unprofitable'. [*] Like many critics of the later Dickens, Simpson would clearly have preferred to see him working to the formulae of past successes rather than moving into a new fictional territory. But the fact remains that 'the depths of social life' and 'the wells of social action' (in Simpson's own phrases) were to become more and more Dickens's province during the remainder of his career. Lord Macaulay characterised the novel in his journal as 'sullen socialism', and indeed much contemporary discussion focussed on its political and social ideas rather than on its literary qualities. Mrs Margaret Oliphant wrote in *Blackwood's Magazine* that it offered only 'the petulant theory of a man in a world of his own making, where he has no fear of being contradicted'. Later an American critic, Edwin Whipple, argued that the book was weakened by its author's lack of intellectual grasp of the political, legal and economic aspects of his topic. [*] Whipple was not the only critic to apply Stephen Blackpool's references to 'muddle' to the thinking of Stephen's creator. An outstanding exception to the chorus of depreciation or indifference was John Ruskin. [*] Not surprisingly, his high praise was deemed extravagant by Whipple and others.

Among later readers there was widespread neglect. George Gissing, one of the most intelligent of Dickens's critics at the turn of the century, called it 'that very poor book'; 'it is practically a forgotten book, and little in it demands attention'. And he also condemned it as showing inadequate knowledge of a manufacturing town. [*] F. G. Kitton, a bibliographer of the same period, classified it among Dickens's minor writings. But the neglect was not universal. G. K. Chesterton, in 1906, took it more seriously [*]; and G. Bernard Shaw, as already mentioned, published vigorous appreciations in 1912 [*] and 1914. However, as late as 1941 it could still be described by Humphry House as 'the least read of all the novels' [*]; and it was almost a hundred years after its first appearance that *Hard Times* received an unexpected revaluation at the hands of F. R. Leavis (in *The Great Tradition*, 1948).

Many of Leavis's readers in 1948 must have received a double shock: first, that Dickens should have made an appearance at all in a study of a tradition of fiction defined in terms of 'marked moral intensity'; and next, that he should have been represented by one of his least known, least regarded and (by general consent) least characteristic novels. More than twenty years were to pass before Leavis (in *Dickens the Novelist*, 1970 written jointly with his wife, Q. D. Leavis) did fuller justice to Dickens. But meanwhile *Hard Times*, as it were, woke up and found itself famous. Leavis's essay is too long for inclusion in the present volume; and, in any case, its repetitive nature permits its argument to be indicated summarily. The novel is, Leavis contends, a masterpiece, though its importance has gone unrecognised. (He seems to be unaware of the praise accorded it by Ruskin, Chesterton, Shaw and others.) Its art is notable for 'flexibility' and 'diversity'; 'by texture, imaginative mode, symbolic method, and the resulting concentration, *Hard Times* affects us as belonging with formally poetic works'; and at the same time it shows 'a clear insight into the English social structure'. Leavis grants that it can be faulted in minor respects: in the handling, for instance, of Stephen Blackpool and of trade unionism; but these are local weaknesses, and over-all its 'packed richness', combining moral seriousness with poetic and symbolic power, invites comparison with Shakespeare and looks forward to D. H. Lawrence.

Leavis's championing of *Hard Times* did not go unchallenged. Some felt that, paradoxically, it did Dickens a disservice by insisting on the superiority of an unrepresentative work. 'What, after all, can be more harmful to a genuinely great author's reputation', objected E. D. Hirsch in 1964, 'than to insist that one of his dullest and least successful works is one of his greatest?'[8] Leavis's account was also queried on minor issues. K. J. Fielding, for instance, disputed the claim that the Gradgrind children were shown as having been brought up 'on the lines of the experiment recorded by John Stuart Mill as being carried out on himself', and suggested that this was unfair to James Mill and not borne out by his son's autobiography. John Holloway's depreciatory essay on the novel provoked a rejoinder from Leavis in the form of an extended note added to the *Hard Times* essay when it was reprinted in *Dickens the Novelist*.[9] But if the 1948 essay has less impact today than when it first appeared, this is partly because the approach to the reading of fiction which Leavis was then urging—an approach involving the kind of close attention to verbal nuance, tone, metaphor and symbol that were more readily associated with the reading of poetry and dramatic verse—has now become widely adopted.

David Lodge's essay of 1966 [*] illustrates the approach to the criticism of fiction through a close examination of the workings of language. From a different scholarly direction, but serving ultimately somewhat similar purposes, the study of Dickens's manuscripts and memoranda by J. Butt and K. Tillotson [*] brings home to us the subtlety and delicacy, so often underestimated, with which he worked within the demanding framework of the Victorian conventions of serialised fiction.

Great Expectations

Between *Hard Times* and *Great Expectations*, Dickens wrote two novels: *Little Dorrit* (serialised 1855–57) and *A Tale of Two Cities* (serialised during 1859). Neither was received with much critical enthusiasm, and those readers of *Hard Times* who had persuaded themselves that the days of Dickens's greatness were over found little reason to change their minds. Few great Victorian novels, indeed, were as grossly under-estimated as *Little Dorrit*; though now acclaimed as one of Dickens's chief masterpieces, it was for many of his contemporaries, as Philip Collins has noted, 'a by-word for the bad Dickens'.[10] As for *A Tale of Two Cities*: though it was later to have popularity thrust upon it in stage and film versions, its original reception was cool. So, by the time publication of *Great Expectations* began, at the end of 1860, the reputation of his most recent work did not stand very high, though the earlier novels retained their devoted following.

After a dispute with his publishers, Dickens had withdrawn from *Household Words* and in April 1859 had launched another weekly magazine, *All the Year Round*, with *A Tale of Two Cities* as the lead-story. It was followed by Wilkie Collins's *The Woman in White*, a huge success. But the next serial, Charles Lever's *A Day's Ride*, proved much less popular, and the magazine's sales figures dropped (in Dickens's words) 'rapidly and continuously'. As J. A. Sutherland has pointed out, the magazine sold for two pence—less than *The Times* newspaper—and carried relatively little advertising matter, so that 'its revenue depended almost entirely on high sales, and these in turn depended on the serial'.[11]

History was about to repeat itself. As *Hard Times* had been published in response to the falling sales of *Household Words*, the new novel was intended to perform a similar rescue-operation for *All the Year Round*. For Dickens, the solution was that he should come to the aid of the magazine himself. With a characteristic absence of false modesty, he recognised that he was the only writer whose name would make a strong enough appeal to the flagging audience. The following extracts from letters written at the time (October 1860) to Forster and Lever recount the decision in Dickens's own words:

I called a council of war at the office on Tuesday. It was perfectly clear that the one thing to be done was, for me to strike in. I have therefore decided to begin a story, the length of the Tale of Two Cities, on the First of December—begin publishing, that is. I must make the most I can out of the book. . . . The name is, GREAT EXPECTATIONS. I think a good name?

The property of All the Year Round is far too valuable, in every way, to be much endangered . . . by dashing in now, I come in when most wanted.

There is but one thing to be done. I had begun a book which I intended for one of my long twenty number serials. I must abandon that design . . . and shape the story for these pages.

The book will be written in the first person throughout, and during these first three weekly numbers you will find the hero to be a boy-child, like David [Copperfield]. Then he will be an apprentice. You will not have to complain of want of humour as in the Tale of Two Cities. I have made the opening, I hope, in its general effect exceedingly droll. I have put a child and a good-natured foolish man, in relations that seem to be very funny. Of course I have got in the pivot on which the story will turn too—and which indeed, as you remember, was the grotesque tragi-comic conception that first encouraged me.[12]

In the previous month he had described, in a letter to Forster [*], the way in which the central idea of the novel had 'opened upon' him. As is indicated by the reference in that letter to 'the whole of a serial' and the more explicit phrase in one of the letter-extracts given above ('one of my long twenty number serials'), his original intention had been to develop the idea into the twenty-part form, published over nineteen months, in which most of his novels were cast; but the demands of the magazine were over-riding, and the shorter, more compressed, form won the day. It is interesting to consider what, in artistic terms, was gained by the enforced use of the more concentrated form. Certainly, the narrative economy of *Great Expectations* compares very favourably with the prolixity of parts of *David Copperfield*. (As the last of the above extracts shows, the comparison between the two novels, which was taken up by reviewers and later critics, was in Dickens's mind from the start.) Also notable is the emphasis on humour: 'exceedingly droll', 'very funny'. Dickens must have known very well that a return to comedy would be welcomed by his readers; but what may surprise us is his description of the 'pivot' of the story (that is, the relationship between Pip and Magwitch) as a 'grotesque tragi-comic conception'.

Publication began on 1 December 1860, and the weekly instalments continued until 3 August of the following year. It was immediately successful—'an immense success' and 'universally liked', as Dickens gleefully wrote soon after it was launched. Composition was completed by early June 1861, and probably during the same summer he prepared

a condensed version of the novel to be used in his public reading tours,
though for some reason the reading was never given.[13]

Great Expectations was not only successful in salvaging the fortunes of
All the Year Round; it also did much to reverse the decline in Dickens's
popularity traced by its three predecessors. The *Saturday Review*, usually
no friend to Dickens, expressed its relief (20 July 1861) that 'after
passing under the cloud of *Little Dorrit* and *Bleak House* . . . he has
written a story that is new, original, powerful, and very entertaining.
. . . *Great Expectations* restores Mr Dickens and his readers to the old
level'; revealingly, the reviewer found it 'quite worthy to stand beside
Martin Chuzzlewit and *David Copperfield*'. [*] Even Mrs Oliphant—
anything but a dedicated Dickensian—was constrained in her
Blackwood's Magazine review [*] to welcome the return to humour,
though she judged the novel as a whole 'feeble, fatigued, and
colourless', and found the story 'exaggerated and impossible'. (She was
much troubled, for example, by the capacity of Miss Havisham's
wedding-dress to survive twenty-five years' continual wear.) As this
example suggests, the chorus of approval was by no means unanimous.
But there was widespread gratification that Dickens appeared to have
returned to the humour and cheerfulness of his earlier manner: a
reaction summed up by E. S. Dallas in *The Times*. [*] For the
American Edwin Whipple, the book seemed to demonstrate that
Dickens had taken a new lease of his creative life. [*] Forster was to go
even further in claiming that that 'Dickens's humour, not less than his
creative power, was at its best in this book'. [*] As these reactions
indicate, Dickens's readers shared his own tendency to stress the comic
elements in the novel: a response worth bearing in mind as one reads the
many modern interpretations which lay emphasis on the seriousness of
its engagement with moral and psychological issues.

The later fortunes of *Great Expectations* have seen a continuation of its
popularity. Its brevity and its blend of humour and melodrama have
made it an attractive choice for schoolroom study, and the success of
film and other adaptations has given it even wider currency. At the
same time it has held its own in critical esteem as the qualities of its
construction and technique, and the depth of its moral penetration,
have become more fully understood and respected. But the modern
critic usually differs markedly from his Victorian counterpart in
judging its tone to be less sunny and optimistic, more disillusioned and
even melancholy.

As early as 1906, G. K. Chesterton praised its psychological and
moral power. [*] G. Bernard Shaw (1937) insisted in an interesting
essay that it was a profoundly serious book. For Shaw, the ending
substituted at Bulwer Lytton's suggestion—see the concluding part of
the Forster extract in Part Two below [*]—was an artistic flaw, for

'Dickens put nearly all his thought' into this novel. 'It is too serious a book to be a trivially happy one. Its beginning is unhappy; its middle is unhappy; and the conventional happy ending is an outrage on it.'[14] Already we have come a long way from the view of it as a mainly comic novel held by many of its early readers and, at least to some extent, by Dickens himself. Apart from the ending, it is for Shaw 'the most perfect of Dickens's works' in its handling of narrative.

Later critics have developed both of these points. The debate on the two endings has found advocates on both sides: Martin Meisel's essay of 1965 [*] offers a fresh perspective on the familiar question. And the skill of the narrative technique has prompted many analyses, represented here by Robert Partlow Jnr's discussion (1961–2) of the handling of the first-person viewpoint. [*] In the essay already mentioned, Shaw also confronts the moral question of Pip's reactions to the discovery of his benefactor's identity. Pip's initial 'inhuman loathing' of Magwitch is illogical, he argues, for 'if Pip had no objection to be a parasite instead of an honest blacksmith, at least he had a better claim to be a parasite on Magwitch's earnings than, as he imagined, on Miss Havisham's property'. We may retort that logic has not much to do with Pip's reactions; but the argument is a challenging one and raises important questions about Dickens's attitude to class and about the conventions of his art. A later and fuller examination of the moral aspects of the novel has been made by Julian Moynahan. [*]

As this outline suggests, criticism of *Great Expectations* has stressed both the moral seriousness and the technical achievement of the novel. The rigid demands of the weekly serial, which caused Dickens so many pains, seem to have had the beneficial effect of imposing a controlling sense of form upon the material. And although it may not be the novel which offers the most comprehensive diagnosis of the ills of society or the most exuberant Dickensian rhetoric, its account of the individual's struggle to come to terms with the world is conveyed in marvellously intimate and direct prose—what Graham Greene has described as 'Dickens's secret prose, that sense of a mind speaking to itself with no one there to listen'.[15]

Our Mutual Friend

As we have seen, *Great Expectations* was published in serial form in 1860–61. *Our Mutual Friend*, Dickens's next novel and the last he was to live to complete, was serialised during 1864 and 1865. The interval of almost three years contrasts strikingly with the rapid succession in which the earlier novels appeared, some of them indeed overlapping in composition and publication. Dickens in the 1860s was not only an older man of uncertain health: he had now moved on to a concept of the novel which called for more premeditation and planning as well as a much more intensive engagement with style. The contrast between the flowing, lightly corrected manuscript of, say, *Oliver Twist* and the crabbed, barely legible and thoroughly worked-over pages of *Our Mutual Friend*, with their multitudinous revisions, cancellations and interpolations, is eloquent of the radical change in his attitude to his art.

After *Great Expectations* Dickens had not been idle. He was constitutionally incapable of idleness. He had given several highly successful, but physically taxing, series of public readings from his work; he had continued the editorship of *All the Year Round*, with its continuous demands on his time and energies; and he had maintained his regular Christmas stories which had become an immensely popular feature of the national festival (the 1863 story, for instance, sold nearly a quarter of a million copies)—all this in spite of periods of ill health and family anxieties. During the composition of *Our Mutual Friend* (on 9 June 1865) he narrowly escaped death in the Staplehurst railway disaster, referred to in the 'Postscript in lieu of Preface'; the experience left him with symptoms of severe shock.

According to Forster, he had settled on the title of his new novel as early as 1861, and a letter written at this time [*] shows that he already had some of the leading situations and characters (including Rokesmith, the Lammles, the Veneerings and Charlie Hexam) firmly established in his mind. Even earlier, in 1850, he had published in *Household Words* an article by R. H. Horne on 'Dust'; as the extracts given in Part Three show, the article—a blend of reporting and invention—contains several ideas that were to be taken up in the novel, including the dust heap, paradoxically combining refuse and wealth, and the drowned man who returns to life. [*]

Dickens had hoped to embark on composition during 1862, but his 'invention', as he called it, stubbornly refused to deliver the goods. 'Alas!', he wrote in the April of that year, 'I have hit upon nothing for a story. Again and again I have tried . . . .' By the end of August 1863 the prospect was more hopeful: 'I am full of notions . . . for the new twenty numbers', he wrote to Forster; and in October he expressed himself as 'exceedingly anxious to begin my book'. But at the same time he evinced some anxiety that he might not be able to sustain the needful creative effort unless the propitious moment were seized: 'I see my opening perfectly, with the one main line on which the story is to turn; and if I don't strike while the iron (meaning myself) is hot, I shall drift off again, and have to go through all this uneasiness once more.'[16] Of critical interest here is the revelation of his intention to make the opening establish 'the one main line on which the story is to turn'.

Composition proceeded during the ensuing winter, and by March

1864 Dickens had completed the first three numbers. (It was a sign of his waning confidence in his stamina that he had determined to have at least five numbers in hand before publication commenced.) Serialisation began in May 1864, and within three days thirty thousand copies had been sold, with 'orders flowing in fast'; the first number was eventually to sell forty thousand. Chapman and Hall, the publishers, had mounted an advertising campaign which cost them the substantial sum of £1000 and included the distribution of a million handbills. Gratifying though this response was, Dickens's troubles were not at an end. On 29 July we find him writing to Forster that 'although I have not been wanting in industry, I have been wanting in invention, and have fallen back with the book. . . . I . . . have a very mountain to climb before I shall see the open country of my work.' The image seems to hint at depression: the peculiarly demanding nature of serial-writing was beginning to take its toll of his spirits. It was to be almost exactly another year before he was able to declare (on 31 July 1865) that 'I am but now finishing Our Mutual Friend', and it seems clear that those who detect in the novel signs of fatigue and a slackening of that extraordinary creative energy which is one of Dickens's outstanding characteristics can find a certain amount of biographical evidence to support their case.[17]

The illustrator for *Our Mutual Friend* was Marcus Stone, and as usual Dickens closely supervised the artist's work. 'Note', he instructed Stone, 'that the dustman's face should be droll, and not horrible'; 'Mrs Boffin, as I judge of her from the sketch, "Very good indeed"'; 'I want Boffin's oddity, without being at all blinked, to be an oddity of a very honest kind, that people will like'; 'the doll's dressmaker is immensely better than she was. I think she should now come extremely well. A weird sharpness not without beauty is the thing I want'.[18] It was Stone who showed Dickens the curious shop in London which suggested to him the character of Mr Venus.

Serial publication continued until November 1865; the novel also appeared in book form, its two volumes appearing in February and November respectively of that year. In spite of satisfactory initial sales, the serial did less well as time went on, the monthly sales of the later numbers dropping to 25,000—an above-average falling away. The critical reception was very mixed. The *Saturday Review*'s verdict (11 November 1865) was that the novel was 'a very tedious performance' and made 'rather hard reading'. On the other side of the Atlantic, the young Henry James described it as 'the poorest of Mr Dickens's works'. [*] In contrast, *The Times*'s reviewer, E. S. Dallas, perceptively recognised that the usual comparisons with *Pickwick* were irrelevant, since Dickens was now doing something entirely different, and doing it with extraordinary power, 'astonishing us with a fertility in which we can trace no signs of repetition'. [*] To Dickens the assertion that he was not played out must have been deeply reassuring; he signalised his gratitude by presenting Dallas with the manuscript of the novel. Yet it was to be a long time before Dallas's emphatic claim that it was 'infinitely better than *Pickwick* in all the higher qualities of a novel' was to find general critical support.

One of the features of *Our Mutual Friend* that the early critics (and not only the early critics) failed to appreciate was the range and flexibility of its prose style: a prose which is, as we can now see, astonishingly experimental by the standards of the 1860s. The *Westminster Review* singled out for consideration, interestingly enough, the chapter entitled 'Podsnappery' (April 1866), but only in order to ridicule its 'sham wit' and 'bad grammar'. The highly original and stylised art, the rhetorical devices such as *anaphora* (repetition), the strongly marked rhythms— these offered a new literary experience which left the conservative critic disconcerted and, in response to his bafflement, contemptuous. *Our Mutal Friend* belongs to the same years as Trollope's *The Small House at Allington*, Mrs Gaskell's *Wives and Daughters*, George Eliot's *Felix Holt* and Wilkie Collins's *Armadale*; but its author's exploitation of the possibilities of written prose proceeds along very different lines from theirs.[19] Thirty years later, George Gissing, inhibited by his own realist expectations and commitments, was to reveal a similar lack of understanding of what Dickens was attempting. He found 'tedious superfluity' in this novel, and observed that 'on many a page dialogue which is strictly no dialogue at all, but mere verbosity in a vein of forced humour, drags its slow length along in caricature of the author at his best'.[20] Again, it was Dallas who showed an understanding well in advance of his time; instead of trying to read *Our Mutual Friend* as if it were *Pickwick*, he recognised it as a major and innovative stylistic achievement.

For a long time critics seem to have been distracted from the central qualities of this novel by lesser considerations. Thus the success of the familiar Dickensian attack on specific abuses has been debated by critics who have failed to grasp that the novel's true centre of gravity lies elsewhere. In the character of Betty Higden, for example, Dickens returns to the criticism of the Poor Law, which had been a favourite target since the publication of *Oliver Twist* a generation earlier. His 'Postscript' throws down the gauntlet, and it was duly picked up by the *Westminster Review*'s anonymous critic, who tartly observed that 'to attempt to alter the Poor Law by a novel is about as absurd as it would be to call out the militia to stop the cattle disease'. Other critics praised the humanity and pathos with which this character is drawn. For example, Swinburne (admittedly an extreme case) writes ecstatically of 'the martyrdom of Betty Higden—the most nearly intolerable tragedy in all the tragic work of Dickens. Even the unsurpassed and unsurpassable grandeur and beauty of the martyred old heroine's character can hardly make the wonderful record of her heroic agony endurable by those who have been so tenderly and so powerfully compelled to love and to revere her.'[21] Yet Betty can be regarded as a heroine only at the sacrifice of a sense of proportion. In a very different mood, and approaching the novel from another direction, Chesterton remarked that there is abundant humour in this 'dark' novel, and the reminder is salutary; but his description of it as 'a sort of Indian summer of [Dickensian] farce' again seems to put the emphasis in the wrong place.[22]

It is not for its local effects of comedy or pathos or social indignation but as a vision of urban society powerfully communicated through poetic symbols that the most responsible modern critics have valued *Our Mutual Friend*. With J. Hillis Miller's statement that 'no other novel by Dickens is so obsessed with death'[23] we have travelled a long way from the Chestertonian highlighting of the comic and the grotesque. To juxtapose Chesterton's and Miller's comments is to be reminded how radical has been the reinterpretation and revaluation of Dickens's novel in our time. And with the recent revelation that T. S. Eliot originally intended to use a quotation from *Our Mutual Friend* as a title for part of *The Waste Land*, we can see the Victorian novel both as anticipating the modernist poem and as being illuminated by it.

NOTES

1. Barbara Hardy, *Dickens: The Later Novels* (London, 1968), p. 14.

2. Humphry House, *The Dickens World* (London, 1941) pp. 134–5.

3. Quoted by J. H. Buckley, *The Triumph of Time: A Study of the Victorian Concepts of Time, History, Progress and Decadence* (Cambridge, Mass., 1967), p. 35

4. George H. Ford, *Dickens and His Readers* (Princeton. N. J., 1955), pp. 101–2.

5. Philip Collins (ed.), *Dickens: The Critical Heritage* (London, 1971), pp. 272, 356, 360.

6. Bernard Shaw, 'On Dickens', *The Dickensian*, x (June 1914), pp. 250–1.

7. Edmund Wilson, *The Triple Thinkers* (New York and London, 1952), Foreword.

8. E. D. Hirsch, '*Hard Times* and F. R. Leavis', *Criticism*, VI (1964), p. 16.

9. K. J. Fielding, 'Mill and Gradgrind', *Nineteenth Century Fiction*, XI (1956), pp. 148–51; John Holloway, '*Hard Times*: A History and a Criticism', in John Gross and Gabriel Pearson (eds), *Dickens and the Twentieth Century* (London, 1962), pp. 159–74; F. R. and Q. D. Leavis, *Dickens the Novelist* (London, 1970).

10. Collins, op. cit., p. 356.

11. J. A. Sutherland, *Victorian Novelists and Publishers* (London, 1976), p. 171.

12. Walter Dexter (ed.), *The Letters of Charles Dickens* (London, 1938), III, pp. 182–4, 186.

13. The condensed version is printed in Philip Collins (ed.), *Charles Dickens: The Public Readings* (Oxford, 1975), pp. 305–63.

14. G. Bernard Shaw, Preface to 'Limited Editions Club' edition of *Great Expectations* (Edinburgh, 1937).

15. Graham Greene, 'The Young Dickens', in his *The Lost Childhood and Other Essays* (London, 1951), p. 53.

16. Dexter (ed.), *Letters*, op. cit., III, pp. 292, 361, 364.

17. Ibid., III, pp. 387, 394, 433.

18. Ibid., III, p. 380.

19. I have developed this point in my *Speech in the English Novel* (London, 1973), pp. 139–43.

20. George Gissing, *Charles Dickens* (London, 1898), p. 59.

21. A. C. Swinburne, *Charles Dickens* (London, 1913), pp. 61–2.

22. G. K. Chesterton, *Appreciations and Criticisms of the Works of Charles Dickens* (London, 1911), p. 207.

23. J. Hillis Miller, *Charles Dickens: The World of His Novels* (Cambridge, Mass., 1958), p. 316.

PART ONE

Hard Times

Hard Times

Serialised weekly in *Household Words*, from 1 April to 12 August 1854; published in book form in 1854 as *Hard Times, For These Times*, in one volume.

I. BACKGROUND

Dickens (1853, 1854, 1866)

I   From 'Frauds on the Fairies' (1853)

We may assume that we are not singular in entertaining a very great
tenderness for the fairy literature of our childhood. . . .

   In an utilitarian age, of all other times, it is a matter of grave
importance that Fairy tales should be respected. Our English red tape is
too magnificently red ever to be employed in the tying up of such trifles,
but every one who has considered the subject knows full well that a
nation without fancy, without some romance, never did, never can,
never will hold a great place under the sun. . . .

   SOURCE: article in *Household Words* (1 Oct. 1853).

II   Extracts from Letters (1854, 1866)

To W. J. de Cerjat, 16 January 1854
The sad affair of the Preston strike remains unsettled; and I hear, on
strong authority, that if that were settled, the Manchester people are
prepared to strike next. . . .

To Miss Burdett Coutts, 23 January 1854
My purpose is among the mighty secrets of the World at present, but
there is such a fixed idea on the part of my printers and co-partners in
Household Words, that a story of me, continued from week to week,
would make some unheard of effect that I am going to write one.

To Mark Lemon, 20 February 1854
Will you note down and send me any slang terms among thè tumblers
and circus-people that you can call to mind? I have noted down some—
I want them in my new story—but it is very probable that you will
recall several which I have not got.

To Charles Knight, 17 March 1854
The English are, so far as I know, the hardest-worked people on whom
the sun shines. Be content if, in their wretched intervals of pleasure, they
read for amusement and do no worse. They are born at the oar, and
they live and die at it. Good God, what would we have of them! . . .

To W. H. Wills, 18 April 1854
I am in a dreary state, planning and planning the story of Hard times
(out of materials for I don't know how long a story), and consequently
writing little . . .

To Thomas Carlyle, 13 July 1854
I am going, next month, to publish in one volume a story now coming
out in Household Words, called Hard Times. . . . It contains what I do
devoutly hope will shake some people in a terrible mistake of these days,
when so presented. I know it contains nothing in which you do not think
with me, for no man knows your books better than I. . . .

To Charles Fechter, 4 September 1866
When I did Hard Times I called the scene Coketown. Everybody knew
what was meant, but every cotton-spinning town said it was the other
cotton-spinning town. . . .

SOURCE: W. Dexter (ed.), *The Letters of Charles Dickens*
(London, 1938): II, pp. 536–7, 542–3, 548, 551–2, 567; III, 483.

2. CONTEMPORARY OPINIONS

Anonymous (1854)

'A poetical conception . . . a prosaic framework'

. . . The idea of Mr Dickens's last story, *Hard Times*, is a good idea:—
but is scarcely wrought out with Mr Dickens's usual felicity. The
purpose is to show that Fact is not everything to man; and that the
spiritual longings of our nature are not to be neglected with impunity.
In its essence, this is a poetical conception; and it required for its due
exhibition an ideal framework. Mr Dickens has been pleased to give it a
prosaic framework and to people it with very repulsive and vulgar
characters. Considered as a work of Art, this is its great defect. A story,
the form of which was poetical, and the characters of which were
removed from commonplace alike in their graces, their humours, and
their pathos—as, for example, are those in *The Tempest* and in the
Midsummer Night's Dream—might have been invented by the literary
artist, in which all the morals proposed by Mr Dickens as a necessary
part of the education of young people could have been established
without the straining and the violence which many persons will
reasonably object to in *Hard Times*. The case of Fancy *versus* Fact is here
stated in prose, but without the fairness which belongs to a prose
argument. A purely ideal treatment was needed for such a purpose.
Many persons—and most certainly those for whose reproof the tale is
written—will fail to see that the education of Fact, as opposed to the
education of Fancy—of the Reason without due notice of the
Emotions—of the Intellect without reference to the Imagination—
leads of necessity to the results pourtrayed in Louisa and Tom
Gradgrind. If not of necessity, why seek to substitute the general by the
incidental? The many will object—unless Mr Dickens goes so far as to
assert that the girl came to the brink of shame, and the boy went over it,
because they had not been allowed to read fairy tales and see strolling
players in their youth—as we think he will scarcely venture to do—that
the story teaches nothing at all, and that therefore the moral machinery
of it fails. That *Hard Times*, like everything that Mr Dickens writes, is
full of humour, observation, knowledge of manhood, will not be

gainsaid. It has the beauties and the vices of his style. It abounds in passages bright and glowing—delicate in their humour—and subtle in their fancy; but these passages are found in close relationship to others coarse, violent, and awkward. Altogether, the tale is readable, though it lacks moral interest; and the puppets of the play move and speak like living creatures, though the mind refuses to allow that they are fitting messengers of the poetical truth with the delivery of which they appear to be charged. Fancy asks an ideal advocate.

SOURCE: review in the *Athenaeum* (12 Aug. 1854).

John Forster (1854)

'No thesis can be argued in a novel'

. . . So far as the purpose of *Hard Times* involves the direct raising of any question of political economy, we abstain from comment upon it. In a tale, especially a very short one, clearly and powerfully written, full of incident and living interest, it is difficult to find room for a sufficiently full expression of opinion upon details, in the working of a given principle. The principle emphatically laid down by Mr Dickens in the story before us is one to which every sound heart responds. We cannot train any man properly unless we cultivate his fancy, and allow fair scope to his affections. We may starve the mind upon hard fact as we may starve the body upon meat, if we exclude all lighter diet, and all kinds of condiment. To enforce this truth has been the object of the story of *Hard Times*, and its enforcement is not argumentative, because no thesis can be argued in a novel; but by a warm appeal from one heart, to a hundred thousand hearts quite ready to respond. The story is not meant to do what fiction cannot do—to prove a case; its utmost purpose is to express forcibly a righteous sentiment. To run anywhere into a discussion of detail would have checked the current of a tale, which, as it stands, does not flag for the space even of a page. Wherever in the course of it any playful handling of a notion of the day suited the artist's purpose, the use made of it has been artistic always, never argumentative.

Hard Times, in fact, is not meant to be fought through, prosed over, conned laboriously, Blue Book in hand. Is the heart touched with a lively perception of the true thought which pervades the work from first to last—then the full moral purpose of it is attained. The very journal in which the novel appeared is itself a complete answer to any man, who, treating in a hard-fact spirit all the fanciful allusions of the novelist, should accuse Mr Dickens of attacking this good movement and the other, or of opposing the search after statistical and other information by which only real light can be thrown on social questions. What is *Household Words* but a great magazine of facts? And what one is there, of all those useful matters of detail which the novelist has by some readers been supposed to treat with disrespect, which he has not, as conductor of that journal, carefully and fully urged upon the public notice? In his character of journalist Mr Dickens has from the first especially laboured to cultivate the kindly affections and the fancy at the same time with the intellect, and that is simply what he asks men in 'these times' to do. But because he knows that facts and figures will not be lost sight of by the world, he leaves them, when he speaks as a novelist, to take care of themselves, and writes his tale wholly in the interests of the affections and the fancy.

SOURCE: extract from review in the *Examiner* (9 Sept. 1854).

Richard Simpson (1854)

The Limitations of Dickens

. . . Here and there we meet with touches not unworthy of the inventor of *Pickwick*; but, on the whole, the story is stale, flat, and unprofitable; a mere dull melodrama, in which character is caricature, sentiment tinsel, and moral (if any) unsound. It is a thousand pities that Mr Dickens does not confine himself to amusing his readers, instead of wandering out of his depth in trying to instruct them. The one, no man can do better; the other, few men can do worse. With all his quickness of perception, his power of seizing salient points and surface-shadows, he has never shown any ability to pierce the depths of social life, to fathom the wells of social action. He can only paint what he sees, and should plan out his canvas accordingly. No doubt great evils exist in

manufacturing towns, and elsewhere; but nevertheless, steam-engines
and power-looms are not the evil principle in material shape, as the folly
of a conventional humanitarian slang insists on making them. The
disease of Coketown will hardly be stayed by an abstinence from facts
and figures; nor a healthy reaction insured by a course of cheap divorce
and the poetry of nature. In short, whenever Mr Dickens and his school
assume the office of instructors, it is, as Stephen Blackpool says, 'aw a
muddle! Fro' first to last, a muddle!'

SOURCE: extract from review in the *Rambler* (Oct. 1854).

Anonymous (1854)

Character and Style

. . . [The characters] have, most of them, the appearance of puppets
which Mr Dickens has constructed expressly for his present purpose. Mr
Bounderby, for example, is a most outrageous character—who can
believe in the possibility of such a man? Brought up carefully, and
pushed on in the world by a poor and devoted mother, he not only
pensions her off on a miserable pittance, and denies her all approach to
him in his full-blown prosperity, but he is never introduced on the scene
without being made to traduce her character, and that of others of his
relatives, and invent lies about the way in which he lived, when he was,
as he ever gave out, thrown helpless on the world. He is made to
entertain his guests with the flavour of the stewed eels he purchased in
the streets at eight years old, and with calculations that he had eaten in
his youth at least three horses, under the guise of polonies and saveloys.
Such things may excite a laugh, perhaps, in a farce spoken at the
Victoria, but will hardly do so with any reader of taste. The whole of the
Gradgrind family are unpleasant enough, but especially we might have
been spared the melancholy spectacle of Mrs Gradgrind's decease. The
death-bed of an inoffensive weak-minded woman should not have been
made ridiculous, especially as it does not in any way assist the plot. The
principal charm of the story is the style, which, aided by his delicate
perception, enables Mr Dickens to take off the fleeting peculiarities of
time and place, in the manner which has gained great part of his literary

reputation. We doubt, however, whether his descriptions will be so intelligible fifty years hence: it is a language which speaks especially to the present generation. It has, however, frequent extravagances, which are indulged in by Mr Dickens and his followers, to a degree that becomes not unfrequently insupportable. The description of Coketown is good—in Mr Dickens's style.

SOURCE: extract from notice in the *Westminster Review* (Oct. 1854).

Hippolyte Taine (1856)

The Two Classes

. . . Take away the grotesque characters, who are only introduced to fill up and to excite laughter, and you will find that all Dickens's characters belong to two classes—people who have feelings and emotions, and people who have none. He contrasts the souls which nature creates with those which society deforms. One of his last novels, *Hard Times*, is an abstract of all the rest. He there exalts instinct above reason, intuition of heart above positive science; he attacks education built on statistics, figures, and facts; overwhelms the positive and mercantile spirit with misfortune and ridicule; combats the pride, hardness, selfishness of the merchant and the aristocrat; falls foul of manufacturing towns, towns of smoke and mud, which fetter the body in an artificial atmosphere, and the mind in a factitious existence. He seeks out poor artisans, mountebanks, a foundling, and crushes beneath their common sense, generosity, delicacy, courage, and sweetness, the false science, false happiness, and false virtue of the rich and powerful who despise them. He satirises oppressive society; praises oppressed nature; and his elegiac genius, like his satirical genius, finds ready to his hand in the English world around him, the sphere which it needs for its development.

SOURCE: extract from article in the *Revue des deux mondes* (1856); later included in Taine's *History of English Literature* (1859; translated into English 1873).

John Ruskin (1860)

The Critic of Society

. . . The essential value and truth of Dickens's writings have been
unwisely lost sight of by many thoughtful persons, merely because he
presents his truth with some colour of caricature. Unwisely, because
Dickens's caricature, though often gross, is never mistaken. Allowing for
his manner of telling them, the things he tells us are always true. I wish
that he could think it right to limit his brilliant exaggeration to works
written only for public amusement; and when he takes up a subject of
high national importance, such as that which he handled in *Hard Times*,
that he would use severer and more accurate analysis. The usefulness of
that work (to my mind, in several respects the greatest he has written) is
with many persons seriously diminished because Mr Bounderby is a
dramatic monster, instead of a characteristic example of a wordly
master; and Stephen Blackpool a dramatic perfection, instead of a
characteristic example of an honest workman. But let us not lose the use
of Dickens's wit and insight, because he chooses to speak in a circle of
stage fire. He is entirely right in his main drift and purpose in every book
he has written; and all of them, but especially *Hard Times*, should be
studied with close and earnest care by persons interested in social
questions. They will find much that is partial, and, because partial,
apparently unjust; but if they examine all the evidence on the other
side, which Dickens seems to overlook, it will appear, after all their
trouble, that his view was the finally right one, grossly and sharply told.

SOURCE: extract from article in the *Cornhill Magazine* (Aug.
1860); published, with the series of which it was a part, in *Unto
This Last* (1862).

Edwin Whipple (1877)

A Reply to Ruskin

. . . It is ridiculous to assert, as Ruskin asserts, that *Hard Times* is Dickens's greatest work; for it is *the* one of all his works which should be distinguished from the others as specially wanting in that power of real characterisation on which his reputation as a vivid delineator of human character and human life depends. The whole effect of the story, though it lacks neither amusing nor pathetic incidents, and though it contains passages of description which rank with his best efforts in combining truth of fact with truth of imagination, is ungenial and unpleasant. Indeed, in this book, he simply intensified popular discontent; he ignored or he was ignorant of those laws the violation of which is at the root of popular discontent; and proclaimed with his favorite ideal workman, Stephen Blackpool, that not only the relation between employers and employed, but the whole constitution of civilised society itself, was a hopeless 'muddle,' beyond the reach of human intelligence or humane feeling to explain and justify. It is to be observed here that all cheering views of the amelioration of the condition of the race come from those hard thinkers whose benevolent impulses push them to the investigation of natural and economic laws. Starting from the position of sentimental benevolence, and meeting unforeseen intellectual obstacles at every step in his progress, Dickens ends 'in a muddle' by the necessity of his method. Had he been intellectually equipped with the knowledge possessed by many men to whom in respect to genius he was immensely superior, he would never have landed in a conclusion so ignominious, and one which the average intellect of well-informed persons of the present day contemptuously rejects. If Dickens had contented himself with using his great powers of observation, sympathy, humor, imagination, and characterisation in their appropriate fields, his lack of scientific training in the austere domain of social, legal, and political science would have been hardly perceptible; but after his immense popularity was assured by the success of *The Pickwick Papers*, he was smitten with the ambition to direct the public opinion of Great Britain by embodying, in exquisitely satirical caricatures, rash and hasty judgements on the whole government of Great Britain in all its departments, legislative, executive, and judicial. He overlooked uses, in order to fasten on abuses. His power to excite, at his will, laughter, or tears, or indignation was so great, that the victims of his mirthful wrath were not at first disposed to resent his debatable fallacies while enjoying his delicious fun. His invasion of the domain of political science with the palpable design of substituting benevolent instincts for established laws was carelessly condoned by the statesmen, legists, and economists whom he denounced and amused.

SOURCE: extract from article in the *Atlantic Monthly* (March 1877).

3. LATER CRITICISM

George Gissing 'Dickens and the Working Class' (1898)

. . . We do not nowadays look for a fervent Christianity in leaders of the people. In that, as in several other matters, Dickens was by choice retrospective. Still writing at a time when 'infidelity'—the word then used—was becoming rife among the populace of great towns, he never makes any reference to it, and probably did not take it into account; it had no place in his English ideal. I doubt, indeed, whether he was practically acquainted with the 'free-thinking' workman. A more noticeable omission from his books (if we except the one novel which I cannot but think a failure) is that of the workman at war with capital. This great struggle, going on before him all his life, found no place in the scheme of his fiction. He shows us poor men who suffer under tyranny, and who exclaim against the hardship of things; but never such a representative wage-earner as was then to be seen battling for bread and right. One reason is plain; Dickens did not know the north of England. With adequate knowledge of a manufacturing town, he would never have written so unconvincingly as in his book *Hard Times*—the opportunity for dealing with this subject. Stephen Blackpool represents nothing at all; he is a mere model of meekness, and his great misfortune is such as might befall any man anywhere, the curse of a drunken wife. The book is a crude attack on materialism, a theme which might, of course, have entered very well into a study of the combatant working-class. But, as I have already pointed out, the working-class is not Dickens's field, even in London. . . .

SOURCE: extract from *Charles Dickens: A Critical Study* (London, 1898), pp. 201–2.

G. B. Shaw   'Dickens's Portrait of England' (1912)

John Ruskin once declared *Hard Times* Dickens's best novel. [See above—Ed.] It is worth while asking why Ruskin thought this, because he would have been the first to admit that the habit of placing works of art in competition with one another, and wrangling as to which is the best, is the habit of the sportsman, not of the enlightened judge of art. Let us take it that what Ruskin meant was that *Hard Times* was one of his special favorites among Dickens's books. Was this the caprice of fancy? or is there any rational explanation of the preference? I think there is.

Hard Times is the first fruit of that very interesting occurrence which our religious sects call, sometimes conversion, sometimes being saved, sometimes attaining to conviction of sin. Now the great conversions of the XIX century were not convictions of individual, but of social sin. The first half of the XIX century considered itself the greatest of all the centuries. The second discovered that it was the wickedest of all the centuries. The first half despised and pitied the Middle Ages as barbarous, cruel, superstitious, ignorant. The second half saw no hope for mankind except in the recovery of the faith, the art, the humanity of the Middle Ages. In Macaulay's *History of England*, the world is so happy, so progressive, so firmly set in the right path, that the author cannot mention even the National Debt without proclaiming that the deeper the country goes into debt, the more it prospers. In Morris's *News from Nowhere* there is nothing left of all the institutions that Macaulay glorified except an old building, so ugly that it is used only as a manure market, that was once the British House of Parliament. *Hard Times* was written in 1854, just at the turn of the half century; and in it we see Dickens with his eyes newly open and his conscience newly stricken by the discovery of the real state of England. In the book that went immediately before, *Bleak House*, he was still denouncing evils and ridiculing absurdities that were mere symptoms of the anarchy that followed the industrial revolution of the XVIII and XIX centuries, and the conquest of political power by Commercialism in 1832. In *Bleak House* Dickens knows nothing of the industrial revolution: he imagines that what is wrong is that when a dispute arises over the division of the plunder of the nation, the Court of Chancery, instead of settling the dispute cheaply and promptly, beggars the disputants and pockets both their shares. His description of our party system, with its Coodle,

Doodle, Foodle, etc., has never been surpassed for accuracy and for penetration of superficial pretence. But he had not dug down to the bed rock of the imposture. His portrait of the ironmaster who visits Sir Leicester Dedlock, and who is so solidly superior to him, might have been drawn by Macaulay: there is not a touch of Bounderby in it. His horrible and not untruthful portraits of the brickmakers whose abject and battered wives call them 'master', and his picture of the now vanished slum between Drury Lane and Catherine Street which he calls Tom All Alone's, suggest (save in the one case of the outcast Jo, who is, like Oliver Twist, a child, and therefore outside the old self-help panacea of Dickens's time) nothing but individual delinquencies, local plague-spots, negligent authorities.

In *Hard Times* you will find all this changed. Coketown, which you can see to-day for yourself in all its grime in the Potteries (the real name of it is Hanley in Staffordshire on the London and North Western Railway), is not, like Tom All Alone's, a patch of slum in a fine city, easily cleared away, as Tom's actually was about fifty years after Dickens called attention to it. Coketown is the whole place; and its rich manufacturers are proud of its dirt, and declare that they like to see the sun blacked out with smoke, because it means that the furnaces are busy and money is being made; whilst its poor factory hands have never known any other sort of town, and are as content with it as a rat is with a hole. Mr Rouncewell, the pillar of society who snubs Sir Leicester with such dignity, has become Mr Bounderby, the selfmade humbug. The Chancery suitors who are driving themselves mad by hanging about the Courts in the hope of getting a judgment in their favor instead of trying to earn an honest living, are replaced by factory operatives who toil miserably and incessantly only to see the streams of gold they set flowing slip through their fingers into the pockets of men who revile and oppress them.

Clearly this is not the Dickens who burlesqued the old song of the Fine Old English Gentleman, and saw in the evils he attacked only the sins and wickednesses and follies of a great civilization. This is Karl Marx, Carlyle, Ruskin, Morris, Carpenter, rising up against civilization itself as against a disease, and declaring that it is not our disorder but our order that is horrible; that it is not our criminals but our magnates that are robbing and murdering us; and that it is not merely Tom All Alone's that must be demolished and abolished, pulled down, rooted up, and made for ever impossible so that nothing shall remain of it but History's record of its infamy, but our entire social system. For that was how men felt, and how some of them spoke, in the early days of the Great Conversion which produced, first, such books as the *Latter Day Pamphlets* of Carlyle, Dickens's *Hard Times*, and the tracts and sociological novels of the Christian Socialists, and later on the Socialist

movement which has now spread all over the world, and which has
succeeded in convincing even those who most abhor the name of
Socialism that the condition of the civilized world is deplorable, and
that the remedy is far beyond the means of individual righteousness. In
short, whereas formerly men said to the victim of society who ventured
to complain, 'Go and reform yourself before you pretend to reform
Society', it now has to admit that until Society is reformed, no man can
reform himself except in the most insignificantly small ways. He may
cease picking your pocket of half crowns; but he cannot cease taking a
quarter of a million a year from the community for nothing at one end of
the scale, or living under conditions in which health, decency, and
gentleness are impossible at the other, if he happens to be born to such a
lot.

    You must therefore resign yourself, if you are reading Dickens's books
in the order in which they were written, to bid adieu now to the light-
hearted and only occasionally indignant Dickens of the earlier books,
and get such entertainment as you can from him now that the
occasional indignation has spread and deepened into a passionate revolt
against the whole industrial order of the modern world. Here you will
find no more villains and heroes, but only oppressors and victims,
oppressing and suffering in spite of themselves, driven by a huge
machinery which grinds to pieces the people it should nourish and
ennoble, and having for its directors the basest and most foolish of us
instead of the noblest and most farsighted.

    Many readers find the change disappointing. Others find Dickens
worth reading almost for the first time. The increase in strength and
intensity is enormous: the power that indicts a nation so terribly is much
more impressive than that which ridicules individuals. But it cannot be
said that there is an increase of simple pleasure for the reader, though
the books are not therefore less attractive. One cannot say that it is
pleasanter to look at a battle than at a merry-go-round; but there can be
no question which draws the larger crowd.

    To describe the change in the readers' feelings more precisely, one
may say that it is impossible to enjoy Gradgrind or Bounderby as one
enjoys Pecksniff or the Artful Dodger or Mrs Gamp or Micawber or
Dick Swiveller, because these earlier characters have nothing to do with
us except to amuse us. We neither hate nor fear them. We do not expect
ever to meet them, and should not be in the least afraid of them if we
did. England is not full of Micawbers and Swivellers. They are not our
fathers, our schoolmasters, our employers, our tyrants. We do not read
novels to escape from them and forget them: quite the contrary. But
England is full of Bounderbys and Podsnaps and Gradgrinds; and we
are all to a quite appalling extent in their power. We either hate and
fear them or else we are them, and resent being held up to odium by a

novelist. We have only to turn to the article on Dickens in the current edition of the *Encyclopedia Britannica* to find how desperately our able critics still exalt all Dickens's early stories about individuals whilst ignoring or belittling such masterpieces as *Hard Times, Little Dorrit, Our Mutual Friend,* and even *Bleak House* (because of Sir Leicester Dedlock), for their mercilessly faithful and penetrating exposures of English social, industrial, and political life; to see how hard Dickens hits the conscience of the governing class; and how loth we still are to confess, not that we are so wicked (for of that we are rather proud), but so ridiculous, so futile, so incapable of making our country really prosperous. *The Old Curiosity Shop* was written to amuse you, entertain you, touch you; and it succeeded. *Hard Times* was written to make you uncomfortable; and it will make you uncomfortable (and serve you right) though it will perhaps interest you more, and certainly leave a deeper scar on you, than any two of its forerunners.

At the same time you need not fear to find Dickens losing his good humor and sense of fun and becoming serious in Mr Gradgrind's way. On the contrary, Dickens in this book casts off, and casts off for ever, all restraint on his wild sense of humor. He had always been inclined to break loose: there are passages in the speeches of Mrs Nickleby and Pecksniff which are impossible as well as funny. But now it is no longer a question of passages: here he begins at last to exercise quite recklessly his power of presenting a character to you in the most fantastic and outrageous terms, putting into its mouth from one end of the book to the other hardly one word which could conceivably be uttered by any sane human being, and yet leaving you with an unmistakable and exactly truthful portrait of a character that you recognize at once as not only real but typical. Nobody ever talked, or ever will talk, as Silas Wegg talks to Boffin and Mr Venus, or as Mr Venus reports Pleasant Riderhood to have talked, or as Rogue Riderhood talks, or as John Chivery talks. They utter rhapsodies of nonsense conceived in an ecstasy of mirth. And this begins in *Hard Times.* Jack Bunsby in *Dombey and Son* is absurd: the oracles he delivers are very nearly impossible, and yet not quite impossible. But Mrs Sparsit in this book, though Rembrandt could not have drawn a certain type of real woman more precisely to the life, is grotesque from beginning to end in her way of expressing herself. Her nature, her tricks of manner, her way of taking Mr Bounderby's marriage, her instinct for hunting down Louisa and Mrs Pegler, are drawn with an unerring hand; and she says nothing that is out of character. But no clown gone suddenly mad in a very mad harlequinade could express all these truths in more extravagantly ridiculous speeches. Dickens's business in life has become too serious for troubling over the small change of verisimilitude, and denying himself and his readers the indulgence of his humor in inessentials. He even calls the schoolmaster M'Choakumchild, which is almost an insult to the serious reader. And it was so afterwards to the end of his life. There are moments when he imperils the whole effect of his character drawing by some overpoweringly comic sally. For instance, happening in *Hard Times* to describe Mr Bounderby as drumming on his hat as if it were a tambourine, which is quite correct and natural, he presently says that 'Mr Bounderby put his tambourine on his head, like an oriental dancer'. Which similitude is so unexpectedly and excruciatingly funny that it is almost impossible to feel duly angry with the odious Bounderby afterwards.

This disregard of naturalness in speech is extraordinarily entertaining in the comic method; but it must be admitted that it is not only not entertaining, but sometimes hardly bearable when it does not make us laugh. There are two persons in *Hard Times*, Louisa Gradgrind and Sissy Jupe, who are serious throughout. Louisa is a figure of poetic tragedy; and there is no question of naturalness in her case: she speaks from beginning to end as an inspired prophetess, conscious of her own doom and finally bearing to her father the judgment of Providence on his blind conceit. If you once consent to overlook her marriage, which is none the less an act of prostitution because she does it to obtain advantages for her brother and not for herself, there is nothing in the solemn poetry of her deadly speech that jars. But Sissy is nothing if not natural, and though Sissy is as true to nature in her character as Mrs Sparsit, she 'speaks like a book' in the most intolerable sense of the words. In her interview with Mr James Harthouse, her unconscious courage and simplicity, and his hopeless defeat by them, are quite natural and right; and the contrast between the humble girl of the people and the smart sarcastic man of the world whom she so completely vanquishes is excellently dramatic; but Dickens has allowed himself to be carried away by the scene into a ridiculous substitution of his own most literary and least colloquial style for any language that could conceivably be credited to Sissy.

> 'Mr Harthouse: the only reparation that remains with you is to leave her immediately and finally. I am quite sure that you can mitigate in no other way the wrong and harm you have done. I am quite sure that it is the only compensation you have left it in your power to make. I do not say that it is much, or that it is enough; but it is something, and it is necessary. Therefore, though without any other authority than I have given you, and even without the knowledge of any other person than yourself and myself, I ask you to depart from this place to-night, under an obligation never to return to it.'

This is the language of a Lord Chief Justice, not of the dunce of an elementary school in the Potteries.

But this is only a surface failure, just as the extravagances of Mrs Sparsit are only surface extravagances. There is, however, one real failure in the book. Slackbridge, the trade union organizer, is a mere figment of the middle-class imagination. No such man would be listened to by a meeting of English factory hands. Not that such meetings are less susceptible to humbug than meetings of any other class. Not that trade union organizers, worn out by the terribly wearisome and trying work of going from place to place repeating the same commonplaces and trying to 'stoke up' meetings to enthusiasm with them, are less apt than other politicians to end as windbags, and sometimes to depend on stimulants to pull them through their work. Not, in short, that the trade union platform is any less humbug-ridden than the platforms of our more highly placed political parties. But even at their worst trade union organizers are not a bit like Slackbridge. Note, too, that Dickens mentions that there was a chairman at the meeting (as if that were rather surprising), and that this chairman makes no attempt to preserve the usual order of public meeting, but allows speakers to address the assembly and interrupt one another in an entirely disorderly way.[1] All this is pure middle-class ignorance. It is much as if a tramp were to write a description of millionaires smoking large cigars in church, with their wives in low-necked dresses and diamonds. We cannot say that Dickens did not know the working classes, because he knew humanity too well to be ignorant of any class. But this sort of knowledge is as compatible with ignorance of class manners and customs as with ignorance of foreign languages. Dickens knew certain classes of working folk very well: domestic servants, village artisans, and employees of petty tradesmen, for example. But of the segregated factory populations of our purely industrial towns he knew no more than an observant professional man can pick up on a flying visit to Manchester.

It is especially important to notice that Dickens expressly says in this book that the workers were wrong to organize themselves in trade unions, thereby endorsing what was perhaps the only practical mistake of the Gradgrind school that really mattered much. And having thus thoughtlessly adopted, or at least repeated, this error, long since exploded, of the philosophic Radical school from which he started, he turns his back frankly on Democracy, and adopts the idealized Toryism of Carlyle and Ruskin, in which the aristocracy are the masters and superiors of the people, and also the servants of the people and of God. Here is a significant passage.

'Now perhaps,' said Mr Bounderby, 'you will let the

gentleman know how you would set this muddle (as you are so
fond of calling it) to rights.'

'I donno, sir. I canna be expecten to't. Tis not me as should
be looken to for that, sir. Tis they as is put ower me, and ower aw
the rest of us. What do they tak upon themseln, sir, if not to do
it?'

And to this Dickens sticks for the rest of his life. In *Our Mutual Friend* he
appeals again and again to the governing classes, asking them with
every device of reproach, invective, sarcasm, and ridicule of which he is
master, what they have to say to this or that evil which it is their
professed business to amend or avoid. Nowhere does he appeal to the
working classes to take their fate into their own hands and try the
democratic plan.

Another phrase used by Stephen Blackpool in this remarkable fifth
chapter is important. 'Nor yet lettin alone will never do it.' It is
Dickens's express repudiation of *laissez-faire*.

There is nothing more in the book that needs any glossary, except,
perhaps, the strange figure of the Victorian 'swell', Mr James
Harthouse. His pose has gone out of fashion. Here and there you may
still see a man—even a youth—with a single eyeglass, an elaborately
boied and weary air, and a little stock of cynicisms and indifferentisms
contrasting oddly with a moral anxiety about his clothes. All he needs is
a pair of Dundreary whiskers, like the officers in Desanges's military
pictures, to be a fair imitation of Mr James Harthouse. But he is not in
the fashion; he is an eccentric, as Whistler was an eccentric, as Max
Beerbohm and the neo-dandies of the *fin de siècle* were eccentrics. It is
now the fashion to be energetic, and hustle as American millionaires are
supposed (rather erroneously) to hustle. But the soul of the swell is still
unchanged. He has changed his name again and again, become a
Masher, a Toff, a Johnny and what not; but fundamentally he remains
what he always was, an Idler, and therefore a man bound to find some
trick of thought and speech that reduces the world to a thing as empty
and purposeless as himself. Mr Harthouse reappears, more seriously
and kindly taken, as Eugene Wrayburn and Mortimer Lightwood in
Our Mutual Friend. He reappears as a club in The Finches of the Grove of
Great Expectations. He will reappear in all his essentials in fact and in
fiction until he is at last shamed or coerced into honest industry and
becomes not only unintelligible but inconceivable.

Note, finally, that in this book Dickens proclaims that marriages are
not made in heaven, and that those which are not confirmed there,
should be dissolved.

SOURCE: Introduction to *Hard Times* (London, 1912).

NOTE

1. See a different reading of the trade-union meeting scenes in the following extract by Humphry House. [Ed.]

Humphry House   'A Novel of Sociological Argument' (1941)

. . . The strange thing is that though most readers find *Hard Times* dry and brain-spun, Dickens said of it himself that he had not meant to write a new story for a year, when the idea laid hold of him by the throat in a very violent manner.

What this central idea was there is no means of knowing; but it is plain that *Hard Times* is one of Dickens's most thought-about books. One of the reasons why, in the 1850s, his novels begin to show a greater complication of plot than before, is that he was intending to use them as a vehicle of more concentrated sociological argument. All his journalism shows too that he was *thinking* much more about social problems, whereas earlier he had been content to feel mainly, and to record a thought, when it occurred, in emotional dress. The objection to such a character as Gradgrind is not just that he is a burlesque and an exaggeration—so are Squeers and Pecksniff—but rather that in him the satire is directed against a kind of thought: he is in fact the only major Dickens character who is meant to be an 'intellectual': 'His character was not unkind, all things considered; it might have been a very kind one indeed if he had only made some round mistake in the arithmetic that balanced it, years ago.' Dickens was caught with the idea of a man living by a certain philosophy, as in the past he had often been caught with the idea of a man living by a master vice such as miserhood or hypocrisy or pride. Such vices he understood, but he did not understand enough of any philosophy even to be able to guy it successfully. But he obviously felt during the 'fifties, when Public Health and Administrative Reform were keeping him so closely to social-political problems, that there must be some essential flaw in the reasoning of such a man as Bright. The creation of Gradgrind is an attempt to track it

down. The despondent atmosphere of the whole book reflects the failure
to do so.

This atmosphere is concentrated in Stephen Blackpool. In him
Dickens tried to rescue the idea of personality in an individual industrial
worker. Stephen's successive defeats by the Law, by the Trade Union,
and by his employer might have become the material of genuine
tragedy, if Dickens had been prepared to accept his death from the
beginning as inevitable and unanswerable; but he was hankering all the
time after a way to avoid the proper tragic solution, and the result is
nothing but a slow record of inglorious misery and defeat. Dickens did
not want to admit that Stephen's bargaining power—whether against
Bounderby, his marriage, or life itself—was negligible, but wrote as if
there might be an unexpected solution at every turn. There is no
difficulty about Stephen's relation to the Law or about his relation to
Bounderby;[1] the true crux is in the part of the plot that deals with the
Trade Union, and in making it so Dickens was apparently trying to
work out, in the actual writing of the book, the implications of his old
ideal of *man to man* benevolence in the relations between employers and
labour in large-scale industry. Three points were emphasised in the
treatment of the Union—Stephen's inexplicable obstinacy in refusing
to join it; Dickens's hatred of Slackbridge; and the difference of mood
and attitude of the other workers towards Stephen as men and as Union
members under Slackbridge's influence.

For the Union meeting itself he did a thing which was very rare for
him—he deliberately went in search of copy, to Preston, to watch the
effects of a strike of the cotton workers there which had dragged on for
weeks. He seems to have gone expecting to find discontent, disorder,
and even rioting, and his first impression caused surprise and a sort of
sentimental gladness that everything was so quiet and the men
generally so well-behaved. When he came to write up the visit for the
article 'On Strike' in *Household Words* (Feb. 11, 1854) there was overlaid
upon this first impression a certain horror at the idleness. He seemed to
be asking whether these were perhaps after all the lazy poor, in whose
existence he had never believed. The article describes the two meetings
of the strikers that he attended, and they are obviously the foundation
for the Union meeting in *Hard Times*: it stresses their order and courtesy,
the efficiency of the business and the competence of the men's local
leaders; it decries the influence of an outside orator who is a prototype of
Slackbridge; it makes clear that the men fully believed in the justice of
their case, but that, at the same time, they had no hatred or resentment
for most of the employers: it does, however, quote one example of a
threatening notice against a particular man, together with various
other placards and verses: the moral approval seems to be all on the side
of the strikers. But the political conclusion is not that the strike is right:

In any aspect in which it can be viewed, this strike and lock-out is a deplorable calamity. In its waste of time, in its waste of a great people's energy, in its waste of wages, in its waste of wealth that seeks to be employed, in its encroachment on the means of many thousands who are laboring from day to day, in the gulf of separation it hourly deepens between those whose interests must be understood to be identical or must be destroyed, it is a great national affliction. But, at this pass, anger is of no use, starving out is of no use—for what will that do, five years hence, but overshadow all the mills in England with the growth of a bitter remembrance?—political economy is a mere skeleton unless it has a little human covering and filling out, a little human bloom upon it, and a little human warmth in it.

The only practical suggestion is that the dispute should be submitted immediately to impartial arbitrators agreed upon by both sides. This paragraph is extremely important and interesting, because in it Dickens accepts the fundamental ethical and political proposition of the political economy he generally so much deplores. The interests of employers and employed must be assumed to be identical or must be destroyed. The doctrine of the identity of interests was common to the utilitarians and the economists: on the question of *theory* there is no real difference between Dickens and W. R. Greg:[2] he is not in the least a Socialist.

This paragraph also helps to explain why the satire of Mr Gradgrind is comparatively ineffective; for Dickens is not even intending to attack the whole philosophy which he thought was represented in the Manchester men; he is only attacking the excessive emphasis on statistics; in fact he is repeating Mr Filer over again, and he seems to have no uneasiness about whether such satire is adequate or important. He is through all these years, however, extremely uneasy in his attempts to find a channel through which the desires and needs of an ordinary decent working man like Blackpool can find expression. Why, when he recognised the capacity of such men for conducting their own business, did he reject the Trade Union solution, and reject it as emphatically as a Manchester man like Greg?

On the whole the 'Combinations' of the 'thirties and 'forties, whether organised locally, by trades, or nationally, had avowed revolutionary aims. The extent to which their members advocated the use of physical force was less important than the fact that they were widely believed to do so; but, physical force aside, they were revolutionary in the sense that they did not accept the doctrine of the natural identity of interests between Capital and Labour, and were in their political activities more or less conscious of a class-struggle; and this consciousness was shared by their opponents. The Chartist failure of '48 meant widespread disillusionment in the possibilities of working-class political action, and the reviving unions of the 'fifties concentrated more on the immediate problem of collective bargaining within particular trades than on the formation of huge amalgamations with political aims.[3] Dickens seems to have realised that this change was happening, but he shared two common popular misconceptions about it; the first was that the leaders of such unions were bound to be demagogic frauds like Gruffshaw and Slackbridge; and the second was that the unions were likely to violate liberty by being exclusive and tyrannical towards workers who refused to join them:[4] both points were heavily underlined in *Hard Times*. The first of these objections was a legacy from the earlier amalgamating, revolutionary period, and was very largely justified. For in the period of Chartism and the large national unions the working-class movement was grotesquely top-heavy and therefore unstable: the middle-class mistrust of 'demagogues' and 'paid agitators', whatever its motives may have been, was justified in the sense that national leadership had not developed out of solidly organised cells of local opinion. Local organisation even in the 'fifties was likely, as in the Preston strike, to be an *ad hoc* affair called into being by a particular dispute; and Dickens was faithful in his reporting, in 'On Strike', of the way that outside influence was likely to be overridden: but in *Hard Times* he regarded local opinion as dynamically inferior to Slackbridge's bluster: he meant to imply that Stephen was socially boycotted in spite of a predominating feeling in his favour, and the other workers bamboozled out of their better selves; and he made the distortion seem more serious by giving Stephen no better reason for not joining them than a mysterious promise. The objection to unions on the ground of exclusiveness and tyranny followed inevitably from the general misunderstanding of their nature: Dickens realised that when Stephen had been both boycotted by his fellow-workers and sacked by Bounderby he had no chance of getting another job; but he did not draw from this the conclusion that an individual worker *cannot* be the equal of an employer in bargaining power, and that the ideal bargaining for labour-price talked of by the economists only had any meaning when the bargaining was done by a unanimous combination. His emotional admiration for the conscientious blackleg was not based on any alternative argument. But he did not abandon all hope of finding some means other than the unions by which such men as Stephen might be politically and socially articulate; he was still groping after it later in the year in the address 'To Working Men' and the other articles on Public Health we have already discussed.

However, the failure of *Hard Times* in two main strands of its plot and in so many of its major characters does not lessen the force of the mixture of fascination and repulsion that Dickens felt for the industrial scene in which the book was set. The fascination, which appears in the descriptions of the night railway journey out from Coketown to

Bounderby's house, of the people surging to the mills in the morning, and returning at night to their various homes, has the interest in life and movement, which is plain everywhere in his work, heightened by greater speed and tension. The repulsion is generally more marked, as it is in the Black Country parts of *The Old Curiosity Shop*; the dismal appearance of the competing chapels, the rigidity of the Bounderby bank and the grim business discipline which intrudes on every detail even of domestic life, express once more the Southerner's dismay at what he could not assimilate; but underlying it there is unresting indignation at the impoverishment of human life that such things implied. This indignation is not crude and immature anger, but rather a disturbed mood that colours every perception, contributing a great deal to the unpopularity of *Hard Times*. The book is ultimately unsatisfying and oddly uncomfortable to nearly all its readers; but this very fact is the main thing that has to be considered in assessing its value as a novel; unanswerable disquiet was normal among the very few who were not misled into the easy optimism in which Bagehot typifies the 'fifties; Ruskin's exaggerated praise of *Hard Times* may be understood as a recognition that a work of art, by conveying this at least to others, might make up for many other imperfections; and even those writers whose economics and social criticism were more solid and thoughtful than Dickens's betray in their own ways shifting of opinion and misplacement of emphasis—Mill, Ruskin, and Arnold are examples—which equally, express the practical embarrassment of the time.

SOURCE: extract from *The Dickens World* (Oxford, 1941; paperback edn, 1960), pp. 204–11.

NOTES

1. Ruskin's judgement that Bounderby was merely a 'dramatic monster, instead of a characteristic example of a worldly master' is probably more or less true if we assume Coketown to be Manchester and Bounderby a man of the local prominence that Dickens gives him. But if Coketown was some smaller place, a monster of that kind might well have got such power over its life. Mr and Mrs Hammond have, for instance, found a possible original (*Town Labourer*, p. 302): 'P——d, the Beggar-maker, who sits on the destinies of the Poor, we have made a Man of him, whose Mother hawked about the Streets a small Basket; on two Spinners being deputed to ask for a small advance of Price, had the audacity to thrust one of them from him with an Umbrella and discharged them both' (Letter from Committee of Manchester Weavers, 1823, *Home Office Papers*, 40, p. 18). Such a man might well have grown into Bounderby by the 'fifties. .

2. See especially Greg's long review of *Mary Barton*, of 1849, reprinted in *Mistaken Aims and Attainable Ideals of the Artizan Class* (1876), and his *English Socialism*, of 1850. Both essays are directed against the impatient philanthropy of 'feeling' as compared with the long-distance philanthropy of the economists. The cures for labour disputes are that the working class should be more provident and should, by the study of political economy, realise the necessary identity of their interests with those of the employers.

3. The Amalgamated Society of Engineers, for instance, was founded in 1851, and played a very important part in the development of Unionism in the next twenty years.

4. Even Kingsley, when calling himself a Socialist, wrote to a Manchester friend, March 28, 1856: 'I admire your boldness in lifting up your voice to expose the tyranny of "Union" Strikes. From my own experience of demagogues . . . I can well believe every word you say as to the "humbug" connected with the inner working of them.'

John Butt and *Kathleen Tillotson*
The Problems of a Weekly Serial (1957)

I

HOUSEHOLD WORDS had been running for some eighteen months when *Bleak House* was completed at the end of August 1853. While Dickens was engaged with his book he had no time to write anything for his magazine more substantial than articles; but once the book was out of the way, he could listen to the persuasions of Forster, Bradbury and Evans, and Wills. 'There is such a fixed idea on the part of my printers and copartners in *Household Words*, that a story of me, continued from week to week, would make some unheard of effect with it that I am going to write one'; so he told Miss Coutts on 23 January 1854.[1] The decision had been taken some time earlier, however. On 20 January he sent Forster a list of fourteen titles for 'the *Household Words* story', begging him to look at them 'between this and two o'clock or so, when I will call. It is my usual day, you observe, on which I have jotted them down—Friday! It seems to me that there are three very good ones among them. I should like to know whether you hit upon the same.'[2] Though he had not yet set himself to write, it would seem that he had already discussed the theme of the novel with Forster; for if he had not,

he could scarcely have expected Forster to choose between titles for a
single story so strictly committing as these: *According to Cocker, Prove it,
Stubborn Things, Mr Gradgrind's Facts, The Grindstone, Hard Times, Two
and Two are Four, Something Tangible, Our Hard-headed Friend, Rust and
Dust, Simple Arithmetic, A Matter of Calculation, A Mere Question of Figures,
The Gradgrind Philosophy*.

These rejected titles and those in the manuscript—*Fact, Hard-headed
Gradgrind, Hard Heads and Soft Hearts, Heads and Tales, Black and White*—
remain of interest, since they seem to indicate the limits within which
the book would move. The irony implicit in *Something Tangible, A Matter
of Calculation*, and *A Mere Question of Figures* suggests that the novel will
open up areas of experience beyond the reach of Mr Gradgrind's
philosophy, and the importance of feelings, disregarded by the political
economists, is represented in *Hard Heads and Soft Hearts*, while *Heads and
Tales* seems to forecast the opposition of fact and fancy so prominent in
the scenes at Sleary's Circus troupe. These titles show that the story
would appropriately appear in the columns of *Household Words*, whose
policy Dickens had defined in an initial address (30 March 1850):

. . . No mere utilitarian spirit, no iron binding of the mind to grim realities, will
give a harsh tone to our *Household Words*. In the bosoms of the young and old, of
the well-to-do and of the poor, we would tenderly cherish that light of Fancy
which is inherent in the human breast; which, according to its nurture, burns
with an inspiring flame, or sinks into a sullen glare, but which (or woe betide
that day!) can never be extinguished.

The same day on which he consulted Forster about the title, Dickens sat
down to plan the book. On a sheet of paper preserved in the manuscript
he wrote first the date and then a memorandum on quantity, which
reads as follows:

One sheet (16 pages of Bleak House) will make 10 pages and a quarter of
Household Words. Fifteen pages of my writing, will make a sheet of Bleak
House.
A page and a half of my writing, will make a page of Household Words.
The Quantity of the story to be published weekly, being about five pages of
Household Words, will require about seven pages and a half of my writing.

and at the head of the first number plan he has, subsequently, written:
'Write and calculate the story in the old monthly N^os.'

These calculations conceal the real difficulty. They amount to saying
that one monthly number is the equivalent of four weeklies; but they do
not emphasise that the weekly number is now the unit, and that within
its brief limits characters must be presented, background sketched, and
atmosphere created. A monthly number of thirty-two pages had been a

convenient unit for two or three episodes; one or two episodes had now to be related in the equivalent of eight pages. It is no wonder that Dickens found himself hampered. In February he wrote to Forster:

The difficulty of the space is CRUSHING. Nobody can have an idea of it who has not had an experience of patient fiction-writing with some elbow-room always, and open places in perspective. In this form, with any kind of regard to the current number, there is absolutely no such thing.[3]

The sense of this restriction never left him: 'I am in a dreary state,' he told Wills on 18 April, 'planning and planning the story of *Hard Times* (out of materials for I don't know how long a story)'[4] and in the end he was forced to enlarge his weekly stints to ten pages of his manuscript.[5]

But though the difficulties of the weekly number exasperated him, and though there is reason to suppose that some material was forcibly excluded, there is no doubt that Dickens was able to adapt his manner to the new conditions, and it might be argued that the discipline was good for him. The necessary shortness of the chapters is matched by an economy in detail, noticeable throughout the novel and especially obvious if the opening chapters of *Hard Times* are compared with the opening chapters of *Bleak House*. It is appropriate, no doubt, that the symbolical fog of *Bleak House* should be more leisurely presented than the symbolical fact of *Hard Times*; but it is difficult to believe that in any monthly novel Dickens would have been content with those mere eight but sufficient words which set the scene, 'a plain, bare, monotonous vault of a schoolroom'. The initial description of Mr Gradgrind's square appearance is conveyed in a traditional manner, but it is considerably shorter than the initial descriptions of Sir Leicester Dedlock and Mr Tulkinghorn in *Bleak House*, chapter ii; and more remarkable still, both in economy and in power, is the symbolically contrasting appearance of Sissy Jupe and Bitzer as the sunlight plays upon them:

whereas the girl was so dark-eyed and dark-haired, that she seemed to receive a deeper and more lustrous colour from the sun, when it shone upon her, the boy was so light-eyed and light-haired that the self-same rays appeared to draw out of him what little colour he ever possessed. His cold eyes would hardly have been eyes, but for the short ends of lashes which, by bringing them into immediate contrast with something paler than themselves, expressed their form. His short-cropped hair might have been a mere continuation of the sandy freckles on his forehead and face. His skin was so unwholesomely deficient in the natural tinge, that he looked as though, if he were cut, he would bleed white.

It is not merely that Bitzer's body has been deprived by Coketown smoke of the life-giving sun, or that his mind has been repressed by a lifeless education, but that he is emptier and shallower than Sissy; there is no depth to him. The monthly novels are not without comparable moments. The juxtaposition of Miss Flite and the young wards at the end of *Bleak House*, chapter iii, is equally well contrived, she suitably enough at the *bottom* of the steep, broad flight of stairs, they looking down upon her, and her words are equally powerful to suggest more than they say,

> 'Youth. And hope. And beauty. And Chancery. And Conversation Kenge! Ha! Pray accept my blessing!'

This, however, is only a small part of a much larger episode. It lacks the rounded completeness of the scene in *Hard Times*.

But though Dickens recognised how his manner required adapting to weekly presentation, he was also determined to 'write and calculate the story in the old monthly N^{os}'. This is shown not only by the memorandum but by the whole appearance of the manuscript. In it the novel is divided into five monthly parts, each separately foliated as his custom was when writing a monthly serial, and each represented by a separate number plan. The first of these makes clear that after deciding what shall happen during the month he arranged this material in chapters before distributing the chapters into weekly issues. He evidently felt the need to see these chapters grouped into units larger than a weekly number, even though the monthly unit could not force itself upon the reader's attention and might not even be apparent to him. These larger monthly units would serve as stages by which to measure the progress made and the distance still to be covered. Thus the opening words of chapter viii, the last of the first monthly 'part'—'Let us strike the key-note again, before pursuing the tune'—seem to indicate that the exposition is completed; and the ending of the second 'part' with Louisa Gradgrind's marriage to Bounderby, the third with Stephen Blackpool leaving Coketown, and the fourth with the breakdown of Louisa's marriage, all mark important stages completed in the development of the story.

Though the reader may appreciate the completion of the stage without observing that a monthly 'part' is completed also, his attention is called to still larger movements in the story by the division of the novel into 'books'. The device had frequently been used since its adoption from the epic by Fielding in *Joseph Andrews*. But Dickens had not hitherto employed it.[6] Perhaps he had taken notice of Thackeray's refinement in *Esmond* (1852) of not merely numbering his books, as the custom was, but of naming them. The second number plan of *Hard Times* shows him considering this device ('republish in 3 books?/1. Sowing/2. Reaping/3. Garnering'). By then it was perhaps too late to adopt it in serial publication: we do not know whether the first weekly issue, without an indication of book number, was already in print when the second monthly 'part' was under consideration. But the notion was kept in mind, and when the novel was reissued in volume form it was divided into books with the titles already determined, the divisions coinciding with what had been the end of the second and fourth monthly 'parts'.

Of earlier novels, only *Dombey and Son* lends itself to a similar division, with well-marked stages reached at the end of Number v (the death of Paul), Number x (Mr Dombey's second marriage), and Number xv (the flight of Florence). But from *Hard Times* onwards each novel, except for *Edwin Drood*, is divided into books even in the serial issues. This is further evidence of the attention which Dickens was now paying to construction. He was quite justified in telling Carlyle that *Hard Times* was 'constructed . . . patiently, with a view to its publication altogether in a compact cheap form'.[7]

II

Dickens's first purpose was to establish the dominion of Fact and of its high priest, Mr Gradgrind. The draft titles show that Mr Gradgrind was to be the representative of a theory. It is therefore appropriate that he should first appear in his own school impressing his theories upon the rising generation, who will show the effect of his teaching as the story develops.

Although Dickens had settled upon the name, opinions, and perhaps the nature of his principal character before beginning to write, he was still undetermined about his supporters. Mr Gradgrind was to have two children—the first number plan specifies 'Louisa Gradgrind' and 'Young Thomas'—who would doubtless exist to disappoint him in different ways; but whether his wife was still alive was not yet decided. Dickens was evidently tempted to produce another repellent widower with a sister in attendance, as Miss Murdstone had attended upon Mr Murdstone, and Mrs Chick upon Mr Dombey. The number plan shows his purpose settling: 'Mrs Gradgrind—or Miss? Wife or Sister? <u>Wife.</u>' Having fixed upon that, he turned to consider the remainder of the household:

Any little Gradgrinds?

Say 3.   Adam Smith ⎫
          Malthus   ⎬ no parts to play
          Jane   ⎭

Jane Gradgrind is later to play a small, yet not unimportant, part; and
Mrs Gradgrind is to become one more of Dickens's ineffectual mothers,
closer in type to Mrs Matthew Pocket in the future than to Mrs
Nickleby in the past. Her entry is carefully timed—postponed from
chapter iii

Mrs Gradgrind—badly done transparency, with not enough light behind it. No
not yet

to chapter iv ('Now, Mrs Gradgrind'). No member of his household
could have had less effect upon Mr Gradgrind or upon his children, and
that was perhaps the reason that she displaced the sister in Dickens's
choice: she serves to emphasise more powerfully than any sister that Mr
Gradgrind alone influenced the course of his children's career.

Gradgrind is to be recognised not only in his house and family, but
also by the company he keeps. He is seen in school with a representative
of the Department of Practical Art, who in his determination to remove
flowers from the design of carpets and foreign birds and butterflies from
the design of crockery, is as anxious as Gradgrind to submit the
imagination to the chains of fact and real circumstance. But the
representative of the Department of Practical Art has served a limited
purpose by the end of chapter ii, and no more is seen of him.[8]

Much more prominent among Gradgrind's friends is Josiah
Bounderby, for whose appearance the reader's expectations are raised
at the end of the first weekly number (chapter iii). 'What would Mr
Bounderby say?' cried Mr Gradgrind on finding his elder children
peeping through a hole in the circus tent. But Dickens himself had not
pronounced the name with equal confidence when meditating his
number: 'What will Mr Bound say?' is the version on the number plan
(and in the manuscript of chapter iii), subsequently altered to
'Bounder' and finally to 'Bounderby'. Dickens may already have
known his man; certainly the very next entry on the number plan shows
that he knew what parts he was to play ('Mr Bounderby, the Bully of
humility. Dawn of Bounderby and Louisa'), and in their partnership
Gradgrind supplies the ethos of heartless calculation in which
Bounderby can oppress the Coketown operatives; but the momentary
hesitation over his name shows that Bounderby was not so prominent in
Dickens's scheme as Gradgrind.

A final entry on the first number plan points to Gradgrind's third
associate: 'The man who, being utterly sensual and careless, comes to
very much the same thing in the end as the Gradgrind school? Not yet.'

This was James Harthouse, who is not introduced until the third month. He is a young man of good family who had found army and diplomatic life a bore, and had now been persuaded by an elder brother in Parliament to 'go in' for statistics, make a place for himself amongst the 'hard Fact fellows', and canvass one of the industrial seats. Finding Coketown as much of a bore as the army and the diplomatic service, he whiles away his time there by attempting to seduce Louisa Bounderby. If Dickens had already foreseen this rôle, it is surprising that he should have contemplated introducing Harthouse in the first month, since he could not perform his function in the plot until Bounderby and Louisa were married. A possible explanation is that Dickens, with his mind on the fable, needed Harthouse as a supporter to Gradgrind; but recognising that Harthouse could best be employed as a seducer of Louisa, he permitted the requirements of the fable to give place temporarily to the requirements of the plot.

Bounderby also has his supporter. Just as Captain Cuttle is incomplete without Mrs MacStinger and Captain Bunsby, and Mr Toots without the Game Chicken, so Bounderby is incomplete without Mrs Sparsit. The distance he has reached from the humblest origins, born in a ditch and abandoned by his mother, is most readily measured by his now employing as a housekeeper this lady of seemingly the highest family connexions. But Mrs Sparsit's aristocratic connexions are of doubtful authenticity, and so are Bounderby's origins. The reader is left to guess this and merely to suspect that the eminently respectable countrywoman, Mrs Pegler, is betraying a suspiciously maternal interest in a most unlovable mill-owner. Dickens is already preparing the ground for the scene of Bounderby's exposure, or rather of his deflation, for at his first appearance he is seen to have

> a great puffed head and forehead, swelling veins in his temples, and such a strained skin to his face that it seemed to hold his eyes open, and lift his eyebrows up. A man with a pervading appearance on him of being inflated like a balloon, and ready to start. [ch. iv]

But though all but the most unsophisticated reader can see that a rich retribution is in store for Bounderby, this assumption of humility on his part and of gentility on Mrs Sparsit's serves a more immediate purpose. Here at the very centre of the dominion of Fact are people indulging in Fancy, a peculiarly repulsive Fancy maybe, but Fancy still. Here, in the punning of one of the rejected titles, is a man proud of his head but flourishing his tale. This apposition of Fact and Fancy is forcibly presented throughout the first three weekly parts. The young Gradgrinds have been brought up on Fact, but when we first meet them they are contriving to satisfy their starved Fancy by peeping through a hole in a circus tent. Coketown too is 'Fact, fact, fact, everywhere in the material aspect of the town; fact, fact, fact, everywhere in the immaterial'; but in an obscure corner of Coketown, Fancy is ensconced in the shape of a circus. The district is so obscure that Mr Gradgrind and Mr Bounderby, like two evil characters in *The Pilgrim's Progress*, do not know where to find it and are forced to enlist the help of the clown's daughter. The circus people are lodged at an inn named, in a suitable frolic of Fancy, the Pegasus's Arms, and are expert in all sorts of fanciful behaviour, in dancing upon rolling casks, standing upon bottles, catching knives and balls, twirling hand-basins, and dancing upon the slack wire and the tight-rope. But for all that they are the salt of the earth:

> there was a remarkable gentleness and childishness about these people, a special inaptitude for any kind of sharp practice, and an untiring readiness to help and pity one another, deserving often of as much respect, and always of as much generous construction, as the every-day virtues of any class of people in the world.

And their leader, Mr Sleary, has a philosophy adapted to the world of Fancy just as Mr Gradgrind's is adapted to the world of Fact:

> 'People must be amuthed, Thquire, thomehow,' continued Sleary, rendered more pursy than ever, by so much talking; 'they can't be alwayth a working, nor yet they can't be alwayth a learning. Make the betht of uth; not the wurtht. I've got my living out of the horthe-riding all my life, I know; but I conthider that I lay down the philothophy of the thubject when I thay to you, Thquire, make the betht of uth: not the wurtht!' [ch. vi]

This is the milieu from which Sissy comes to be an inmate of the Gradgrind household, there to be educated in Mr Gradgrind's system. It is some measure of the man's inherent goodness that he receives her as an inmate. He is redeemable, and the course of the novel shows that he will be redeemed by Sissy. He fails to educate her head, but she succeeds in educating his heart.

III

Within a week of setting to work, Dickens had paid a visit to Preston.

The Lancashire towns had been suffering from a succession of strikes, and *The Times* had kept its readers fully informed about them by frequent reports, leading articles, and correspondence. The Preston strike, which had begun in the summer, had been especially stubborn. Forster relates that the choice of subject for *Hard Times* made Dickens anxious to observe it at first hand; but he was disappointed, and reported to Forster 'I am afraid I shall not be able to get much here'.[9] If his intention had ever been to introduce a strike into the novel, he changed his mind and recorded his resolution in a letter (21 April) to Mrs Gaskell, who was also at work on an industrial novel and interested in avoiding an overlap:

I have no intention of striking. The monstrous claims at domination made by a certain class of manufacturers, and the extent to which the way is made easy for working men to slide down into discontent under such hands, are within my scheme; but I am not going to strike.[10]

If a strike was ever entertained, the decision not to strike must have been taken early. The only position for a strike in the novel as we have it would have been in the second or the third month; a strike could have made no difference to the course of the plot or to the relations of the principal characters; but the number plans never canvass the possibility. They are not even concerned with industrial unrest. 'Mill Pictures' are indeed mentioned, and Bounderby's slander upon the operatives is rehearsed ('Turtle and Venison & a gold spoon. "That's what the Hands want Sir!"—'); but the subject of principal importance here is 'Law of Divorce' and the name of the sufferer, first 'John Prodge?' then in succession 'Stephen? George? old Stephen?' and eventually, the notion of martyrdom winning approval, 'Stephen Blackpool'. Another memorandum keeps Harthouse in mind but still defers his entry ('Man of Nº 1?—Not yet'). These are the principal memoranda; the others remind him to 'carry on' Tom, Louisa, and Sissy, the last designated as 'Power of affection'.

The weekly numbers in the second month confirm this impression. Four of the eight chapters, ix, xiv, and the whole of the eighth weekly number, are devoted to the children: Sissy, a mere child in matters of political economy and statistics but uttering such wisdom as is given only to babes and sucklings, and ingratiating herself so effectively with the family that Mr Gradgrind, though disappointed in her development, freely admits that she is 'an affectionate, earnest, good young woman—and—and we must make that do'; Tom selfishly pressing Louisa upon Bounderby; Louisa coldly accepting Bounderby's proposal made through her father, and eliciting from Sissy a look of wonder, pity, sorrow, and doubt.

The remaining four chapters 'open the Law of Divorce', in the words of the number plan.[11] The Matrimonial Causes Act came into force three years after the novel was written, and permitted a husband to obtain a decree in a divorce court on the ground of his wife's adultery. Hitherto a divorce could only be obtained by Act of Parliament, and was therefore so expensive as to lie beyond a poor man's reach: Bounderby in fact reckoned it to cost 'from a thousand to fifteen hundred pound. Perhaps twice the money'. The plight of the poor man is depicted in Stephen's interview with Bounderby and in the two subsequent chapters which illustrate Stephen's married life. It is a plea for greater latitude than the Act of 1857 was to permit. Stephen's wife may have been an adulteress, but more emphasis is laid upon her habitual drunkenness, a condition chosen perhaps because it permits a more harrowing scene of martyrdom to be displayed. As for Bounderby and Mrs Sparsit, they are not merely scandalised by Stephen's wish to be free to marry again, but they point out that the law cannot help such as Stephen is. There is one law for the rich and one for the poor. If Dickens had in mind at this stage to point the contrast between Stephen and Bounderby, he takes no pains to press it upon the reader. Bounderby is not yet married to Louisa, and the time is still far ahead— twenty chapters, in fact—when Bounderby, like Stephen, will feel that he 'mun be ridded o' her', and will take the law into his own hands by returning Louisa to her father. The ironic foreshadowing of an event is characteristic of Dickens's art at this period, but there is no premonition in chapter xi of the power which Bounderby will possess over his wife but which Stephen does not possess, and in chapter iii of Book III he offers no reminder of chapter xi of Book I. A novelist so adept at linking his episodes is unlikely to have overlooked such a favourable opportunity of pointing at least one of the morals in his story. It is more probable that the crushing demands of the weekly serial compelled him to leave it out.

The Law of Divorce is 'opened' in Weekly Number VI (chapters xi and xii). It is not until Weekly Number XI that Dickens approaches the question of industrial unrest. In the first chapter of that number [Bk II, ch. iv] we find the 'hands' assembled to listen to the popular leader, Slackbridge. 'Stephen won't join', adds the number plan, 'and is sent to Coventry'. Here without doubt Dickens was drawing upon his Preston experiences, for he had attended just such a meeting and had noted the attitude of the strikers as they listened to a delegate from another district. He was inevitably contributing to the knowledge of his south-country readers in describing the scene, and he was also exercising their sympathies for the Lancashire operatives both here and in other scenes where the Coketown landscape is described; but he made little attempt to discuss the problems of industrial unrest. In fact he scarcely went beyond the comments of *The Times* reporter who, in an article of 8 November 1853, found in the Preston operatives 'a certain rough vigour and independence of thought and feeling which one cannot help respecting', and blamed the masters 'for a generally stern and unbending demeanour towards their operatives, which freezes their sympathy, and lays the groundwork for constant suspicion and occasional violent ruptures, like the present'. These characteristics are exhibited in Bk II, ch. v, the second chapter of Weekly Number XI, where Stephen expounds 'the Slackbridge question' (in the words of the number plan) to an unsympathetic Bounderby, who proceeds to discharge him. Stephen's exposition is certainly rough, vigorous, and independent, but it contributes little to the problem and perhaps was not intended to contribute much. Why Stephen was sent to Coventry by his fellows we are not informed—perhaps there was insufficient space to offer a reason; it is enough that he suffers a further degree of martyrdom by first adopting an independent line and then defending it before Bounderby. That is the limited service of this theme; Coketown with its troubles is merely the purgatory in which individuals suffer. After a scene in which Tom Gradgrind projects his robbery of Bounderby's bank and arranges for suspicion to fall upon Stephen, Dickens provides (in the words of the number plan) a 'Morning picture of Stephen going away from Coketown out of the cruel ashes on to the country dust'. So ends the twelfth weekly and the third monthly number, and at that point Stephen and the industrial theme walk out of the novel until Weekly Number XIX.

IV

Meanwhile Dickens was occupied in developing that much-favoured theme, the education of the heart. At the beginning of the third month [Bk II, ch. i], Bounderby has set up house in the country with Louisa,[12] and the stage is set in the number plans for the destruction of this nominal marriage:

Mrs Sparsit's life at the Bank?   Yes

Bitzer, Light Porter   Yes

Tom's Progress   Yes

Louisa's married life—Dawn of knowledge of her immaterial self—Too late   Scarcely yet.

Man dropped in Nº 1?   Yes.   Percy Harthouse
                                Jem
                                James

Here are the means by which Louisa will return to her father's home at the end of the fourth month [Bk II, ch. xii], and say to him

> 'I do not know that I am sorry, I do not know that I am ashamed, I do not know that I am degraded in my own esteem. All that I know is, your philosophy and your teaching will not save me. Now, father, you have brought me to this. Save me by some other means.'

The movement in the third month is somewhat slow. One weekly number and much of another had to be devoted to Stephen's isolation; but two entries on the number plan suggest some infirmity of purpose

Lover for Sissy?   <u>No. Decide on no love at all</u>

Sissy and Rachael to become acquainted?   <u>No.</u>

and the time to show the 'dawn of knowledge' of Louisa's 'immaterial self' was deemed to be not yet ripe. In the event Dickens did little more during this month than establish Harthouse in a convenient relationship with Tom Gradgrind, and place Mrs Sparsit and Bitzer in a strategic position to watch what is to come.

The stream of action moves rapidly once more in the fourth month and reaches the climax at the end of the sixteenth weekly number without apparent hesitation. We should have suspected none had it not been for the number plan. The first three entries for the fourth month are confirmatory:

Tom to rob Bounderby?   <u>Yes</u>

Louisa to be acted on by Harthouse, through Tom?   <u>Yes</u>

<u>Louisa's danger slowly drawn about her.   Yes.</u>

Since these plans had already been sketched in the previous month, the entries here can only mean that now was the time to put them into force. But the following entries betray some doubt where else the course of the story might stray during this important month:

<u>Sissy?   No?</u>
Rachael?

Bring her with Louisa again?   <u>No.</u>

Stephen?   <u>No</u>

It is not surprising that Sissy, whose healing powers will prove so valuable, should be passed in review at this point, though reflection must soon have shown that her time was not yet;[13] and to consider at least a passing reference to a now distant Stephen is equally understandable. But that there should ever have been a question of bringing Rachael to Louisa in her distress seems to imply some doubt of the final issue of Louisa's actions which the firm control of the narrative denies. A visit from Rachael before Louisa's flight could only have been distracting, for it is essential that Tom and Harthouse alone have power to direct the course she takes. A visit to Rachael after the flight, or even a chance encounter, could only have delayed the inevitable return to Mr Gradgrind with its decisive effect upon his belief in his system. Though we cannot tell how long these entries were deliberated, their rejection would seem to have been inevitable, and the remaining entries return to the heart of the action:

To show Louisa, how alike in their creeds, her father and Harthouse are?—How the two heartless things come to the same in the end?
                    Yes,   But almost imperceptibly.
Louisa
        'You have brought me to this, father.   Now, save me!'

Louisa is therefore to be denied such guidance as Sissy or as Rachael (another fount of affectionate guidance) might have offered in a matter where the heart must decide. Tom had been the subject of all the little tenderness of her life;[14] Harthouse had used Tom to gain her confidence and having gained it had shown that he recognised the emptiness of her marriage. Louisa is to be reduced by degrees to a situation in which she can bear her marriage no longer; she seeks refuge in flight, and returns a broken creature to her father's house. Weekly instalments were desperately short for representing these degrees; and to help us in recognising them, Dickens offers his readers almost apologetically the image of Mrs Sparsit's staircase:

> Now, Mrs Sparsit was not a poetical woman; but she took an idea in the nature of an allegorical fancy, into her head. Much watching of Louisa, and much consequent observation of her impenetrable demeanour, which keenly whetted and sharpened Mrs Sparsit's edge, must have given her as it were a lift, in the way of inspiration. She erected in her mind a mighty Staircase, with a dark pit of shame and ruin at the bottom; and down those stairs, from day to day and hour to hour, she saw Louisa coming.
>
> It became the business of Mrs Sparsit's life, to look up at her staircase, and to watch Louisa coming down. Sometimes slowly,

sometimes quickly, sometimes several steps at one bout, sometimes stopping, never turning back. If she had once turned
back, it might have been the death of Mrs Sparsit in spleen and
grief. [Bk 2, ch. x]

Mrs Sparsit, so often likened to a bird of prey, is an appropriate observer
of this gradual descent, and the arrangement by which the reader views
the relationship of Louisa and Harthouse through her eyes is admirably
managed, for while he relishes her misapprehension of it, he is
prevented from regarding it as a romance.

Yet there is something ambiguous in the relationship. Louisa is
attracted to Harthouse, and in her final confession to her father she finds
herself unable to say whether or not she loves him. Those 'almost
imperceptible' steps by which Dickens hoped to show her recognition of
the identity of Harthouse's and Gradgrind's creeds are difficult to
discover. Were they too jettisoned because the difficulties of space were
crushing? The equation of Harthouse with Gradgrind suggested in the
number plan is neither clear nor satisfactory.[15] He is closer to
Bounderby. Gradgrind is honestly persuaded of the truth of his system,
and for him there is hope as the next monthly part will show; but
Bounderby and Harthouse merely use the system for their own ends,
and for them there is no hope.

                                    v

The fifth month is co-extensive with the third and last book named
'Garnering'. Gradgrind, of whom little has been seen, except in the last
chapter, during the two previous months, is now to return to the centre
of the action. He was first observed at the beginning of the novel
impressing the system upon the rising generation; it is time to see how
the system has worked. The reader has been made fully aware of its
failure both in Louisa and in Tom, and in that premonitory scene of Mrs
Gradgrind's death he has received some hint of another force at work in
Stone Lodge during Mr Gradgrind's absence; but it is only in the last
chapter of the fourth month [Bk II, ch. xii], when he sees Louisa 'the
pride of his heart and the triumph of his system, lying, an insensible
heap, at his feet' that Gradgrind himself begins to recognise the failure
and its cause. The requirements of the weekly serial[16] ensure that the
recognition is both swift and clear. Gradgrind meets his daughter the
morning after her return, and confides to her:

'It would be hopeless for me, Louisa, to endeavour to tell you
how overwhelmed I have been, and still am, by what broke

upon me last night. The ground on which I stand has ceased to
be solid under my feet. The only support on which I leaned, and
the strength of which it seemed, and still does seem, impossible
to question, has given way in an instant. I am stunned by these
discoveries. I have no selfish meaning in what I say; but I find
the shock of what broke upon me last night, to be very heavy
indeed.'

and later in the same chapter:

'Louisa, I have a misgiving that some change may have been
slowly working about me in this house, by mere love and
gratitude: that what the Head has left undone and could not do,
the Heart may have been doing silently . . .'

Of course it had. The reader, who has previously seen what 'the Heart'
had done even for Mrs Gradgrind, has already noticed its effect upon
Jane Gradgrind, or rather has seen its effect through Louisa's eyes:

'What a beaming face you have, Jane!' said Louisa, as her young
sister—timidly still—bent down to kiss her.
'Have I? I am very glad you think so. I am sure it must be
Sissy's doing.'

Of course it is; and before the chapter is over, Sissy, the representative of
'the Heart', has begun to exert her influence over Louisa too:

'Forgive me, pity me, help me! Have compassion on my great
need, and let me lay this head of mine upon a loving heart!'
'O lay it here!' cried Sissy. 'Lay it here, my dear.' [Bk 3,
ch. i]

The remaining chapter of Weekly Number XVII [Bk III, ch. ii]
completes the victory of Heart over Head, or at least is so intended.
Sissy, like Jack the Giant-killer, goes resolutely forth to dispose of James
Harthouse and succeeds in touching him 'in the cavity where his heart
should have been'. Both Harthouse and the reader agree that it is 'very
ridiculous' that a stroller's child should succeed in evicting a parliamentary candidate from his prospective constituency; but that is how things
happen in fairy tales, and Dickens could never entirely resist the
satisfaction of giving the victory over the forces of evil to the children of
light. Another consideration might also have influenced him. If, as he
supposed he had made clear, Gradgrind and Harthouse were alike in
their creeds, it was appropriate that Sissy, who had penetrated

Gradgrind's complacency, should succeed in wounding Harthouse also.

After the scene to which reference has already been made, where Bounderby repudiates his marriage with Louisa, the story returns to the robbery of the bank, and therefore to the suspected Stephen and his reappearance, and to Tom the real culprit.[17] The suspense—'Still no Stephen' is thrice repeated in the number plans—is admirably contrived.[18] It is not merely a question of what can have happened to Stephen. That is perplexing enough when the bills have been posted offering Twenty Pounds reward for the apprehension of a man whom the reader knows to be innocent, and of whose innocence many characters in the story are convinced. But his disappearance has also an important bearing upon Tom. The reader knows him to be guilty, Louisa and Sissy darkly suspect his guilt, but as yet their suspicions are not shared by Mr Gradgrind, who does not therefore recognise what further humiliations may be in store for him.

Stephen's discovery is presented in one of Dickens's most allegorically lurid scenes. His hat is found by Rachael and Sissy at the mouth of an abandoned mineshaft. The faith and hope of Rachael are insufficient and she gives him up as lost, but Sissy's charity is equal to the situation; she controls Rachael, and fetches help. After several hours, Stephen is brought to the surface, still alive, and makes a dying statement before the large throng which has collected in the torchlight. It seems that he had set out immediately to vindicate his innocence, had taken the nearest cross-country route to Bounderby's villa, and had fallen down Old Hell Shaft, a mine whose foul air had formerly killed many who worked in it:

> 'When it were in work,' [Stephen comments,] 'it killed wi'out need; when 'tis let alone it kills wi'out need. See how we die an' no need, one way an' another—in a muddle—every day!'

He had begun his journey in anger with Louisa and Tom for plotting against him as he thought; but while in Hell a star shone down upon him ('I thowt it were the star as guided to our Saviour's home'), and by its light he saw more clearly and therefore more charitably, making it his dying prayer

> 'that aw th'world may on'y coom toogether more, an' get a better unnerstan'in o' one another, than when I were in 't my own weak seln;'

and commending Mr Gradgrind to clear his name—'Yor son will tell yo how', the martyr dies with the appropriate reflection (picked out in the number plan) 'in our judgments, like as in our doins, we mun bear and forbear'.

The utter failure of his system has its physical effect upon Mr Gradgrind, as a similar failure had had upon Mr Dombey: 'aged and bent he looked, and quite bowed down; and yet he looked a wiser man, and a better man, than in the days when in this life he wanted nothing but Facts' [Bk III, ch. vii]. But the system does not invariably fail, and almost as appalling as its failure is its success. Tom is to be smuggled abroad through the agency of Sleary and his circus troupe, and all is going well with their plans when Bitzer appears and arrests the culprit. We have now come full circle. In the first weekly number, the reader had seen Bitzer a model pupil returning model answers to Mr Gradgrind's questions; now in the last number Bitzer is 'true to his bringing up', as the number plan remarks, and once more returns model answers to the questions put to him:

'Bitzer,' said Mr Gradgrind, broken down, and miserably submissive to him, 'have you a heart?'

'The circulation, Sir,' returned Bitzer, smiling at the oddity of the question, 'couldn't be carried on without one. No man, Sir, acquainted with the facts established by Harvey relating to the circulation of the blood, can doubt that I have a heart.'

'Is it accessible,' cried Mr Gradgrind, 'to any compassionate influence?'

'It is accessible to Reason, Sir,' returned the excellent young man. 'And to nothing else.'

In response to a final appeal to the sense of gratitude for schooling received, Bitzer dismisses this 'untenable position' with the comment that his schooling was paid for and the bargain ended when he left. Dickens's point is made; but he cannot leave a dying story like that, and he cannot consent to the further punishment of a reforming character. Besides, Gradgrind in his unreformed days had taken pity upon Sissy and now he is to garner the reward which, by her presence in his house, he had already begun to reap. 'The Thquire thtood by you, Thethilia,' says Sleary, 'and I'll thtand by the Thquire'; Sleary knows a trick worth two of Bitzer's, and Tom escapes.

It is the end, except for that dip into the characters' future with which Dickens always assuages the curiosity of his readers. But before the epilogue is reached, he gives the last word to Mr Sleary, who had had to apologise on a previous occasion for being 'too muth of a Cackler'. The payment which he accepts for services rendeřd is altogether appropriate. It was a fundamental principle of the Gradgrind philosophy that everything was to be paid for; and Mr Gradgrind pays. Five pounds, it is true, went to Mr Childers, who had assisted Tom's escape; but Childers was a family man, and the money 'mightn't be unactheptable'. Apart from that, the philosopher of Fact 'very willingly undertook' to stand a collar for the dog, 'a thet of bellth for the horthe', brandy and water for Mr Sleary, and 'a little thpread for the company'. After so willingly paying in kind, and agreeing, it would seem, to 'give a Hortheriding, a bethpeak' whenever he could, the exponent of calculable Fact has to listen to a tale about the instinct of the faithful dog Merrylegs, and we can readily accept his giving tacit assent to the moral which Mr Sleary sees in the depths of his brandy and water:

> 'one, that there ith a love in the world, not all Thelf-interetht after all, but thomething very different; t'other, that it hath a way of ith own of calculating or not calculating, whith thomehow or another ith at leatht ath hard to give a name to, ath the wayth of the dogth ith!'

What remains for this brandy-sodden Fairy Queen to do but to pronounce a benediction and repeat the philosophy of fancy:

> 'People muth be amuthed. They can't be alwayth a learning, nor yet they can't be alwayth a working, they an't made for it. You *mutht* have uth, Thquire. Do the withe thing and the kind thing too, and make the betht of uth; not the wurtht!'

Source: extract from *Dickens at Work* (London, 1957), pp. 201–21.

NOTES

1. Walter Dexter (ed.), *Letters of Charles Dickens* (London, 1938), II, p. 537.
2. Ibid.
3. *Letters*, II, p. 543.
4. *Letters*, II, p. 551.
5. See below, note 16.
6. Except in the serial version of *Oliver Twist*, of which ch. xxii in Part XI is numbered the first of the Second Book. The Book-division of this novel was abandoned in the first 'volume' edition.
7. *Letters*, II, p. 567.
8. See further K. J. Fielding, 'Charles Dickens and the Department of Practical Art', *Modern Language Review*, 48 (1953), pp. 270–77.

9. *Letters*, II, p. 538.

10. *Letters*, II, p. 554.

11. The subject was topical. In 1853 a Royal Commission had reported on the Ecclesiastical Courts, one of whose functions was to try divorce petitions before their submission to Parliament, and had recommended transferring their functions to other bodies. A second reading was given in the House of Lords to a Divorce and Matrimonial Causes Bill on 13 June 1854, seven weeks after Dickens's fifth weekly number where the Law of Divorce was 'opened'. In the Debate the Lord Chancellor admitted that Divorce on other grounds than adultery had been suggested in various quarters, but that he considered that the Bill should be confined to adultery. Lord Redesdale, opposing the Bill, allowed that a divorce could at present be obtained only by the rich, but denied that there was 'the least expression of a desire for a cheap tribunal for granting divorces'. See *Parliamentary Debates*, 3rd ser.cxxxiv (1854), coll. 1–20. The Bill never reached the House of Commons.

12. In moving Bounderby out into the country, Dickens was doubtless describing what many a millowner was doing at that time. Though he does not specifically condemn the action, it may be assumed that he would disapprove since it would tend to separate the master still farther from his men. But the move to the country is convenient in several other ways: the bank is more readily robbed; Harthouse and Louisa are more clearly isolated; and Tom, the betrayer of the sister who loved him, is more suitably shown (in 2, vii) biting and tearing rosebuds, the emblems of love.

13. She makes a brief appearance at the end of 2, ix, the scene of Mrs Gradgrind's death. But though we see little of her in that scene, we are made to feel her presence both in the difference which Louisa notices in her sister and in the thought with which the dying Mrs Gradgrind struggles, a thought more effectively presented in the number plan than in the text itself: ' "Mr Gradgrind must have forgotten some ology. Can't have had them all taught".' Though nothing in Mrs Gradgrind's life became her like the leaving of it, we recognise that the scene really belongs to Sissy.

14. The words are Louisa's (2, xii).

15. The best that Dickens offers to convince his readers of the likeness of the two men is a passage at the beginning of the first chapter of this month (2, vii):

The not being troubled with earnestness was a grand point in his favour, enabling him to take to the hard Fact fellows with as good a grace as if he had been born one of the tribe, and to throw all other tribes overboard, as conscious hypocrites.

'Whom none of us believe, my dear Mrs Bounderby, and who do not believe themselves. The only difference between us and the professors of virtue or benevolence, or philanthropy—never mind the name—is, that we know it is all meaningless, and say so; while they know it equally and will never say so.'

Why should she be shocked or warned by this reiteration? It was not so unlike her father's principles, and her early training, that it need startle her. Where was the great difference between the two schools, when each chained her down to material realities, and inspired her with no faith in anything else? What was there in her soul for James Harthouse to destroy, which Thomas Gradgrind had nurtured there in its state of innocence!

16. The demands of the story required additional space for this last monthly number. Dickens's note at the head of the number plan reads: 'Weekly N^{os} to be enlarged to 10 of my sides each—about', i.e., an extension of about two and a half sheets of manuscript for each weekly number.

17. The anxiety which Dickens experienced in the composition of these episodes is reflected in a letter to Forster of which, alas, Forster (VII i) transcribed only an extract:

> Tavistock House. Look at that! Boulogne, of course. Friday, 14th of July, 1854. I am three parts mad, and the fourth delirious, with perpetual rushing at *Hard Times*. I have done what I hope is a good thing with Stephen, taking his story as a whole; and hope to be over in town with the end of the book on Wednesday night . . . I have been looking forward through so many weeks and sides of paper to this Stephen business, that now—as usual—it being over, I feel as if nothing in the world, in the way of intense and violent rushing hither and thither, could quite restore my balance.

Weekly No. XIX, in which Stephen is at last found, is endorsed in the number plan 'The great effect'.

18. It may be remarked that the suspense is scarcely interrupted by the capital scene of Mr Bounderby's deflation, for when Mrs Sparsit brings Mrs Pegler into Bounderby's presence she supposes that she has captured a material witness to the robbery and to Stephen's disappearance.

David Lodge   'The Rhetoric of *Hard Times*' (1966)

. . . On every page *Hard Times* manifests its identity as a polemical work, a critique of mid-Victorian industrial society dominated by materialism, acquisitiveness, and ruthlessly competitive capitalist economics. To Dickens, at the time of writing *Hard Times*, these things were represented most articulately, persuasively, (and therefore

dangerously) by the Utilitarians. It is easy to abstract the argument
behind the novel, and to demonstrate its logical and practical
weaknesses. The argument has two stages: (1) that the dominant
philosophy of Utilitarianism, particularly as it expresses itself in
education, results in a damaging impoverishment of the moral and
emotional life of the individual; and (2) that this leads in turn to social
and economic injustice, since individuals thus conditioned are incapable of dealing with the human problems created by industrialism. On
the level of plot (1) is expounded in terms of the Nemesis which
punishes Gradgrind through his children and (2) is expounded in
terms of Stephen Blackpool's sufferings. That Dickens makes a
connection between the two propositions and the two areas of the plot is
made clear in the scene where Blackpool confronts Bounderby and
Harthouse, and is challenged to offer a solution for the 'muddle' he is
always complaining about. Stephen expresses himself negatively. He
repudiates the employers' exploitation of their power ('the strong hand
will never do't'); their reliance on *laissez faire* ('lettin alone will never
do't'); their withdrawal from social contact with the working classes
('not drawin nigh to fok, wi' kindness and patience an' cheery
ways . . . will never do't'); and, 'most o' aw', their mental habit of
regarding the workers as soulless units in the economic machine while
inconsistently accusing them of ingratitude if they protest:

> 'Most o' aw, rating 'em as so much Power, and reg'lating 'em as
> if they was figures in a soom, or machines; wi'out loves and
> likens, wi'out memories and inclinations, wi'out souls to weary
> and souls to hope—when aw goes quiet draggin' on wi' 'em as if
> they'd nowt o' th'kind, and when aw goes onquiet, reproachin'
> 'em for their want o' sitch humanly feelins in their dealins wi'
> yo—this will never do't, Sir, till God's work is onmade.' [Bk II,
> ch. v]

It is clear that Dickens is speaking through Stephen here, and what the
speech amounts to in positive terms is a plea for generosity, charity,
imaginative understanding of the spiritual and emotional needs of
humanity.

While these values have an obvious relevance to the field of personal
relations (the Gradgrind-Bounderby circle) they are less viable as a
basis for reform of the body politic, because there are no sanctions to
ensure their application. They are not—apart from Louisa's abortive
attempt to help Stephen—shown in action in the novel vertically
through the class structure: Stephen's martyr-like death bears witness to
this. Yet Dickens could only offer a disembodied and vaguely defined
benevolence as a cure for the ills of Coketown because he had rejected

all the alternatives. In his hostile portrait of Gradgrind, Dickens repudiated not only the narrowest kind of Utilitarian rationalism, but also, as House and others have pointed out, the processes by which most of the great Victorian reforms were carried out—statistical enquiry, commissions, reports, acted on by Parliamentary legislation.[1] In his hostile portrait of Slackbridge, and his account of Stephen's ostracism because of his refusal to join the Trade Union, Dickens repudiated the workers' claim to secure justice by collective bargaining. Dickens is, then, opposed to any change in the political and economic structure of society, and places his hopes for amelioration in a change of heart, mind, and soul in those who possess power, who will then disseminate the fruits of this change over the lower echelons of society. Dickens's ideal State would be one of 'benevolent and genial anarchy'.[2]

This is an insecure basis from which to launch a critique of society, and its insecurity becomes all the more obvious when we look outside *Hard Times* to Dickens's journalism of the same period, and find him enthusing over the wonders of Victorian manufacture[3] and expressing surprised admiration for the Preston cotton-workers' conduct of their strike in 1854.[4]

And yet, when all this has been said, and the contradictions, limitations, and flaws in Dickens's argument extrapolated, *Hard Times* remains a novel of considerable polemical effectiveness. The measure of this effectiveness, it seems to me, can only be accounted for in terms of Dickens's rhetoric. This approach should recommend itself to the author of *The Victorian Sage*, a study which shows how many key Victorian writers, disarmed of logic by their opponents, resorted to non-logical methods of persuasion in order to communicate their ideas. In the criticism of fiction we have learned, notably from Wayne Booth, to use 'rhetoric' as a term for all the techniques by which a novelist seeks to persuade us of the validity of his vision of experience, a vision which cannot usually be formulated in abstract terms. But in a novel like *Hard Times*, which can be called a *roman à thèse*, rhetoric functions very nearly in its traditional rôle as the vehicle of an argument.

There is another reason why rhetoric seems a particularly useful term in discussing Dickens's work. Not only is the 'author's voice' always insistent in his novels, but it is characteristically a public-speaking voice, an oratorical or histrionic voice; and it is not difficult to see a connection between this feature of his prose and his fondness for speech-making and public reading of his works.

I shall try to show that *Hard Times* succeeds where its rhetoric succeeds and fails where its rhetoric fails; and that success and failure correspond fairly closely to the negative and positive aspects, respectively, of the argument inherent in the novel.

The very first chapter of *Hard Times* affords an excellent illustration of Dickens's rhetoric, and it is short enough to be quoted and analysed in its entirety.

HARD TIMES

BOOK THE FIRST, SOWING

CHAPTER I

THE ONE THING NEEDFUL

'Now, what I want is, Facts. Teach these boys and girls nothing but Facts. Facts alone are wanted in life. Plant nothing else, and root out everything else. You can only form the minds of reasoning animals upon Facts: nothing else will ever be of any service to them. This is the principle on which I bring up my own children, and this is the principle on which I bring up these children. Stick to Facts, Sir!'

The scene was a plain, bare, monotonous vault of a schoolroom, and the speaker's square forefinger emphasised his observations by underscoring every sentence with a line on the schoolmaster's sleeve. The emphasis was helped by the speaker's square wall of a forehead, which had his eyebrows for its base, while his eyes found commodious cellarage in two dark caves, overshadowed by the wall. The emphasis was helped by the speaker's mouth, which was wide, thin, and hard set. The emphasis was helped by the speaker's voice, which was inflexible, dry, and dictatorial. The emphasis was helped by the speaker's hair, which bristled on the skirts of his bald head, a plantation of firs to keep the wind from its shining surface, all covered with knobs, like the crust of a plum pie, as if the head had scarcely warehouse-room for the hard facts stored inside. The speaker's obstinate carriage, square coat, square legs, square shoulders—nay, his very neckcloth, trained to take him by the throat with an unaccommodating grasp, like a stubborn fact, as it was—all helped the emphasis.

'In this life, we want nothing but Facts, Sir; nothing but Facts!'

The speaker, and the schoolmaster, and the third grown person present, all backed a little, and swept with their eyes the inclined plane of little vessels then and there arranged in order, ready to have imperial gallons of facts poured into them until they were full to the brim.

This chapter communicates, in a remarkably compact way, both a description and a judgement of a concept of education. This concept is defined in a speech, and then evaluated—not in its own terms, but in terms of the speaker's appearance and the setting. Dickens, of course, always relies heavily on the popular, perhaps primitive, assumption that there is a correspondence between a person's appearance and his character; and as Gradgrind is a governor of the school, its design may legitimately function as a metaphor for his character. Dickens also had a fondness for fancifully appropriate names, but—perhaps in order to stress the representativeness of Gradgrind's views—he does not reveal the name in this first chapter.*

Because of the brevity of the chapter, we are all the more susceptible to the effect of its highly rhetorical patterning, particularly the manipulation of certain repeated words, notably *fact, square,* and *emphasis.* The kind of education depicted here is chiefly characterised by an obsession with facts. The word occurs five times in the opening speech of the first paragraph, and it is twice repeated towards the end of the second, descriptive paragraph to prepare for the reintroduction of Gradgrind speaking—' "we want nothing but Facts, sir—nothing but Facts" '; and it occurs for the tenth and last time towards the end of the last paragraph. In Gradgrind's speeches the word is capitalised, to signify his almost religious devotion to Facts.

Gradgrind's concept of education is further characterised in ways we can group into three categories, though of course they are closely connected:

(1) It is authoritarian, fanatical and bullying in its application.
(2) It is rigid, abstract and barren in quality.
(3) It is materialistic and commercial in its orientation.

The first category is conveyed by the structure of the second paragraph, which is dominated by 'emphasis'. This paragraph comprises six sentences. In the first sentence we are told how the 'speaker's square forefinger emphasised his observations'. The next four, central sentences are each introduced, with cumulative force, by the clause 'The emphasis was helped', and this formula, translated from the passive to the active voice, makes a fittingly 'emphatic' conclusion to the paragraph in the sixth sentence: 'all helped the emphasis'. This rhetorical pattern has a dual function. In one way it reflects or imitates

* Mary McCarthy has suggested that an anonymous 'he' at the beginning of a novel usually moves the reader to sympathetic identification.[5] That the effect is quite the reverse in this example shows that the effect of any narrative strategy is determined finally by the narrator's language.

Gradgrind's own bullying, over-emphatic rhetoric, of which we have an example in the first paragraph; but in another way it helps to *condemn* Gradgrind, since it 'emphasises' the narrator's own pejorative catalogue of details of the speaker's person and immediate environment. The narrator's rhetoric is, as it must be, far more skilful and persuasive than Gradgrind's.

The qualities in category (2) are conveyed in a number of geometrical or quasi-geometrical terms, *wide, line, thin, base, surface, inclined plane* and, particularly, *square* which recurs five times; and in words suggestive of barren regularity, *plain, bare, monotonous, arranged in order, inflexible*. Such words are particularly forceful when applied to human beings—whether Gradgrind or the children. The metamorphosis of the human into the non-human is, as we shall find confirmed later, one of Dickens's main devices for conveying his alarm at the way Victorian society was moving.

Category (3), the orientation towards the world of commerce, is perhaps less obvious than the other categories, but it is unmistakably present in some of the boldest tropes of the chapter: *commodious cellarage, warehouse room, plantation, vessels, imperial gallons*.

The authoritarian ring of '*imperial*' leads us back from category (3) to category (1), just as '*under-scoring* every sentence with a *line*' leads us from (1) to (2). There is a web of connecting strands between the qualities I have tried to categorise: it is part of the rhetorical strategy of the chapter that all the qualities it evokes are equally applicable to Gradgrind's character, person, ideas, his school and the children (in so far as he has shaped them in his own image).

Metaphors of growth and cultivation are of course commonplace in discussion of education, and we should not overlook the ironic invocation of such metaphors, with a deliberately religious, prophetic implication (reinforced by the Biblical echo of the chapter heading, 'The One Thing Needful'[6]) in the title of the Book, 'SOWING', later to be followed by Book the Second, 'REAPING', and Book the Third, 'GARNERING'. These metaphors are given a further twist in Gradgrind's recommendation to 'Plant nothing else and root out everything else' (except facts).

If there is a flaw in this chapter it is the simile of the plum pie, which has pleasant, genial associations alien to the character of Gradgrind, to whose head it is, quite superfluously, applied. Taken as a whole, however, this is a remarkably effective and densely woven beginning of the novel.

The technique of the first chapter of *Hard Times* could not be described as 'subtle'. But subtle effects are often lost in a first chapter, where the reader is coping with the problem of 'learning the author's language'. Perhaps with some awareness of this fact, sharpened by his sense of addressing a vast, popular audience, Dickens begins many of his novels by nailing the reader's attention with a display of sheer rhetorical power, relying particularly on elaborate repetition. One thinks, for instance, of the fog at the beginning of *Bleak House* or the sun and shadow in the first chapter of *Little Dorrit*. In these novels the rhetoric works to establish a symbolic atmosphere; in *Hard Times*, to establish a thematic Idea—the despotism of Fact. But this abstraction—Fact—is invested with a remarkable solidity through the figurative dimension of the language.

The gross effect of the chapter is simply stated, but analysis reveals that it is achieved by means of a complex verbal activity that is far from simple. Whether it represents fairly any actual educational theory or practice in mid-nineteenth-century England is really beside the point. It aims to convince us of the *possibility* of children being taught in such a way, and to make us recoil from the imagined possibility. The chapter succeeds or fails as rhetoric; and I think it succeeds.

Dickens begins as he means to continue. Later in the novel we find Gradgrind's house, which, like the school-room, is a function of himself, described in precisely the same terms of fact and rigid measurement, partly geometrical and partly commercial.

> A very regular feature on the face of the country, Stone Lodge was. Not the least disguise toned down or shaded off that uncompromising fact in the landscape. A great square house, with a heavy portico darkening the principal windows, as its master's heavy brows over-shadowed his eyes. A calculated, cast up, balanced and proved house. Six windows on this side of the door, six on that side; a total of twelve in this wing, a total of twelve in the other wing; four and twenty carried over to the back wings. A lawn and garden and an infant avenue, all ruled straight like a botanical account-book. [Bk i, ch. iii]

It has been observed[7] that Dickens individualises his characters by making them use peculiar locutions and constructions in their speech, a technique which was particularly appropriate to serial publication in which the reader's memory required to be frequently jogged. This technique extends beyond the idiosyncratic speech of characters, to the language in which they are described. A key-word, or group of key-words, is insistently used when the character is first introduced, not only to identify him but also to evaluate him, and is invoked at various strategic points in the subsequent action. Dickens's remarkable metaphorical inventiveness ensures that continuity and rhetorical emphasis are not obtained at the expense of monotony. The application of the key-words of the first chapter to Mr Gradgrind's house gives the same delight as the development of a metaphysical conceit. The observation that Mrs Gradgrind, 'whenever she showed a sympton of coming to life, was invariably stunned by some weighty piece of fact tumbling on her' [I, iv], affords a kind of verbal equivalent of knock-about comedy, based on a combination of expectancy (we know the word will recur) and surprise (we are not prepared for the particular formulation).

Bounderby offers another illustration of Dickens's use of key-words in characterisation. He is first introduced as 'a big, loud man, with a stare, and a metallic laugh' [I, iv]. The metallic quality is shortly afterwards defined as 'that brassy speaking-trumpet of a voice of his' [ibid.]. His house has a front door with 'BOUNDERBY (in letters very like himself) upon a brazen plate, and a round brazen door-handle underneath it, like a brazen full stop' [I, xi]. Bounderby's bank 'was another red brick house, with black outside shutters, green inside blinds, a black street door up two white steps, a brazen door-plate, and a brazen door-handle full-stop' [II, i]. The buildings Bounderby inhabits take their character from him, as Gradgrind's do from him. But here the emphasis is on the brass embellishments which, by the use of the word *brazen* (rather than *brass* used adjectivally) epitomise several facets of his characters: his hardness, vanity, crude enjoyment of wealth, and, most important of all, the fact that he is a brazen liar. (We do not know for certain that he is a liar until the end of the novel; 'brazen' fittings reinforce other hints which prepare us for the revelation.)

The failures of characterisation in *Hard Times* are generally failures in using rhetorical strategies which Dickens elsewhere employs very successfully. The portrait of Slackbridge, the trade union demagogue, for instance, seeks to exploit a relationship between character and appearance in a way which is familiar in Dickens and well exemplified in the first chapter; but it does so crudely and clumsily:

> Judging him by Nature's evidence, he was above the mass in very little but the stage on which he stood. In many respects he was essentially below them. He was not so honest, he was not so manly, he was not so good-humoured; he substituted cunning for their simplicity, and passion for their safe solid sense. An ill-made, high shouldered man, with lowering brows, and his features crushed into an habitually sour expression, he contrasted most unfavourably, even in his mongrel dress, with the great body of his hearers in their plain working clothes. [Bk II, ch. iv]

Apart from the vividness of 'crushed', the description of Slackbridge is carelessly vague, and we miss the metaphorical inventiveness that characterises Dickens's best descriptions of people. But the main error of the passage is the ordering of its material. The rhetorical strategy announced by the opening sentence is that Slackbridge's character is to be read in his appearance. But in fact the character is read *before* we are given the appearance. It is as if Dickens has so little confidence in his own imaginative evidence that he must inform us, over-explicitly, what conclusions we are to draw, before we come to the evidence. We know from external sources that Dickens was in a confused state of mind about the trade union movement at the time of writing *Hard Times*,[8] and we can rarely expect to receive a balanced account of organised labour from any middle-class Victorian novelist. However, the failure of understanding here reveals itself in the first place as a failure of expression; the portrait of Gradgrind, on the other hand, though it probably derives from an equivalent misunderstanding of Utilitarianism, succeeds.

Another, more significant failure of Dickens's rhetoric is to be observed in the treatment of Tom Gradgrind. In this connection, I must register my disagreement with John Holloway's opinion that 'the gradual degeneration of Tom . . . is barely (as in fact it is treated) related to Dickens's major problems in the book, though it is one of its best things'.[9] It is gradual (though not very extensively treated) up to the beginning of Book II, by which point we have gathered that Tom, so far from drawing strength of character from his repressive and rationalist upbringing, is turning into a selfish young man prepared to exploit others for his own advantage. He is still a long way, however, from the depravity that allows him to connive at the seduction of his own sister and to implicate an innocent man (Stephen Blackpool) in his own crime. This moral gap is rather clumsily bridged by Dickens in the second chapter of Book II, where he suddenly introduces a key-word for Tom: 'whelp'.

The Bounderbys are entertaining James Harthouse to dinner. Louisa does not respond to Harthouse's attempts to flirt, but when Tom comes in, late, 'She changed . . . and broke into a beaming smile. . . .'

> 'Ay, ay?' thought the visitor. 'This whelp is the only creature she cares for. So, so!'
> The whelp was presented, and took his chair. The appellation was not flattering, but not unmerited. [Bk II, ch. ii]

The chapter ends very shortly afterwards, but Dickens contrives to use the word 'whelp' three more times, and the title of the following chapter [II, iii], in which Tom betrays Louisa's situation to Harthouse, is entitled 'The Whelp'.

'Whelp' is a cliché, and it will be noticed that the word is first used by Harthouse, and then adopted by the novelist in his authorial capacity. When a novelist does this, it is usually with ironical intent, suggesting some inadequacy in the speaker's habits of thought.* Dickens plays on Gradgrind's 'facts' to this effect. But in the case of Harthouse's 'whelp' he has taken a moral cliché from a character who is morally unreliable, and invested it with his own authority as narrator. This gives away the fact that Tom is being forced into a new rôle halfway through the book. For Tom's degeneration *should* be related to the major problems with which Dickens is concerned in *Hard Times*. According to the overall pattern of the novel, Tom and Louisa are to act as indices of the failure of Mr Gradgrind's philosophy of education, and should thus never be allowed to stray outside the area of our pity, since they are both victims rather than free agents. But Tom's actions do take him beyond our pity, and diminish the interest of his character.

Perhaps Dickens was misled by feeling the need to inject a strong crime-interest into his story, of which Tom was a handy vehicle; or perhaps he lost his head over the preservation of Louisa's purity (the somewhat hysterical conclusion to chapter iii, Book II, 'The Whelp', seems to suggest this). Whatever the explanation, 'the whelp', unlike those key-words which organise and concentrate the represented character of individuals and places, acts merely as a slogan designed to generate in the reader such a contempt for Tom that he will not enquire too closely into the pattern of his moral development—a pattern that will not, in fact, bear very close scrutiny.

---

* Compare E. M. Forster, a master of this device, in *A Room with a View* (George Emerson has been indiscreet enough to mention in company that his father is taking a bath):

> 'Oh dear!' breathed the little old lady, and shuddered as if all the winds of heaven had entered the apartment. 'Gentlemen sometimes do not realise——' Her voice faded away. But Miss Bartlett seemed to understand, and a conversation developed in which gentlemen who did not realise played a principal part.' (I, I)

Much later in the novel. Lucy, engaged to another, is desperately fighting off the advances of George. 'What does a girl do when she comes across a cad?' she asks Miss Bartlett.

> 'I always said he was a cad, dear. Give me credit for that at all events. From the very first moment—when he said his father was having a bath.' . . . She moved feebly to the window, and tried to detect the cad's white flannels among the laurels. (II, 16)

In the conduct of his central argument, Dickens explicitly calls our attention to a 'key-note'. The first occasion on which he does so is when introducing the description of Coketown, in chapter v of Book I, entitled 'The Key-note':

> COKETOWN, to which Messrs. Bounderby and Gradgrind now walked, was a triumph of fact; it had no greater taint of fancy in it than Mrs Gradgrind herself. Let us strike the keynote, Coketown, before pursuing our tune.
>
> It was a town of red brick, or of brick that would have been red if the smoke and ashes had allowed it; but as matters stood it was a town of unnatural red and black and the painted face of a savage. It was a town of machinery and tall chimneys, out of which interminable serpents of smoke trailed themselves for ever and ever, and never got uncoiled. It had a black canal in it, and a river that ran purple with ill-smelling dye, and vast piles of building full of windows where there was a rattling and a trembling all day long, and where the piston of the steam engine worked monotonously up and down like the head of an elephant in a state of melancholy madness. It contained several large streets all very like one another, and many more small streets still more like one another, inhabited by people equally like one another, who all went in and out at the same hours, with the same sound upon the same pavements, to do the same work, and to whom every day was the same as yesterday and tomorrow, and every year the counterpart of the last and the next.

Dorothy Van Ghent has commented on the effects Dickens gains by investing the inanimate with animation and vice versa. 'The animation of inanimate objects suggests both the quaint gaiety of a forbidden life, and an aggressiveness that has got out of control. . . . The animate is treated as if it is a thing. It is as if the life absorbed by things had been drained out of people who have become incapable of their humanity.'[10] The description of Coketown illustrates this process. The buildings and machinery of Coketown are invested with a sinister life of their own, the life of savages, serpents, and elephants (the serpent and elephant images are reiterated at least five times in the novel).[11] The people of Coketown, on the other hand, take their character from the architecture of the town non-metaphorically conceived—'large streets all very like one another, and many small streets still more like one another'. They are reduced to indistinguishable units caught up in a mindless, monotonous, mechanical process, superbly represented in the droning repetition of sound and syntax in the last sentence of the passage quoted.

In the rest of this chapter Dickens goes on to say that, despite the efficiency of the town, it was afflicted by *malaise*, social and moral: drunkenness, idleness, irreligion. 'Is it possible,' he asks, 'that there was any analogy between the case of the Coketown populace and the little Gradgrinds?' He goes on to suggest that in both 'there was fancy in them demanding to be brought into healthy existence instead of struggling on in convulsions'.

The antithesis of 'fact and fancy' introduces the chapter (see the quotation above). It has been previously introduced in the school-room chapters, where Sissy Jupe's words, 'I would fancy——', are rudely interrupted by the government official:

> 'Ay, ay, ay! But you mustn't fancy,' cried the gentleman, quite elated by coming so happily to his point. 'That's it! You are never to fancy. . . . You are to be in all things regulated and governed . . . by fact. . . . You must discard the word Fancy altogether.' [Bk i, ch. ii]

A very similar interruption establishes the same antithesis in slightly different terms in chapter viii, Book i, 'Never Wonder', where Dickens again proposes to strike the key-note:

> Let us strike the key-note again, before pursuing the tune.
>
> When she was half a dozen years younger, Louisa had been overheard to begin a conversation with her brother one day, by saying 'Tom, I wonder'—upon which Mr Gradgrind, who was the person overhearing, stepped forth into the light, and said, 'Louisa, never wonder!'
>
> Herein lay the spring of the mechanical art and mystery of educating the reason without stooping to the cultivation of the sentiments and affections. Never wonder. By means of addition, subtraction, multiplication and division, settle everything somehow, and never wonder. Bring to me, says M'Choakumchild, yonder baby just able to walk, and I will engage that it shall never wonder.

The antithesis between fact and fancy (or wonder), is, then, the dominant key-note of *Hard Times*. It relates the public world of the novel to the private world, the *malaise* of the Gradgrind—Bounderby circle to the *malaise* of Coketown as a social community; and it draws together the two stages of the central argument of the book; the relationship between education in the broad sense and social health. In this respect Dickens is not so very far removed from the position of the Romantic critics of industrialist society. Compare Shelley:

We have more moral, political and historical wisdom than we know how to reduce into practice; we have more scientific and economical knowledge than can be accommodated to the just distribution of the produce which it multiples. The poetry, in these systems of thought, is concealed by the accumulations of facts and calculating processes. . . . We want the creative faculty to imagine that which we know. . . . To what but a cultivation of the mechanical arts in a degree disproportioned to the presence of the creative faculty, which is the basis of all knowledge, is to be attributed the abuses of all invention for abridging and combining labour, to the exasperation of the inequality of mankind? From what other cause has it arisen that the discoveries which should have lightened, have added a weight to the curse of Adam? Poetry, and the principle of Self, of which money is the visible incarnation, are the God and Mammon of the world.[12]

There is a real community of feeling between Shelley and Dickens here: one might almost think that *Hard Times* takes its cue for the criticism of 'the accumulation of facts', 'calculating processes', and 'the principle of Self' from the *Defence of Poetry*. But whereas Shelley opposes to these things poetry, imagination, the creative faculty, Dickens can only offer Fancy, wonder, sentiments—though he does so with the same seriousness and the same intentions as Shelley, as a panacea for the ills of modern society. It is tempting to relate the inadequacy of Dickens's concept of Fancy[13] to the discussions familiar in Romantic criticism of Fancy and Imagination. But it is on the rhetorical level that the inadequacy of Dickens's concept manifests itself. In the first 'key-note' chapter, the authorial voice inquiries, with heavy irony, whether we are to be told 'at this time of day'

> that one of the foremost elements in the existence of the Coketown working-people had been for scores of years deliberately set at nought? That there was any Fancy in them demanding to be brought into healthy existence instead of struggling on in convulsions? That, exactly in the ratio as they worked long and monotonously, the craving grew within them for some physical relief—some relaxation, encouraging good humour and good spirits, and giving them a vent—some recognized holiday, though it were but for an honest dance to a stirring band of music—some occasional light pie in which even M'Choakumchild had no finger—which craving must and would be satisfied aright, or must and would inevitably go wrong, until the laws of the Creation were repealed? [Bk I, ch. v]

The rhetorical questions here impede and confuse the argument. The parallelism of 'which craving must and would be satisfied aright, or must and would inevitably go wrong' is tired and mechanical. A mathematical image is enlisted in arguing *against* the mathematical, calculating faculty: it is precisely Dickens's case in the novel as a whole that the 'laws of Creation' are not accountable in terms of 'ratios'. The vagueness of '*some* relaxation', '*some* recognised holiday' is by no means clarified by the unexciting offer of an 'honest dance' or a 'light pie' as specific palliatives for the people of Coketown.

Dickens is struggling to assert, here, the existence of a universal need in humanity, a need which arises from quite a different side of man's nature from that which is occupied with the mechanical processes of industrialism, a need which must be satisfied, a need distantly related to that need for poetry which Shelley asserts. But whereas Shelley's 'poetry' is a faculty which involves and enhances and transforms the total activity of man—'We must imagine that which we know'— Dickens's Fancy is merely a temporary escape from what is accepted as inevitably unpleasant. It is 'relief', 'a vent', 'a holiday'. To be cruel, one might say that Dickens offers the oppressed workers of Coketown bread and circuses: bread in the metaphorical 'light pie' and circuses in the 'honest dance'—and, of course, in Mr Sleary's circus.

The realm of Fancy is most vividly evoked by the rhetoric of *Hard Times* in what might be called the 'fairy-tale' element of the novel.[14] Many of the characters and events are derived from the staple ingredients of the fairy-tale, and this derivation is clearly revealed in the language.

Louisa and Tom first figure as the brother and sister who often appear in fairy-tales as waifs, exiles, victims of circumstance, hedged about with dangers (the Babes in the Woods, etc.). As they sit by the fire of their room, 'Their shadows were defined upon the wall, but those of the high presses in the room were all blended together on the wall and on the ceiling, as if the brother and sister were overhung by a dark cavern' [I, viii]. In their childhood their father wears the aspect of an 'Ogre':

> Not that they knew, by name or nature, anything about an Ogre. Fact forbid! I only use the word to express a monster in a lecturing castle, with Heaven knows how many heads manipulated into one, taking childhood captive, and dragging it into gloomy statistical dens by the hair. [Bk I, ch. iii]

Later, Louisa becomes the enchanted princess with a heart of ice, while Tom takes on the rôle of the knave. Harthouse is the demon king, popping up suddenly in the action with mischievous intent, in a cloud of (cigar) smoke:

James Harthouse continued to lounge in the same place and attitude, smoking his cigar in his own easy way, and looking pleasantly at the whelp, as if he knew himself to be a kind of agreeable demon who had only to hover over him, and he must give up his whole soul if required. [Bk II, ch. iii]

Sissy tells Mrs Gradgrind that she used to read to her father 'About the fairies, sir, and the dwarf, and the hunchback, and the genies' [I, vii]; and the circus folk in *Hard Times* are comparable to the chorus of benevolent, comic, grotesque, half-supernatural creatures who inhabit the world of romance and fairy-tale. They are persistently associated with legend and myth—Pegasus [I, v], Cupid [ibid.], Jack the Giant Killer [III, vii], etc. Mr Bounderby's mother, Mrs Pegler, 'the mysterious old woman' [III, v] is the crone who figures in many fairy tales and who brings about a surprising turn in the action. Mr Bounderby refers to her as 'an old woman who seems to have been flying into the town on a broomstick now and then' [II, viii]. But the proper witch of the story, and Dickens's most effective adaptation of a stock-figure from fairy-tale, is Mrs Sparsit. 'Mrs Sparsit considered herself, in some sort, the Bank Fairy', we are told, but the townspeople 'regarded her as the Bank Dragon, keeping watch over the treasures of the mine'. Her heavy eyebrows and hooked nose are exploited for vivid effects of cruelty:

> Mr Bounderby sat looking at her, as, with the points of a stiff, sharp pair of scissors, she picked out holes for some inscrutable purpose, in a piece of cambric. An operation which, taken in connexion with the bushy eyebrows and the Roman nose, suggested with some liveliness the idea of a hawk engaged upon the eyes of a tough little bird. [Bk I, ch. xvi]

She flatters Bounderby to his face, but secretly insults his portrait. She wills Louisa into Harthouse's clutches, figuring Louisa's progress as the descent of a 'Giant's Staircase', on which she keeps anxious watch [II, x]. The boldest treatment of Mrs Sparsit as a witch occurs in the scene where she steals through the grounds of Mr Gradgrind's country house, hoping to catch Louisa and Harthouse together.

> She thought of the wood and stole towards it, heedless of long grass and briers: of worms, snails, and slugs, and all the creeping things that be. With her dark eyes and her hook nose warily in advance of her, Mrs Sparsit softly crushed her way through the thick undergrowth, so intent upon her object that she would

probably have done no less, if the wood had been a wood of
adders.

Hark!

The smaller birds might have tumbled out of their nests,
fascinated by the glittering of Mrs Sparsit's eyes in the
gloom. . . . [Bk II, ch. xi]

When a thunderstorm bursts immediately afterwards, Mrs Sparsit's
appearance becomes still more grotesque:

It rained now, in a sheet of water. Mrs Sparsit's white stockings
were of many colours, green predominating; prickly things were
in her shoes; caterpillars slung themselves, in hammocks of their
own making, from various parts of her dress; rills ran from her
bonnet, and her Roman nose. [Bk II, ch. xi]

Traditionally, witches are antipathetic to water. It is appropriate,
therefore, that the frustration of Mrs Sparsit's spite, when she loses track
of Louisa, is associated with her ludicrous, rain-soaked appearance (see
the conclusion to II, xi).

We may add to these examples of the invocation of fairy tale, the
repeated description of the factories illuminated at night as 'fairy
palaces' [I, x; I, xi; II, i; and generally], and Mr Bounderby's often
expressed conviction that his men 'expect to be set up in a coach and six,
and to be fed on turtle soup and venison and fed with a gold spoon' [I, xi;
I, vi; II, i; and generally]. These phrases contrast ironically with the
actual drab environment and existence of the Coketown people.

It is, indeed, as an *ironic* rhetorical device that the fairy-tale element
operates most successfully. On one level it is possible to read the novel as
an ironic fairy-tale, in which the enchanted princess is released from her
spell but does not find a Prince Charming, in which the honest,
persecuted servant (Stephen) is vindicated but not rewarded, and in
which the traditional romantic belief in blood and breeding, confirmed
by a discovery, is replaced by the exposure of Bounderby's inverted
snobbery.

In other respects, however, the fairy-tale element sets up unresolved
tensions in the novel. It encourages a morally-simplified, non-social,
and non-historical view of human life and conduct, whereas Dickens's
undertaking in *Hard Times* makes quite opposite demands. Mr Sleary's
ruse for releasing Tom from the custody of Bitzer, for instance [III, viii],
is acceptable on the level of fairy-tale motivation: he returns Mr
Gradgrind's earlier good deed (the adoption of Sissy) and scores off an
unsympathetic character (Bitzer). But the act is essentially lawless, and
conflicts with Dickens's appeals elsewhere in the novel for justice and

social responsibility. As long as the circus-folk represent a kind of life that is anarchic, seedy, socially disreputable, but cheerful and humane, they are acceptable and enjoyable. But when they are offered as agents or spokesmen of social and moral amelioration, we reject them. The art they practice is Fancy in its tawdriest form, solemnly defended by Mr Sleary in terms we recognise as the justification of today's mass entertainers:

> 'People mutht be amuthed. They can't be alwayth a learning, nor yet they can't be alwayth a working, they an't made for it. You *mutht* have uth, Thquire. [Bk III, ch. viii]

Sissy is meant to represent a channel through which the values of the circus folk are conveyed to the social order. But her one positive act, the dismissal of Harthouse [III, ii], depends for its credibility on a simple faith in the superiority of a good fairy over a demon king.

In other words, where Dickens invokes the world of fairy-tale ironically, to dramatise the drabness, greed, spite and injustice which characterise a society dominated by materialism, it is a highly effective rhetorical device; but where he relies on the simplification of the fairy-tale to suggest means of redemption, we remain unconvinced.

If Dickens's notion of Fancy was attached mainly to fairy-tale and nursery rhyme (cf. the allusions to the cow with the crumpled horn and Peter Piper in I, iii), his own art is very much one of Fancy in the Coleridgean sense: 'Fancy has no other counters to play with, but fixities and definites. The Fancy is indeed no other than a mode of Memory emancipated from the order of time and space. . . .'[15] This seems an appropriate description of Dickens's method in, for instance, the first chapter of *Hard Times*, or in the description of Coketown, or in the treatment of Mrs Sparsit as a witch. To appreciate this, is to feel that Coleridge was wrong to depreciate Fancy as a literary mode; but it is also to understand why Dickens's greatest achievement as a novelist was his depiction of a disordered universe in which the organic and the mechanical have exchanged places, rather than in his attempts to trace moral and emotional processes within the individual psyche.

In *Hard Times*, Dickens expounds a diagnosis of the ills of modern industrial society for which no institutions can supply a cure: society, represented by a group of characters, must therefore change itself, learning from a group outside the social order—the circus. But Dickens's characters are incapable of change: the language in which they are embodied fixes them in their 'given' condition. They can only die (like Stephen Blackpool) or be broken (like Mr Bounderby). Mr

Gradgrind may lose his 'squareness', but he is left a shadow: he cannot become a Michelin Man, all circles and spheres. Louisa when her heart has been melted is a far less convincing character than Louisa with a heart of ice. (This can be quickly seen by comparing the scene of her interview with Gradgrind to discuss Bounderby's proposal [I, xv], rightly singled out for praise by Leavis, with the parallel scene at the end of the book where she returns to her father to reproach him for her upbringing, and where she is given the most embarrassing lines in the novel to speak [III, xii].) Dickens faiters in his handling of the character of Tom Gradgrind precisely because he uses a device for fixing character (*whelp*) to express a process of change.

If *Hard Times* is a polemical novel that is only partially persuasive, it is because Dickens's rhetoric is only partially adequate to the tasks he set himself.

SOURCE: extract from *The Language of Fiction* (London, 1966), pp. 145–63.

NOTES

[Shortened and renumbered from the original—Ed.]

1. For example: Mr Gradgrind 'then returned with promptitude to the national cinder-heap, and resumed his sifting for the odds and ends he wanted, and his throwing of the dust into the eyes of other people who wanted other odds and ends — in fact, resumed his parliamentary duties' [II, xi].

2. Cf. Humphry House, commenting on H. T. Buckle's *History of Civilisation* (1857–61), a work quoted with approval by Dickens in 1869: 'From one point of view Buckle's book can be seen as an attempt to erect the doctrine of *laissez-faire* into a philosophy of history, and to defend civilised society as a state of benevolent and genial anarchy': *The Dickens World* (Oxford, 1941; paperback 1960), pp. 173–4.

3. See ibid, p. 166.

4. See note 8 below.

5. Mary McCarthy, 'Characters in Fiction', *The Partisan Review Anthology* (New York, 1962), pp. 260–1.

6. Ch. ii of Book I is called 'Murdering the Innocents'.

7. Randolph Quirk, 'Some Observations on the Language of Dickens', *Review of English Literature*, II (1961), pp. 20–1.

8. House (op. cit., pp. 206–8) says that Dickens deliberately went to Preston to observe the cotton strike there early in 1854, in order to gather material for *Hard Times*, and notes that his report in *Household Words* . . . shows a somewhat surprised respect for the orderly and efficient conduct of the strikers. [See excerpt from House, above—Ed.] K. J. Fielding, in his *Charless Dickens: A Critical Introduction* (London, 1958), argues (pp. 134–5) that 'the

conditions described in *Hard Times* are much closer to the engineering strike of 1852 than to the dispute at Preston' and quotes a contemporary letter of Dickens:

> As to the Engineers . . . I believe the difficulty in the way of compromise, from the very beginning, is not so much with the masters as with the men. Honourable, generous and free-spirited themselves, they have fallen into an unlucky way of trusting their affairs to contentious men, who work them up into a state of conglomeration and irritation, and are the greatest pests that their own employers can encounter upon earth.

This is certainly the attitude Dickens adopts in *Hard Times*. But on a more fundamental level he also distrusted the trade unions as a threat to the liberty of the individual. He weakens his own case, however, by making Stephen Blackpool refuse to join the union because of a mysterious and apparently meaningless promise he has made to Rachael [II, vi]. See Raymond Williams, *Culture and Society, 1780–1950* (London, 1958; Penguin edn 1961), pp. 99–100, for a discussion of the distrust of organised labour by Victorian novelists who sympathised with the oppressed working classes.

9. John Holloway, '*Hard Times*: A History and a Criticism', in John Gross and Gabriel Pearson (eds), *Dickens in the Twentieth Century* (London, 1962), p. 171.

10. Dorothy Van Ghent, 'The Dickens World: A View from Todgers's', in George H. Ford and Lauriat Lane Jnr (eds), *The Dickens Critics* (Ithaca, N.Y., 1161), p. 214.

11. See I, xi; I, xii; II, i; III, v.

12. H. F. B. Brett-Smith (ed.), *Peacock's 'Four Ages of Poetry', Shelley's 'Defence of Poetry', Browning's 'Essay on Shelley'* (Oxford, 1921), p. 52.

13. Dickens's commitment to 'Fancy' is not restricted to *Hard Times*, as P. A. W. Collins shows in his very thorough study of Dickens's use of the word: 'Queen Mab's Chariot among the Steam Engines: Dickens and Fancy', *English Studies*, XLII (1961), pp. 78–90.

14. My attention was first directed to this (apart from the characterisation of Mrs Sparsit) by a Birmingham undergraduate, Miss Margaret Thomas. Possibly it has been observed before, but I have not been able to find it in Dickens criticism.

15. Coleridge, *Biographia Literaria*, ch. XIII.

PART TWO

Great Expectations

Great Expectations

Serialised weekly in *All the Year Round*, from 1 December 1860 to 3
August 1861; published in book form in 1861, in three volumes.

I. BACKGROUND

Dickens (1860, 1861)

Extracts from Letters

To John Forster, September 1860

. . . For a little piece I have been writing—or am writing; for I hope to
finish it to-day—such a very fine, new, and grotesque idea has opened
upon me, that I begin to doubt whether I had not better cancel the little
paper, and reserve the notion for a new book. You shall judge as soon as
I get it printed. But it so opens out before *me* that I can see the whole of a
serial revolving upon it, in a most singular and comic manner. . . .

To John Forster, April 1861

. . . It is a pity that the third portion cannot be read all at once, because
its purpose would be much more apparent; and the pity is the greater,
because the general turn and tone of the working out and winding up,
will be away from all such things as they conventionally go. But what
must be, must be. As to the planning out from week to week, nobody can
imagine what the difficulty is, without trying. . . .

> SOURCE: W. Dexter (ed.), *The Letters of Charles Dickens*
> (London, 1938), III, pp. 182, 216–17.

John Forster (1874)

'The grotesque tragi-comic conception'

[Forster quotes the passage from Dickens' letter of September 1860 given above.] . . . This was the germ of Pip and Magwitch, which at first he intended to make the groundwork of a tale in the old twenty-number form, but for reasons perhaps fortunate brought afterwards within the limits of a less elaborate novel. 'Last week', he wrote on 4 October, 1860, 'I got to work on the new story. I had previously very carefully considered the state and prospects of *All the Year Round*, and, the more I considered them, the less hope I saw of being able to get back, *now*, to the profit of a separate publication in the old 20 numbers.' (A tale, which at the time was appearing in his serial, had disappointed expectation.) 'However, I worked on, knowing that what I was doing would run into another groove; and I called a council of war at the office on Tuesday. It was perfectly clear that the one thing to be done was, for me to strike in. I have therefore decided to begin the story as of the length of the *Tale of Two Cities* on the first of December—begin publishing, that is. I must make the most I can out of the book. You shall have the first two or three weekly parts to-morrow. The name is GREAT EXPECTATIONS. I think a good name?' Two days later he wrote: 'The sacrifice of *Great Expectations* is really and truly made for myself. The property of *All the Year Round* is far too valuable, in every way, to be much endangered. Our fall is not large, but we have a considerable advance in hand of the story we are now publishing, and there is no vitality in it, and no chance whatever of stopping the fall; which on the contrary would be certain to increase. Now, if I went into a twenty-number serial, I should cut off my power of doing anything serial here for two good years—and that would be a most perilous thing. On the other hand, by dashing in now, I come in when most wanted; and if Reade and Wilkie follow me, our course will be shaped out handsomely and hopefully for between two and three years. A thousand pounds are to be paid for early proofs of the story to America.' A few more days brought the first instalment of the tale, and explanatory mention of it. 'The book will be written in the first person throughout, and during these first three weekly numbers you will find the hero to be a boy-child, like David. Then he will be an apprentice. You will not have to complain of the want of humour as in the *Tale of Two Cities*. I have made the opening, I hope, in its general effect exceedingly droll. I have put a child and a good-natured foolish man, in relations that seem to me very funny. Of course I have got in the pivot on which the story will turn too—and which indeed, as you remember, was the grotesque tragi-comic conception that first encouraged me. To be quite sure I had fallen into no unconscious repetitions, I read *David Copperfield* again the other day, and was affected by it to a degree you would hardly believe.' . . .

Sending the chapters . . . which open the third division of the tale, he wrote thus: 'It is a pity that the third portion cannot be read all at once, because its purpose would be much more apparent; and the pity is the greater, because the general turn and tone of the working out and winding up, will be away from all such things as they conventionally go. But what must be, must be. As to the planning out from week to week, nobody can imagine what the difficulty is, without trying. But, as in all such cases, when it is overcome the pleasure is proportionate. Two months more will see me through it, I trust. All the iron is in the fire, and I have 'only' to beat it out.' One other letter throws light upon an objection taken not unfairly to the too great speed with which the heroine, after being married, reclaimed, and widowed, is in a page or two again made love to, and remarried by the hero. This summary proceeding was not originally intended. But, over and above its popular acceptance, the book had interested some whose opinions Dickens specially valued (Carlyle among them, I remember); and upon Bulwer Lytton objecting to a close that should leave Pip a solitary man. Dickens substituted what now stands. 'You will be surprised', he wrote, 'to hear that I have changed the end of *Great Expectations* from and after Pip's return to Joe's, and finding his little likeness there. Bulwer, who has been, as I think you know, extraordinarily taken by the book, so strongly urged it upon me, after reading the proofs, and supported his view with such good reasons, that I resolved to make the change. You shall have it when you come back to town. I have put in as pretty a little piece of writing as I could, and I have no doubt the story will be more acceptable through the alteration.' This turned out to be the case; but the first ending nevertheless seems to be more consistent with the drift, as well as natural working out, of the tale.

SOURCE: extracts from *The Life of Charles Dickens* (London, 1872–74), Book Ninth, ch. 3.

2. CONTEMPORARY OPINIONS

H. F. Chorley (1861)

'The imaginative book of the year'

... Whether the library of English fiction contains a romance comparable with *Great Expectations* is a matter which admits of doubt— because with the breathless interest of a tale of mystery and adventure, with descriptions in which familiar and tame scenery is wrought up so as to exceed in picturesqueness the Apennine landscapes of a Radcliffe, or the deep-sea storms of a Fenimore Cooper, are combined such variety of humour, such deep and tender knowledge of the secrets of a yearning human heart, as belong to a novel of the highest order. Grant the two leading inventions of the tale as romantic, but not impossible; grant a certain exaggeration, so artfully distributed over the whole work as to amount to nothing more than a high tone of colour, and *Great Expectations* can be charged with only one fault — that of being too short. It stands the test of collection, too, as few tales published in its fragmentary fashion can. Every week almost, as it came out, we were artfully stopped at some juncture which made Suspense count the days till the next number appeared—again to be baulked, and anew to count. Yet, on reading through the romance as a whole, there is no feeling of shock or spasm, still less any impression of 'dropped stitches', but a sense that we have to do with a work of Art arranged from the first moment of conception with power, progress, and a minuteness consistent with the widest apparent freedom. Trying Mr Dickens by himself, we find in this his last tale as much force as in the most forcible portions of *Oliver Twist*, as much delicacy as in the most delicate passages of *David Copperfield*, as much quaint humour as in *Pickwick*. In short, that this is the creation of a great artist in his prime we have felt from the very first moment of its appearance, and can deliberately sign and seal the conviction, even though the catastrophe is before us, and though we have been just devouring the solution of *Great Expectations.* . . .

Most admirable is the manner in which the plot of the tale winds round the wretched hunted jail-bird. Those who from the first understood the delusion of the boy's great expectations—who felt or saw that they had nothing to do with the ghastly recluse in the deserted house, and her brooding revengeful sense of the wicked wrong which had laid her woman's life waste—were, therefore, all the more terribly held in thrall by the knowledge that the convict would return some day, and the air-castle be blown into fragments as by a whirlwind. It is much to say, that the suspense so strongly excited is followed by a catastrophe as fearfully and forcibly outdoing expectation as if it had not been foreseen. There is nothing in English fiction, not even 'the print of the man's foot in the sand' in *Robinson Crusoe*, fuller of engrossing and legitimate terror than the night scene of the convict's return, dogged from its first moment by Death. From this point to its close, the interest of the romance increases with a resistless and steady power never before attained by Mr Dickens. Nor has he ever used his own language with such poignant muscular force as here. Not an epithet is lost; not a touch is laid on carelessly; not a sentence is mannered. Adventure follows adventure—each one more riveting than the last—each one, too, adding some softening and redeeming light to the character of the poor hunted 'warmint', without making the close of his sad story maudlin or sentimental. Everything is as it should be, great and small—from the tremendous murder-scene in the limekiln down to Wemmick's lamentation over 'the portable property'.

There are those who will say that Miss Havisham's strange mad life is overdrawn; but such have not been conversant with the freaks and eccentricities which a haughty spirit in agony can assume: nor the manner in which a resolution once taken becomes a law never to be broken. We have no doubt, that, even now, in remote places of England, rich old mansions might be found as strangely peopled as the deserted brewery—with its spectre in white. Satis House, with its dank and weed-grown garden and the mouldering bridal feast, is as real, to us, as the lonely church on the marshes, or as the wonderful estate in Walworth, with its works of art and ingenuity—the original of which, by the way, we have heard claimed for half-a-dozen different localities.

One word more. In no late fiction has Mr Dickens been so happy in his group of what may be called accessory characters. Mr Jaggers, with his handkerchief; Mr Wopsle, with his dramatic instincts; the greedy, sycophantish seedsman; that wonderful thorn in everyone's side, Trabb's boy—are all capital. We fancy that at the outset he may have meant to make more of Mr and Mrs Matthew Pocket, but they are not missed. Herbert is as fresh and genial an *Horatio* as a hero could desire; and most particularly are we grateful for the uncertainty in which the tale closes, as we interpret it. We do not believe that Pip *did* marry Estella, though there are two opinions on the subject.

We part from this tale with as much reluctance as if we had never before known the dear delight of reading a romance. So strong a sensation of pleasure is too rarely received in this wilderness of dubious literature of ours. *Great Expectations*, we are satisfied, will add to Mr Dickens's reputation, and is the imaginative book of the year.

SOURCE: review in the *Athenaeum* (13 July 1861).

Anonymous (1861)

A Qualified Success

Mr Dickens may be reasonably proud of these volumes. After the long series of his varied works—after passing under the cloud of *Little Dorrit* and *Bleak House*—he has written a story that is new, original, powerful, and very entertaining. It has its weaknesses, as most compositions have, but it is astonishing that a writer who has written so much should still have so much novelty to offer us. He does not serve up the hashes of his old entertainments, and live on repeated resuscitations of his defunct creation. He does not bring in David Copperfield at every stage of his life, and David Copperfield's sons and grand-daughters. He thinks of new characters, makes new jokes, contrives new incidents. He ought to have the thanks of the wearied public, and the admiration of those who know how hard it is to observe when the first zest of observation is passed away, and how much courage and resolution it demands to note the comic in life and manners amid the tragedy and farce of declining years. *Great Expectations* restores Mr Dickens and his readers to the old level. It is in his best vein, and although unfortunately it is too slight, and bears many traces of hasty writing, it is quite worthy to stand beside *Martin Chuzzlewit* and *David Copperfield*. It has characters in it that will become part of common talk, and live even in the mouths of those who do not read novels. Wemmick strikes us as the great creation of the book, and his marriage as the funniest incident. . . .

Mr Dickens has always had one great fault, and it was not to be supposed that he would suddenly shake this fault off. *Great Expectations* is strongly marked with it. This fault is that of exaggerating one particular set of facts, a comic side in a character, or a comic turn of expression, until all reality fades away, and the person who is the centre of the extravagance becomes a mere peg or clothes-horse on which the rags of comedy hang loosely and flutter backwards and forwards. Miss Havisham is one of Mr Dickens' regular pieces of melodramatic exaggeration. She is represented as having lived for a quarter of a century in a room never dusted or cleaned, and always lighted with candles. During all this time she has worn her bridal dress, and everything on her and in the room has remained exactly the same and exactly in the same position for this enormous length of time. Human life cannot go on in this way. We cannot, indeed, prove a negative. We cannot show that no woman ever lived in this manner. But even if it were possible, the manner of living would be too exceptional, too nearly bordering on the monstrous and loathsome, to be appropriately introduced in the midst of a story of ordinary English life. Pumblechook, again, is an instance of the personages in Mr Dickens' novels who only exist to say one set of things, and who do say it, and persist in saying it, until they are equally wearisome and unreal. . . .

But if this new tale is marked with the faults of its predecessors, it appears to us to surpass them in one point. There are passages and conceptions in it which indicate a more profound study of the general nature of human character than Mr Dickens usually betrays. The hero writes an autobiography of his own life, tells the story of his childhood, of his struggles with poverty, and of his gradual rise in the world until he attains what, in Mr Dickens's novels, is the very vague position of a gentleman. Every one is a gentleman there who is not a comic servant or labourer or tradesman on the one hand, or a bloated aristocrat on the other. The adventures of Pip, therefore, threaten to trespass very closely on the adventures of David Copperfield, and the power of novel creation which Mr Dickens possesses is shown in nothing more than that he should have succeeded in keeping two stories of a boy's childhood so wholly distinct. The method he has adopted to create the distinction lies not only in the contrivance of an entirely different set of incidents, but also in making Pip a much more thorough study of character than David Copperfield was. . . .

SOURCE: extracts from review in the *Saturday Review* (20 July 1861).

Edwin Whipple (1861)

Dickens's Best Plot

. . . We have read it, as we have read all Mr Dickens's previous works, as it appeared in instalments, and can testify to the felicity with which expectation was excited and prolonged, and to the series of surprises which accompanied the unfolding of the plot of the story. In no other of his romances has the author succeeded so perfectly in at once stimulating and baffling the curiosity of his readers. He stirred the dullest minds to guess the secret of his mystery; but, so far as we have learned, the guesses of his most intelligent readers have been almost as wide of the mark as those of the least apprehensive. It has been all the more provoking to the former class, that each surprise was the result of art, and not of trick; for a rapid review of previous chapters has shown that the materials of a strictly logical development of the story were freely given. Even after the first, second, third, and even fourth of these surprises gave their pleasing electric shocks to intelligent curiosity, the *dénouement* was still hidden, though confidentially foretold. The plot of the romance is therefore universally admitted to be the best that Dickens has ever invented. Its leading events are, as we read the story consecutively, artistically necessary, yet, at the same time, the processes are artistically concealed. We follow the movement of a logic of passion and character, the real premises of which we detect only when we are startled by the conclusions.

The plot of *Great Expectations* is also noticeable as indicating, better than any of his previous stories, the individuality of Dickens's genius. Everybody must have discerned in the action of his mind two diverging tendencies, which, in this novel, are harmonised. He possesses a singularly wide, clear, and minute power of accurate observation, both of things and of persons; but his observation, keen and true to actualities as it independently is, is not a dominant faculty, and is opposed or controlled by the strong tendency of his disposition to pathetic or humorous idealisation. . . .

SOURCE: extract from review in the *Atlantic Monthly* (Sept. 1861).

E. S. Dallas (1861)

A Return to Humour

Mr Dickens has good-naturedly granted to his hosts of readers the desire of their hearts. They have been complaining that in his later works he has adopted a new style, to the neglect of that old manner which first won our admiration. Give us back the old *Pickwick* style, they cried, with its contempt of art, its loose story, its jumbled characters, and all its jesting that made us laugh so lustily; give us back Sam Weller and Mrs Gamp and Bob Sawyer, and Mrs Nickleby, Pecksniff, Bumble, and the rest, and we are willing to sacrifice serious purpose, consistent plot, finished writing, and all else. Without calling upon his readers for any alarming sacrifices, Mr Dickens has in the present work given us more of his earlier fancies than we have had for years. *Great Expectations* is not, indeed, his best work, but it is to be ranked among his happiest. There is that flowing humour in it which disarms criticism, and which is all the more enjoyable because it defies criticism. Faults there are in abundance, but who is going to find fault when the very essence of the fun is to commit fault? . . .

The public insist upon seeing in Mr Dickens chiefly the humourist; and, however great he may be in other directions, they count all as nothing beside his rare faculty of humour. To those who may not be satisfied with a work of this author's unless humour superabounds most, we can heartily commend *Great Expectations*. . . .

SOURCE: extracts from review in *The Times* (17 Oct. 1861)

Mrs Margaret Oliphant (1862)

A Product of Fatigue

. . . So far as *Great Expectations* is a sensation novel, it occupies itself with incidents all but impossible, and in themselves strange, dangerous, and exciting; but so far as it is one of the series of Mr Dickens's works, it is feeble, fatigued, and colourless. One feels that he must have got tired of it as the work went on, and that the creatures he had called into being, but who are no longer the lively men and women they used to be, must have bored him unspeakably before it was time to cut short their career, and throw a hasty and impatient hint of their future to stop the tiresome public appetite. Joe Gargery the blacksmith alone represents the ancient mood of the author. He is as good, as true, patient, and affectionate, as ungrammatical and confused in his faculty of speech, as could be desired; and shields the poor little Pip when he is a child on his hands, and forgives him when he is a man too grand for the blacksmith, with all that affecting tenderness and refinement of affection with which Mr Dickens has the faculty of making his poor blacksmiths and fishermen much more interesting than anything he has ever produced in the condition of gentleman. . . .

> SOURCE: extract from review in *Blackwood's Magazine* (May 1862).

John Forster (1874)

Character and Comedy

. . . It may be doubted if Dickens could better have established his right to the front rank among novelists claimed for him, than by the ease and mastery with which, in these two books of *Copperfield* and *Great Expectations*, he kept perfectly distinct the two stories of a boy's childhood, both told in the form of autobiography. A subtle penetration into character marks the unlikeness in the likeness; there is enough at once of resemblance and of difference in the position and surroundings of each to account for the divergences of character that arise; both children are good-hearted, and both have the advantage of association with models of tender simplicity and oddity, perfect in their truth and quite distinct from each other; but a sudden tumble into distress steadies Peggotty's little friend, and as unexpected a stroke of good fortune turns the head of the small protégé of Joe Gargery. What a deal of spoiling nevertheless, a nature that is really good at the bottom of it will stand without permanent damage, is nicely shown in Pip; and the way he reconciles his determination to act very shabbily to his early friends, with a conceited notion that he is setting them a moral example, is part of the shading of a character drawn with extraordinary skill. . . .

The characters generally afford the same evidence as those two that Dickens's humour, not less than his creative power, was at its best in this book. The Old Bailey attorney Jaggers, and his clerk Wemmick (both excellent, and the last one of the oddities that live in everybody's liking for the goodheartedness of its comic surprises), are as good as his earliest efforts in that line; the Pumblechooks and Wopsles are as perfect as bits of *Nickleby* fresh from the mint; and the scene in which Pip, and Pip's chum Herbert, make up their accounts and schedule their debts and obligations, is original and delightful as Micawber himself. . . .

SOURCE: extracts from *The Life of Charles Dickens*, Book Ninth, ch. 3.

3. LATER CRITICISM

G. K. Chesterton   'A Heavier Reality'
(1906)

... This fine story is told with a consistency and quietude of
individuality which is rare in Dickens. But so far had he travelled along
the road of a heavier reality, that he even intended to give the tale an
unhappy ending, making Pip lose Estella for ever; and he was only
dissuaded from it by the robust romanticism of Bulwer Lytton. But the
best part of the tale—the account of the vacillations of the hero between
the humble life to which he owes everything, and the gorgeous life from
which he expects something, touches a very true and somewhat tragic
part of morals; for the great paradox of morality (the paradox to which
only the religions have given an adequate expression) is that the very
vilest kind of fault is exactly the most easy kind. We read in books and
ballads about the wild fellow who might kill a man or smoke opium, but
who would never stoop to lying or cowardice or to 'anything mean'. But
for actual human beings opium and slaughter have only occasional
charm; the permanent human temptation is the temptation to be mean.
The one standing probability is the probability of becoming a cowardly
hypocrite. The circle of the traitors is the lowest of the abyss, and it is
also the easiest to fall into. That is one of the ringing realities of the
Bible, that it does not make its great men commit grand sins; it makes
its great men (such as David and St Peter) commit small sins and
behave like sneaks.

Dickens has dealt with this easy descent of desertion, this silent
treason, with remarkable accuracy in the account of the indecisions of
Pip. It contains a good suggestion of that weak romance which is the
root of all snobbishness: that the mystery which belongs to patrician life
excites us more than the open, even the indecent virtues of the humble.
Pip is keener about Miss Havisham, who may mean well by him, than
about Joe Gargery, who evidently does. All this is very strong and
wholesome; but it is still a little stern. . . .

SOURCE: extract from *Charles Dickens* (London, 1906), pp.
168–9.

Julian Moynahan   The Hero's Guilt: The Case of *Great Expectations* (1960)

I

Two recent essays on *Great Expectations* have stressed guilt as the dominant theme. They are Dorothy Van Ghent's 'On Great Expectations' (*The English Novel: Form and Function*, New York, 1953) and G. R. Stange's 'Dickens's Fable for his Time' (*College English*, xvi, October 1954). Mr Stange remarks *inter alia* that 'profound and suggestive as is Dickens's treatment of guilt and expiation in this novel, to trace its remoter implications is to find something excessive and idiosyncratic'; and he has concluded that 'compared with most of the writers of his time the Dickens of the later novels seems to be obsessed with guilt'. He does not develop this criticism, if it is a criticism, but one might guess he is disturbed by a certain discrepancy appearing in the narrative between the hero's sense of guilt and the actual amount of wrong-doing for which he may be said to be responsible. Pip has certainly one of the guiltiest consciences in literature. He not only suffers *agenbite of inwit* for his sin of snobbish ingratitude toward Joe and Biddy, but also suffers through much of the novel from what can only be called a conviction of criminal guilt. Whereas he expiates his sins of snobbery and ingratitude by ultimately accepting the convict Magwitch's unspoken claim for his protection and help, by willingly renouncing his great expectations, and by returning in a chastened mood to Joe and Biddy, he cannot expiate—or exorcise—his conviction of criminality, because it does not seem to correspond with any real criminal acts or intentions.

Snobbery is not a crime. Why should Pip feel like a criminal? Perhaps the novel is saying that snobbery of the sort practised by Pip in the second stage of his career is not very different from certain types of criminal behaviour. For instance, a severe moralist might point out that snobbery and murder are alike in that they are both offences against persons rather than property, and both involve the culpable wish to repudiate or deny the existence of other human beings. On this view, Pip reaches the height of moral insight at the start of the trip down the river, when he looks at Magwitch and sees in him only 'a much better man than I had been to Joe'. By changing places with the convict here, he apparently defines his neglectful behaviour toward Joe as criminal. Does this moment of vision objectify Pip's sense of criminality and prepare the way for expiation? Perhaps, but if so, then Pip's pharisaic rewording of the publican's speech, which occurs a few pages later while he is describing Magwitch's death in the prison, must somehow be explained away:

> Mindful, then, of what we had read together, I thought of the two men who went up into the Temple to pray, and I thought I knew there were no better words that I could say beside his bed, than 'O Lord, be merciful to him, a sinner!'

Even Homer nods, and Dickens is not, morally speaking, at his keenest in deathbed scenes, where his love of the swelling organ tone is apt to make him forget where he is going. Still, we ought not to explain anything away before the entire problem of Pip's guilt has been explored at further length.

Other answers to the question I have raised are possible. Consider the following passage, wherein Pip most fully expresses his sense of a criminal 'taint'. He has just strolled through Newgate prison with Wemmick and is waiting near a London coach office for the arrival of Estella from Miss Havisham's:

> I consumed the whole time in thinking how strange it was that I should be encompassed by all this taint of prison and crime; that, in my childhood out on our lonely marshes on a winter evening I should have first encountered it; that, it should have reappeared on two occasions, starting out like a stain that was faded but not gone; that, it should in this new way pervade my fortune and advancement. While my mind was thus engaged, I thought of the beautiful young Estella, proud and refined, coming toward me, and I thought with absolute abhorrence of the contrast between the jail and her. I wished that Wemmick had not met me, or that I had not yielded to him and gone with him, so that, of all days in the year, on this day I might not have had Newgate in my breath and on my clothes. I beat the prison dust off my clothes as I sauntered to and fro, and I shook it out of my dress, and I exhaled its air from my lungs. So contaminated did I feel, remembering who was coming, that the coach came quickly after all, and I was not yet free from the soiling consciousness of Mr Wemmick's conservatory, when I saw her face at the coach window and her hand waving at me.

Without question, Pip here interprets the frequent manifestations in his experience of criminal elements—the runaway prisoner on the marshes, the man with the two pound notes, the reappearance of the same man in chains on the coach going down into the marsh country, the reappearance of Magwitch's leg iron as the weapon which fells Mrs Joe, the accident making the criminal lawyer Jaggers, whose office is beside Newgate prison, the financial agent of his unknown patron—as signs that indicate some deep affinity between him and a world of criminal violence. But a question that the reader must face here and elsewhere in the novel is whether to accept Pip's interpretation. If we conclude that Pip is in fact tainted with criminality, we must rest our conclusion on a kind of symbolic reading of the coincidences of the plot. Through these coincidences and recurrences, which violate all ordinary notions of probability, Dickens, so this argument must go, weaves together a net in whose meshes his hero is entrapped. Regardless of the fact that Pip's association with crimes and criminals is purely adventitious and that he evidently bears no responsibility for any act or intention of criminal violence, he must be condemned on the principle of guilt by association.

Nevertheless, if the reader is himself not to appear a bit of a pharisee, he must be able to show good reason for accepting the principle of guilt by association in settling the question of the hero's criminality. Both Mr Stange and Miss Van Ghent present readings of the guilt theme which are an attempt to validate this principle. Mr Stange decides that 'the last stage of Pip's progression is reached when he learns to love the criminal and to accept his own implication in the common guilt'. He believes that one of Dickens's major points is that 'criminality is the condition of life'. Pip, therefore, feels criminal guilt because he is criminal as we are all criminal. Along similar lines, Miss Van Ghent remarks, 'Pip . . . carries the convict inside him, as the negative potential of his 'great expectations'—Magwitch is the concretion of his potential guilt.' The appearance of Magwitch at Pip's apartment in the Temple is 'from a metaphysical point of view . . . that of Pip's own unwrought deeds'. Finally, she maintains that Pip bows down before Magwitch, who has been guilty towards him, instead of bowing down before Joe, toward whom Pip has been guilty. In so doing Pip reveals by a symbolic act that he takes the guilt of the world on his shoulders— rather in the style of Father Zossima in *The Brothers Karamazov*. This is shown particularly by the fact that Pip assumes culpability in a relationship where he is, in fact, the innocent party.

Objections to these metaphysical readings can be raised. If criminality is the condition of life, and if guilt is universal in the world of the novel, what world may Joe Gargery, Biddy, and Herbert Pocket be said to inhabit? Miss Van Ghent's theory of Pip's guilt as the negative potential of his great expectations is more promising, because it seems to exempt humble people from the guilt attaching itself to a society of wealth and power which thrives on the expropriation of the fruits of labour of its weaker members. But in her description of Pip's redemptory act, Miss Van Ghent insists upon the pervasiveness of guilt throughout the Dickens world. Less disturbing than this contradiction but still questionable is her assumption that Magwitch has been guilty of great wrong-doing towards Pip. Metaphysics aside, how badly has he treated Pip? Does his wrong-doing stand comparison with the vicious practices of an Orlick or even a Miss Havisham? Who, in the light of the virtues of faithfulness and love, virtues which the novel surely holds up for admiration, is the better, Magwitch or his daughter Estella?

My final objection to these interpretations is Pip's language at Magwitch's deathbed. Pip, after all, tells his own story. Evidence that he has attained an unflawed moral grasp of experience in which the distinction between criminal and non-criminal forms of evil is transcended through the confession *mea culpa* must come, at least partly, from Pip himself. On the strength—on the weakness rather—of his biblical flight, this reader is not convinced that the evidence is clear.

Miss Van Ghent's and Mr Stange's efforts to demonstrate Pip's metaphysical involvement in the criminal milieu of *Great Expectations* are dictated, rightly enough, by their concern for the unifying and inclusive significance of the guilt theme. Their readings provide a means of bridging the gulf between Pip's social sins and the more drastic phenomena of criminality presented in the novel—attempts to moralise the melodrama, as it were, attempts to make the complete narrative presentation revolve around the crucial question of Pip's moral nature. Sensitive readers of the novel will sympathise with this effort, but I do not believe they will agree that the gulf *is* bridged by making criminal guilt a universal condition and by insisting that this is what Pip comes to understand by the time his story is told.

II

In my opinion, Pip's relation to the criminal milieu of *Great Expectations* is not that of an Everyman to a universal condition. It is rather a more concrete and particularised relation than the metaphysical approach would indicate, although the novel defines that relation obliquely and associatively, not through discursive analysis. Miss Van Ghent has suggested a metaphoric connection between Magwitch and Pip. Her proposal of such implicit relations between character and character, even though they do not become rationalised anywhere, is an illuminating insight into the artistic method of the mature Dickens. But her principle can be applied differently and yield rather different results.

I would suggest that Orlick rather than Magwitch is the figure from the criminal milieu of the novel whose relations to him come to define

Pip's implicit participation in the acts of violence with which the novel abounds. Considered by himself, Orlick is a figure of melodrama. He is unmotivated, his origins are shrouded in mystery, his violence is unqualified by regret. In this last respect he is the exact opposite of Pip, who is, of course, filled with regret whenever he remembers how he has neglected his old friends at the forge.

On the other hand, if we consider Orlick in his connections with Pip, some rather different observations can be made. In the first place, there is a peculiar parallel between the careers of the two characters. We first encounter Orlick as he works side by side with Pip at the forge. Circumstances also cause them to be associated in the assault on Mrs Joe. Orlick strikes the blow, but Pip feels, with some justification, that he supplied the assault weapon. Pip begins to develop his sense of alienation from the village after he has been employed by Miss Havisham to entertain her in her house. But Orlick too turns up later on working for Miss Havisham as gatekeeper. Finally, after Pip has become a partisan of the convict, it turns out that Orlick also has become a partisan of an ex-convict, Compeyson, who is Magwitch's bitter enemy.

Up to a point, Orlick seems not only to dog Pip's footsteps, but also to present a parody of Pip's upward progress through the novel, as though he were in competitive pursuit of some obscene great expectations of his own. Just as Pip centres his hopes successively on the forge, Satis House, and London, so Orlick moves his base of operations successively from the forge, to Satis House, and to London. From Pip's point of view, Orlick has no right to interest himself in any of the people with whom Pip has developed close ties. For instance, he is appalled when he discovers that his tender feeling for Biddy is given a distorted echo by Orlick's obviously lecherous interest in the same girl. And when he discovers that Orlick has the right of entry into Satis House he warns Jaggers to advise Miss Havisham to get rid of him. But somehow he cannot keep Orlick out of his affairs. When Magwitch appears at Pip's London lodging half-way through the novel, Orlick is crouching in darkness on the landing below Pip's apartment. And when Pip is about to launch the escape attempt down the Thames, his plans are frustrated by the trick which brings him down to the marshes to face Orlick in the hut by the limekiln. Its lurid melodrama and the awkwardness of its integration with the surrounding narrative has made many readers dismiss this scene as a piece of popular writing aimed at the less intelligent members of Dickens's audience. But the confrontation of Orlick and Pip on the marshes is crucial for an understanding of the problem I am discussing, because it is the scene in which Dickens comes closest to making explicit the analogy between the hero and the novel's principal villain and criminal.

Orlick inveigles Pip to the limepit not only to kill him but to overwhelm him with accusations. Addressing Pip over and over again as 'Wolf', an epithet he might more readily apply to himself, he complains that Pip has cost him his place, come between him and a young woman in whom he was interested, tried to drive him out of the country, and been a perpetual obstacle in the path of his own uncouth ambitions. But the charge he makes with the greatest force and conviction is that Pip bears the final responsibility for the assault on Mrs Joe:

> 'I tell you it was your doing—I tell you it was done through you', he retorted, catching up the gun and making a blow with the stock at the vacant air between us. 'I come upon her from behind, as I come upon you to-night. I giv' it to her! I left her for dead, and if there had been a limekiln as nigh her as there is now nigh you, she shouldn't have come to life again. But it warn't old Orlick as did it; it was you. You was favoured, and he was bullied and beat. Old Orlick bullied and beat, eh? Now you pays for it. You done it; now you pays for it.'

The entire scene has a nightmare quality. This is at least partly due to the weird reversal of rôles, by which the innocent figure is made the accused and the guilty one the accuser. As in a dream the situation is absurd, yet like a dream it may contain hidden truth. On the one hand Orlick, in interpreting Pip's character, seems only to succeed in describing himself—ambitious, treacherous, murderous, and without compunction. On the other hand, several of Orlick's charges are justified, and it is only in the assumption that Pip's motives are as black as his own that he goes wrong. We know, after all, that Pip is ambitious, and that he has repudiated his early associates as obstacles to the fulfilment of his genteel aspirations. Another interesting observation can be made about Orlick's charge that 'it was you as did for your shrew sister'. Here Orlick presents Pip as the responsible agent, himself merely as the weapon. But this is an exact reversal of Pip's former assumptions about the affair. All in all, Orlick confronts the hero in this scene, not merely as would-be murderer, but also as a distorted and darkened mirror-image. In fact, he presents himself as a monstrous caricature of the tender-minded hero, insisting that they are two of a kind with the same ends, pursued through similarly predatory and criminal means. This is what his wild accusations come down to.

III

Is Orlick mistaken in representing himself in this scene as a sort of double, *alter ego*, or shadow of Pip? Is he merely projecting his own qualities upon him, or do Orlick's accusations, in any sense, constitute a partially or wholly valid comment on Pip's actions? In order to answer these questions we shall have to begin by analysing the fantasy of great expectations which gives the book so much of its universal appeal. This fantasy, so the psychologists tell us, is a well-nigh universal imaginative flight of childhood. By creating for himself a fiction wherein the world is made to conform to his desire and will, the child succeeds in compensating himself for the fact that his real position is without power and that the quantity of love and nurture to which he believes himself entitled is greatly in excess of the amount he actually receives. Out of this unbalance between an unbounded demand and a limited supply of love and power proceed the fairy godmothers as well as the vicious step-parents and bad giants in which world legend abounds. The fantasy element *Great Expectations* shares with such stories as *Cinderella* and *Jack and the Beanstalk* contains, then, two implicit motives: the drive for power and the drive for more mother-love. However, of the two, the power motive, since it involves the aggressive wish to push beyond the authoritarian figures who hold the child powerless, is apt to be more productive of guilt and, consequently, is likely to be expressed with a certain amount of concealment. Thus, Jack in the folk tale conquers authority in the fictional guise of killing the wicked giant. But there is no attempt to disguise the fact that he steals from the giant in order to live in affluence with his widowed mother, enjoying her undivided love and admiration. We might add that the type of love sought in this fantasy is a childish version of mature love. It is largely passive. It is associated with a super-abundance of the good things of life, often with the enjoyment of great wealth.

In *Great Expectations*, the second motive is clearly represented in the early stages of Pip's career. His early experiences follow the fairy-tale pattern. Circumstances magically conspire to rescue him from the spartan rigours of Mrs Joe. In taking him up, Miss Havisham plays the rôle of fairy godmother, and later permits him to continue in his belief that she is also the sponsor of his luxury in London—until he is brought up short by the rough figure of Magwitch. Until the real world breaks in on him, Pip allows himself to be pushed along, never challenging the requirement that he must not look too closely into the sources of his good fortune. Likewise, he is passive in his longing for Estella, who, in her metaphoric associations with precious jewels and lofty stars, comes to symbolise to him the final goal of his dreams of love, luxury, and high position. Instead of trying to capture her through an aggressive courtship he simply pines, assuming on very little evidence that one day she will be bestowed upon him by Miss Havisham as everything else has been.

Upon the return of Magwitch, Pip is forced to wake up and recognise that life is not, after all, a fairy tale. He learns that his own wealth comes from a criminal, that even the magical figures of Satis House, Miss Havisham and Estella have criminal connections, and, as we have seen, that his callous treatment of Joe Gargery was essentially criminal. This linking up of the criminal milieu and the milieu of wealth and high position is a way of drawing the strongest possible contrast between Pip's regressive fantasy-world, where wealth and good luck have seemed unremitting and uncompromised, and a real world where the dominant moral colouring is at best a dirty grey.

In terms of what we have called the love-motive, then, Dickens has shown fantasy in collision with reality. Pip learns that the world is not a vast mammary gland from which he can draw rich nourishment with moral impunity. He finds that he must hunger and struggle like all the rest. Furthermore, he must accept the unhappy fact that his participation in the old dream of great expectations has hurt real people. With his awakening to reality he develops a capacity for active, self-bestowing love. But the mature tough-minded perspective from which the hero's development is viewed does not permit him to move on into happiness and fulfilment. In the final chapters of *Great Expectations* Pip wants to give himself, but there is no longer anyone in a position to accept his gift. Magwitch's fate is upon him; the circumstance of marriage has carried both Biddy and Estella beyond his reach. In bestowing himself upon the family of Herbert Pocket, Pip comes to rest in a kind of limbo. The book seems to imply that Pip is doomed to a lifetime of vicarious experience, because he lingered too long in his condition of alienation from the real.

This is not a complete account of Dickens's critique of the great expectations fantasy, that dream of huge and easy success which has always haunted the imagination of children and also haunted the imaginations of adults in the increasingly commercial and industrial society of nineteenth-century England. In *Great Expectations*, as in its legendary prototypes, the theme of ambition is treated under the two aspects of desire and will, the search for a superabundance of love and the drive for power. And it is in his presentation of the theme in the latter aspect that Dickens makes the more profound analysis of the immoral and criminal elements in his hero's (and the century's) favourite dream.

But Pip's ambition is passive. He only becomes active and aggressive after he has ceased to be ambitious. How then does *Great Expectations* treat the theme of ambition in terms that are relevant to the total action of which Pip is the centre? I have already begun to suggest an answer to the question. Ambition as the instinct of aggression, as the pitiless drive for power directed against what we have called authority-figures is both coalesced and disguised in the figure of Orlick. And Orlick is bound to the hero by ties of analogy as double, *alter ego* and dark mirror-image. We are dealing here with an art which simultaneously disguises and reveals its deepest implications of meaning, with a method which apparently dissociates its thematic materials and its subject matter into moral fable-*cum*-melodramatic accompaniment, yet simultaneously presents through patterns of analogy a dramatic perspective in which the apparent opposites are unified. In *Great Expectations* criminality is displaced from the hero on to a melodramatic villain. But on closer inspection that villain becomes part of a complex unity—we might call it Pip-Orlick—in which all aspects of the problem of guilt become interpenetrant and co-operative. The only clue to this unity which is given at the surface level of the narrative is Pip's obsession of criminal guilt. Pip tells us over and over again that he feels contaminated by crime. But we do not find the objective correlative of that conviction until we recognise in the insensate and compunctionless Orlick a shadow image of the tender-minded and yet monstrously ambitious young hero.

What is the rationale of this elusive method? In my opinion it enabled Dickens to project a radical moral insight which anticipated the more sophisticated probings of novelists like Dostoievsky and Gide without abandoning the old-fashioned traditions of melodrama and characterisation in which he had worked for more than a quarter of a century before *Great Expectations* was published. Pip, by comparison with Raskolnikov, is a simple young man. But through the analogy Pip—Orlick, *Great Expectations* makes the same point about ambition as *Crime and Punishment*, and it is a very penetrating point indeed. In the *Brothers Karamazov* Ivan comes to recognise during the course of three tense interviews with his half-brother, Smerdyakov, how he shares with that brother a criminal responsibility for the murder of their father, although Smerdyakov alone wielded the weapon. The comparable scene in *Great Expectations* is the limekiln scene. Orlick even adopts the tone of a jealous sibling during the interview, as in the remark, 'You was favoured, and he was bullied and beat.' But Dickens is not a Dostoievsky. Pip does not recognise Orlick as a blood-relation, so to speak. The meaning remains submerged and is communicated to the reader through other channels than the agonised confession of a first-person narrator. Indeed, the profoundest irony of the novel is not reached until the reader realises he must see Pip in a much harsher moral perspective than Pip ever saw himself.

IV

Recognition that Pip's ambition is definable under the aspect of aggression as well as in terms of the regressive desire for passive enjoyment of life's bounty depends upon the reader's willingness to work his way into the narrative from a different angle than the narrator's. The evidence for the hero's power-drive against the authority-figures, the evidence of his 'viciousness' if you will, is embodied in the story in a number of ways, but a clear pattern of meaning only emerges after the reader has correlated materials which are dispersed and nominally unrelated in the story *as told*. Orlick, thus far, has been the figure whose implicit relations to the hero have constituted the chief clue to the darker meaning of Pip's career. He continues to be important in any attempt to set forth the complete case, but there are also some significant correlations to be made in which he does not figure. This is fortunate, if only to forestall the objection that the whole case depends upon an imputed resemblance between two characters whom generations of devoted readers have not, after all, found very much alike. Let us, then, present the rest of the evidence, and see whether Pip, in any sense, stands self-indicted as well as indicted for the bad company he occasionally—and most reluctantly— keeps.

We might begin with the apparently cynical remark that Pip, judged on the basis of what happens to many of the characters closely associated with him, is a very dangerous young man. He is not accident-prone, but a great number of people who move into his orbit decidedly are. Mrs Joe is bludgeoned, Miss Havisham goes up in flames, Estella is exposed through her rash marriage to vaguely specified tortures at the hands of her brutal husband, Drummle. Pumblechook has his house looted and his mouth stuffed with flowering annuals by a gang of thieves led by Orlick. All of these characters, with the exception of Estella, stand at one time or another in the relation of patron, patroness, or authority-figure to Pip the boy or Pip the man. (Pumblechook is, of course, a parody patron, and his comic chastisement is one of the most satisfying things in the book.) Furthermore, all of these characters, including Estella, have hurt, humiliated, or thwarted Pip in some important way. All in some way have stood between him and the attainment of the full measure of his desires. All are punished.

Let us group these individual instances. Mrs Joe, the cruel foster-mother, and Pumblechook, her approving and hypocritical relation by marriage, receive their punishment from the hands of Orlick. Mrs Joe hurts Pip and is hurt in turn by Orlick. Pip has the motive of revenge—a lifetime of brutal beatings and scrubbings inflicted by his sister—but Orlick, a journeyman who does not even lodge with the Gargerys, bludgeons Mrs Joe after she has provoked a quarrel between him and his master. If we put together his relative lack of motive with his previously quoted remarks at the limekiln and add to these Pip's report of his own extraordinary reaction upon first hearing of the attack—

> With my head full of George Barnwell, I was at first disposed to
> believe that *I* must have had some hand in the attack upon my
> sister, or at all events that as her near relation, popularly known
> to be under obligations to her, I was a more legitimate object of
> suspicion than anyone else—

we arrive at an anomalous situation which can best be resolved on the
assumption that Orlick acts merely as Pip's punitive instrument or
weapon.

With regard to Pumblechook's chastisement, the most striking
feature is not that Orlick should break into a house, but that he should
break into Pumblechook's house. Why not Trabb's? One answer might
be that Trabb has never stood in Pip's light. Pumblechook's punishment is nicely proportioned to his nuisance value for Pip. Since he has
never succeeded in doing him any great harm with his petty slanders, he
escapes with a relatively light wound. Although we are told near the
end of the novel that Orlick was caught and jailed after the burglary, we
are never told that Pip reported Orlick's murderous assault on him or
his confessions of his assault on Mrs Joe to the police. Despite the fact
that there is enough accumulated evidence to hang him, Orlick's end is
missing from the book. Actually, it seems that Orlick simply evaporates
into thin air after his punitive rôle has been performed. His case needs
no final disposition because he has only existed, essentially, as an aspect
of the hero's own far more problematic case.

Estella receives her chastisement at the hands of Bentley Drummle.
How does this fit into the pattern we have been exploring? In the first
place, it can be shown that Drummle stands in precisely the same
analogical relationship to Pip as Orlick does. Drummle is a re-
duplication of Orlick at a point higher on the social-economic scale up
which Pip moves with such rapidity through the first three-quarters of
the novel. Drummle, like Orlick, is a criminal psychopath. At Jaggers's
dinner party the host, a connoisseur of criminal types, treats Drummle
as 'one of the true sort', and Drummle demonstrates how deserving he is
of this distinction when he tries to brain the harmless Startop with a
heavy tumbler.

But the most impressive evidence that Orlick and Drummle are
functional equivalents is supplied by the concrete particulars of their
description. To an extraordinary degree, these two physically powerful,
inarticulate, and dark-complexioned villains are presented to the
reader in terms more often identical than similar. Orlick, again and
again, is one who lurks and lounges, Drummle is one who lolls and lurks.
When Pip, Startop, and Drummle go out rowing, the last 'would always

creep in-shore like some uncomfortable amphibious creature, even
when the tide would have sent him fast on his way; and I always think of
him as coming after us in the dark or by the back-water, when our own
two boats were breaking the sunset or the moonlight in mid-stream'.
When Startop walks home after Jaggers's party, he is followed by
Drummle but on the opposite side of the street, 'in the shadow of the
houses, much as he was wont to follow in his boat'. The other creeper,
follower and amphibian of *Great Expectations* is Orlick, whose natural
habitat is the salt marsh, who creeps his way to the dark landing below
Pip's apartment to witness the return of Magwitch from abroad, who
creeps behind Biddy and Pip as they walk conversing on the marshes
and overhears Pip say he will do anything to drive Orlick from the
neighbourhood, who appears out of the darkness near the turnpike
house on the night Pip returns from Pumblechook's to discover that his
sister has been assaulted, and who, finally, creeps his way so far into
Pip's private business that he ends by acting as agent for Compeyson,
Magwitch's—and Pip's—shadowy antagonist.

Like Orlick, Drummle is removed from the action suddenly; Pip is
given no opportunity to settle old and bitter scores with him. In the last
chapter we hear that he is dead 'from an accident consequent on ill-
treating a horse'. This is the appropriate end for a sadist whose crimes
obviously included wife-beating. But more important to the present
argument is our recognition that Drummle has been employed to break
a woman who had, in the trite phrase, broken Pip's heart. Once he has
performed his function as Pip's vengeful surrogate he can be assigned to
the fate he so richly deserves.

Mrs Joe beats and scrubs Pip until she is struck down by heavy blows
on the head and spine. Pumblechook speaks his lies about him until his
mouth is stuffed with flowers. Estella treats his affections with cold
contempt until her icy pride is broken by a brutal husband. In this series
Orlick and Drummle behave far more like instruments of vengeance
than like three-dimensional characters with understandable grudges of
their own. In terms of my complete argument, they enact an aggressive
potential that the novel defines, through patterns of analogy and linked
resemblances, as belonging in the end to Pip and to his unconscionably
ambitious hopes.

When Miss Havisham bursts into flames, there is no Orlick or
Drummle in the vicinity to be accused of having set a match to her. In
the long series of violence which runs through *Great Expectations* from the
beginning to end, this is one climax of violence that can be construed as
nothing more than accidental. And yet it is an accident which Pip, on
two occasions, has foreseen. Before Miss Havisham burns under the eye
of the horror-struck hero, she has already come to a violent end twice in
his hallucinated fantasies—in Pip's visionary experiences in the

abandoned brewery, where he sees Miss Havisham hanging by the neck from a beam. He has this vision once as a child, on the occasion of his first visit to Satis House, and once as an adult, on the occasion on his last visit, just a few minutes before Miss Havisham's accident occurs. What are we to make, if anything, of these peculiar hallucinatory presentiments and of the coincidence by which they come true?

The child first sees his patroness hanging from a beam after his first hour of service with her. At this point the novel dwells at length on his keen awareness that he has been cruelly treated, generalises on the extreme sensitiveness of children to injustice, and describes how Pip in utter frustration vents his injured feelings by kicking a wall and twisting his own hair. In these passages it seems to me that the reader is being prepared to interpret Pip's immediately ensuing hallucination as the child's further attempt to discharge his anger and grief against his adult tormenter. In fantasy Pip punishes a woman whom in fact he cannot disturb in any way, and, by hanging her, attempts to destroy the threat to his peace and security which she represents. This interpretation excludes the possibility of a supernatural element in the experience; the novel provides abundant evidence that the imagination of a child operating under a great stress of emotion is possessed of a hallucinatory power. When Pip carries stolen provisions to Magwitch on the marshes, his guilt-ridden imagination effects a transformation of the countryside through which he passes, until even gates, dykes, banks, cattle and a signpost seem to him to be pursuing him and crying out his guilt. Pip's hallucination, then, is an imaginative fantasy which both projects and disguises the boy's desire to punish his employer and to destroy her baleful power over him.

Pip experiences no recurrence of the hallucination during the long years of an association with Miss Havisham based on his mistaken assumption that she is the sole author of his good fortunes. The fantasy returns only after his eyes have been opened to the fact that nothing has come to him from Miss Havisham except unhappiness. On the last visit to Satis House he learns definitely of Estella's marriage. With this information the last link between him and his former employer snaps. The false fairy godmother kneels to ask forgiveness for her crimes against him, and the duped hero offers forgiveness sincerely, if sadly. Nevertheless, as Pip strolls through the ruins of the estate he is not able to refrain from brooding over Miss Havisham's 'profound unfitness for this earth', and when he walks into the chilly, twilit brewery building he is not able to prevent the return of the old hallucination of Miss Havisham hanging from the beam. We are told that this was owing to the revival of a childish association. But surely the episode represents more than a curious psychological detail. It is profoundly right that the fantasy should return at a time when he can see in complete clarity and detail how his connection with Miss Havisham has hurt him. It is profoundly right that he should forgive the false patroness and yet not forgive her, behave generously toward her and yet feel deeply that she has no right to live, treat her with some degree of melancholy affection, yet hate her also in the depths of his being.

We need not deny Dickens the insight necessary to the imagining of so ambivalent a response in the hero of his great novel. And we should not commit the anachronism of demanding that this response be defined in the novel analytically and self-consciously—that the hero should tell us, 'I forgave Miss Havisham as fully as I could, but continued to think how well it would have been for me if she had never set foot on this earth.' Pip's ambivalence is embodied dramatically. It must be known not as it is talked about, but as enacted. A man forgives a woman, then hallucinates her death by hanging. A man watches a woman burst into flames, then leaps bravely to her rescue, but in the course of describing this rescue is forced to remark, 'We were on the ground struggling like desperate enemies.'

How do these hallucinations, the second followed immediately by Miss Havisham's fatal accident, add to the burden of the hero's guilt? The answer is obvious. Because Pip's destructive fantasy comes true in reality, he experiences the equivalent of a murderer's guilt. As though he had the evil eye, or as though there were more than a psychological truth in the old cliché, 'if looks could kill', Pip moves from the brewery, where he has seen Miss Havisham hanging, to the door of her room, where he gives her one long, last look—until she is consumed by fire. But here the psychological truth suffices to establish imaginative proof that Pip can no more escape untainted from his relationship to the former patroness than he can escape untainted from any of his relationships to characters who have held and used the power to destroy or hamper his ambitious struggles. In all these relationships the hero becomes implicated in violence. With Estella, Pumblechook, and Mrs Joe, the aggressive drive is enacted by surrogates linked to the hero himself by ties of analogy. With Miss Havisham the surrogate is missing. Miss Havisham falls victim to the purely accidental. But the 'impurity' of Pip's motivation, as it is revealed through the device of the recurrent hallucination, suggests an analogy between that part of Pip which wants Miss Havisham at least punished, at most removed from this earth for which she is so profoundly unfit, and the destroying fire itself.

V

In this essay I have argued that Dickens's novel defines its hero's dream of great expectations and the consequences stemming from indulgence in that dream under the two aspects of desire and will, of regressive longing for an excess of love and of violent aggressiveness. In the unfolding of the action these two dramas are not presented separately. Instead they are combined into Dickens's most complex representation of character in action. Pip is Dickens's most complicated hero, demonstrating at once the traits of criminal and gull, of victimiser and victim. He is victimised by his dream and the dream itself, by virtue of its profoundly anti-social and unethical nature, forces him into relation with a world in which other human beings fall victim to his drive for power. He is, in short, a hero sinned against and sinning: sinned against because in the first place the dream was thrust upon the helpless child by powerful and corrupt figures from the adult world; a sinner because in accepting for himself a goal in life based upon unbridled individualism and indifference to others he takes up a career which *Great Expectations* repeatedly, through a variety of artistic means, portrays as essentially criminal.

After Magwitch's death, Pip falls a prey to brain fever. During his weeks of delirium it seems to me that his hallucinations articulate the division in his character between helpless passivity and demonic aggressiveness. Pip tells us he dreamed

> that I was a brick in the house wall, and yet entreating to be released from the giddy place where the builders had set me; that I was a steel beam of a vast engine clashing and whirling over a great gulf, yet that I implored in my own person to have the engine stopped, and my part in it hammered off.

It is tempting to read these images as dream logic. The hero-victim cries for release from his unsought position of height and power, but cannot help himself from functioning as a moving part of a monstrous apparatus which seems to sustain itself from a plunge into the abyss only through the continuous expenditure of destructive force. In the narrative's full context this vast engine can be taken to represent at one and the same time the demonic side of the hero's career and a society that maintains its power intact by the continuous destruction of the hopes and lives of its weaker members. In the latter connection we can think of Magwitch's account of his childhood and youth, and of the judge who passed a death sentence on thirty-two men and women, while the sun struck in through the courtroom windows making a 'broad shaft of light between the two-and-thirty and the judge, linking them both together'. But to think of the engine as a symbol of society is still to think of Pip. For Pip's career enacts his society's condition of being—its guilt, its sinfulness, and in the end, its helplessness to cleanse itself of a taint 'of prison and crime'.

When Pip wakes up from his delirium he finds himself a child again, safe in the arms of the angelic Joe Gargery. But the guilt of great expectations remains inexpiable, and the cruelly beautiful original ending of the novel remains the only possible 'true' ending. Estella and Pip face each other across the insurmountable barrier of lost innocence. The novel dramatises the loss of innocence, and does not glibly present the hope of a redemptory second birth for either its guilty hero or the guilty society which shaped him. I have already said that Pip's fantasy of superabundant love brings him at last to a point of alienation from the real world. And similarly Pip's fantasy of power brings him finally to a point where withdrawal is the only positive moral response left to him.

The brick is taken down from its giddy place, a part of the engine is hammered off. Pip cannot redeem his world. In no conceivable sense a leader, he can only lead himself into a sort of exile from his society's power centres. Living abroad as the partner of a small, unambitious firm, he is to devote his remaining life to doing the least possible harm to the smallest number of people, so earning a visitor's privileges in the lost paradise where Biddy and Joe, the genuine innocents of the novel, flourish in thoughtless content.

SOURCE: *Essays in Criticism*, 10 (1960), pp. 60–79.

Robert B. Partlow Jnr.   The Moving I:
A Study of the Point of View in *Great
Expectations* (1961)

Articles like Norman Friedman's (1955 *PMLA*) are reminders that critical discussions and analyses of point of view in fiction have, in the last half century, become steadily more subtle and penetrative. Henry James, James Joyce, Joseph Warren Beach, Percy Lubbock, E. M. Forster, and Mark Schorer, to mention only the most significant, have made clear the strategic importance of the author's choice of a center (his focus, his position **in** relation to events) and his choices of narrator and listener (his mode of transmission). Professor Friedman asks the questions that must be answered about such choices and outlines the range of possible modes of transmission from editorial omniscience through neutral omniscience, 'I' as witness, 'I' as protagonist, multiple selective omniscience and selective omniscence, to the dramatic mode and the camera method. Within the limits of a short article, he marks out the major categories and hints at some of the possible variations, combinations, and overlappings. He also provides us with the critical terminology needed for a close study of a specific novel, *Great Expectations* for example.

Assuming—perhaps gratuitously—that the characters, story line, and theme had been established in mind and that Dickens had chosen to write autobiographically, in the 'I' as protagonist mode, what specific problems would necessarily have cropped up at once? Certainly these, at the least: (1) What is to be the position of the narrator in time: contemporary throughout with the events of the story proper, contemporary only with the later sections of the story, posterior to the story events, or shifting? To what extent are the characters and events of the story to be presented as history? Is the narrator to be seated in front of a panorama or is he to take his place in events as they are happening? (2) If the historical or panoramic method is chosen, is the narrator to act as an interpreter or merely as a cameraman or recorder? What degree of omniscience, if any, is to be shown? (3) What will be the relationship between narrator and author? (4) What audience is to be selected? (5) Which of all the possible means of presentation (including dialogue, interior monologue, pictured action, description of people and events, and external comment) shall be used? What is to be the relative proportion and balance among these means? The answers to these and similar questions, whether made with full awareness or not, will determine the structure and, to some extent, the tone of the novel.

In *Great Expectations*, the narrator is neither Pip nor Mr Pip, but Mr Pirrip, a moderately successful, middle-aged businessman, a *petit bourgeois* who has risen in life by his own exertions and a fine bit of luck. Now home from his work overseas, he is telling his life story many years after all the events have occurred. Unlike the Pip of all except the last two chapters, he is a mature man, sober, industrious, saddened, aware of his own limitations, and possessed of a certain calm wisdom—the wisdom of a Cinderella who learned the shoe did not fit and the fairy godmother was psychotic and criminal. He also has a keen sense of the ludicrous and the grotesque which cannot be ascribed to himself when younger. As we read the story, it becomes more and more evident that he cannot entirely grasp what Pip was or why the young fellow acted as he did. The narrator, in fact, feels a kind of alienation from Pip. The boy and the young man did, after all, act according to motives and feelings

which the older man sees not directly, but through a film of memory. In
chapter 6, for example, the narrator remarks about young Pip:

> My state of mind regarding the pilfering from which I had been
> so unexpectedly exonerated, did not impel me to frank dis-
> closure; but I hope it had some dregs of good at the bottom of it.
> I do not recall that I felt any tenderness of conscience to Mrs Joe,
> when the fear of being found out was lifted off me. But I loved
> Joe—perhaps for no better reason in those early days than
> because the dear fellow let me love him—and, as to him, my
> inner self was not so easily composed . . . The fear of losing Joe's
> confidence, and of thenceforth sitting in the chimney-corner at
> night staring drearily at my for ever lost companion and friend,
> tied my tongue. I morbidly represented to myself that if Joe
> knew it, I never afterwards could see him at the fireside feeling
> his fair whisker, without thinking that he was meditating on
> it. . . . In a word, I was too cowardly to do what I knew to be
> right, as I had been too cowardly to avoid doing what I knew to
> be wrong. I had had no intercourse with the world at that time,
> and I imitated none of its many inhabitants who act in this
> manner. Quite an untaught genius, I made the discovery of the
> line of action for myself.

This passage, which is a typical one, suggests that the narrator does not
feel identified with Pip. Sympathetic, yes, and amused—but these are
feelings associated with others, not one's self. Even more, the narrator
judges Pip's fear from an adult position, with a sophistication impossible
for a seven-year-old boy, directs his gaze forward a dozen years later to
Pip's subsequent experiences, and comments sardonically on customary
human behavior. Even more, the diction and turn of phrase are those of
a skillful writer, not those of an untaught blacksmith's boy. But all this is
exactly in keeping with the position and character of the narrator and is
part of Dickens's admirable control of his technique in this novel. The
choice of point of view almost obviates the interior monologue, except
at a remove; neither are we taken very deeply into Pip's mind. In this
and other passages the narrator is neither Pip nor an omniscient author;
he is an older man trying, not always with complete success, to recall the
exact dimensions of an emotion formerly felt and the real motives for an
action far back in time. Occasionally he reminds the reader, especially
in the early chapters, that the view is down a long corridor only fitfully
lighted. In chapter 12, for instance, while he is discussing the boy's
relations with the other characters, he stops to say:

> I reposed complete confidence in no one but Biddy; but, I told
> poor Biddy everything. Why it came natural for me to do so, and
> why Biddy had a deep concern in everything I told her, I did not
> know then, though I think I know now.

And in chapter 38 there are three passages which remind the reader of
the gap between the present telling and past events:

> It is impossible to turn this leaf of my life without putting Bentley
> Drummle's name upon it; or, I would, very gladly. . . . I tell
> this lightly, but it was no light thing to me. For, I cannot
> adequately express what pain it gave me to think that Estella
> should show any favour to a contemptible, clumsy, sulky booby,
> so very far below the average. . . . And now that I have given
> the one chapter to the theme that so filled my heart, and so often
> made it ache and ache again, I pass on, unhindered, to the event
> that had impended over me longer yet.

The scrupulous attention to tenses and tense sequences in these and
other chapters is also noteworthy. All events in the main story line are
placed in one of the past tenses; in all except the dramatic scenes present
and future tenses are reserved for the narrator's use. Once the reader has
recognised the point of view being used, this practice is not obtrusive or
distracting; it provides, indeed, an economical means of keeping the
narrator's observations and emotions distinct from those of Pip.

Dickens was not—perhaps could not be—equally scrupulous in his
use of the pronoun *I*. As a result the reader does not always know at once
if it means 'I-the-narrator, as I am now' or 'I-as-Pip, as I was'. In this
novel the two are so different that separate pronouns might well have
been used, perhaps in the manner that the French distinguish between
tu and *vous*. If the reader is very attentive, he will get this effect anyway:
there is often such a great difference between the two *I*'s that the latter,
the 'I-as-I-was', becomes virtually 'he'. Thus we may say that the point
of view seems to combine the first person protagonist method with third
person selective omniscient. Perhaps an image would make the point
clearer. Consider a man showing sound moving pictures of his early life
and explaining them for the benefit of his guests. He watches the action
with them, and comments lovingly or sadly or ironically about events
and people; occasionally he refers to something that has not yet
appeared in the time sequence of the film; he speeds up the dull parts
and slows down the moving or humorous parts, mentioning, as he does
so, that the characters were not playing roles and certainly took
themselves seriously, not as actors working to evoke tears or laughter; he
feels himself an especially knowledgeable member of the present

audience and so looks at himself as he was, in the film, from a distance, as half a stranger.

But not always. Dickens was too competent a novelist merely to tell a story and too confirmed a dramatist not to let the sound-film speak for itself at least part of the time. Almost every chapter, therefore, combines the distant and close views, the narrative and the dramatic modes of presentation, telling and showing—all very smoothly. Take as example chapter 4, that delightful account of the Christmas dinner at Joe Gargery's. Paragraph 1 is narrative, an adult commentary upon the action going on in the moving picture; notice the un-Pippian 'reaping' in the last sentence. In the next three paragraphs the presentation is dramatic: Mrs Joe is allowed to speak for herself. Paragraphs 5 through 16 are a complex mixture of modes of presentation: they set the scene for the dinner, describe Joe and Wopsle both externally and in terms of Pip's reactions, photograph certain actions, and include comments by the narrator from his vantage point outside of and superior to the action. Paragraphs 17 through 40 are very largely dramatic and immediate, with only brief intrusions by the narrator. Paragraphs 41 through 55 combine the dramatic and narrative modes, but the narrative is unlike that used earlier in the chapter in that the narrator identifies himself with Pip for the moment, so closely indeed that we see events through the boy's eyes; we get, not a statement or a re-capitulation, but the almost direct expression of the boy's emotions, even though the diction and the wit are the narrator's.

Thus, though it is true that the narrator occupies a fixed position in time, in the now, and has to look back at earlier events, we get the impression that the point of view shifts. This impression derives partly from the frequent use of dramatic scenes, which are necessarily immediate, and even more importantly from what is often called psychological distance. As the term suggests, the narrator sometimes feels very close to the events that happened and to Pip's feelings at the time, so close that they no longer have to be called up from the memory but are immediately given. When, for example, the narrator tells of the death of Magwitch in chapter 56, he is not merely looking at Pip through the blur of time; he is not remembering or recounting the young man's experience so much as he is reliving it. At such times the narrator and Pip seem to merge. It is almost as if, to revert to the image of the host showing pictures to guests, the narrator occasionally forgets his audience and his present position in society, drops down into the depths of his mind, and there repeats the original experience in something like its original intensity. At other times, especially when Pip is acting the fool, the narrator reassumes his role as polished adult. Of this type is the ironic passage in chapter 30 during which Pip's newly-budded self-esteem is sadly wounded by Trabb's boy. The whole episode is observed from a great psychological distance by a judge who is at once amused, scornful, and a little disgusted. Although the point of view is apparently Pip's (we seem to be looking through his eyes and we are told about his reactions), neither reader nor narrator is close to him; Pip, like a gaudy and rather pathetic butterfly, is being held up to inspection. At other times, however, the narrator gives the curious impression both of being with Pip, or of reliving the experience, and of being withdrawn, or of being superior to it. In chapter 8, to cite only one example, narrator and reader are *with* Pip in Satis House playing cards with Estella under the watchful eyes of Miss Havisham, but at least part of our minds is outside the actions and the interplay of emotions, in some god-like, detached position above and away from the scene.

We get this effect because of the psychological distance between Mr Pirrip and Pip, signalised by the technical devices already noted (the handling of tenses, the ambiguity in the use of the pronoun *I*, and the interweaving of the different means of transmitting information), and also because the narrator does not hesitate to break the illusion of immediacy and contemporaneity, as when he interrupts the first conversation of Pip and Estella to remark: 'I think it will be conceded by my most disputatious reader that she could hardly have directed an unfortunate boy to do anything in the wide world more difficult to be done under the circumstances.' In other chapters the narrator forgets exactly what happened or cannot remember precisely how Pip felt at a given moment, as in the beginning of chapter 43, just after Pip has heard Magwitch's life story. 'Why', asks the narrator,

> Why should I pause to ask how much of my shrinking from Provis might be traced to Estella? Why should I loiter on my road, to compare the state of mind in which I had tried to rid myself of the stain of the prison before meeting her at the coach-office, with the state of mind in which I now reflected on the abyss between Estella in her pride and beauty, and the returned transport whom I now harboured? The road would be none the smoother for it, the end would be none the better for it; he would not be helped, nor I extenuated.

The psychological distance is even more obvious in those scenes in which the tone is not that which the reader might expect of Pip or Mr Pip, but that of the adult narrator. The Christmas dinner in chapter 4 was actually a long torture of mind and body for the boy, but it is presented as immensely amusing. Pip's pain and anger are mentioned, but they are not realised. Even when mentioned, they are reduced in size and their significance is modified because the narrator, from his adult vantage point, no longer feels the direct force of the cruelty and violence, though he does understand the comic nature of the event and the characters as none of the real actors ever could. In such a paragraph as the following, there is a sizeable psychological difference between the 'I-as-I-was' and the 'I-as-I-am-now':

> Among this good company I should have felt myself, even if I hadn't robbed the pantry, in a false position. Not because I was squeezed in at an acute angle of the table-cloth, with the table in my chest, and the Pumblechookian elbow in my eye, nor because I was not allowed to speak (I didn't want to speak), nor because I was regaled with the scaly tips of the drumsticks of the fowls, and with those obscure corners of the pork of which the pig, when living, had had the least reason to be vain. No; I should not have minded that if they would only have left me alone. But they wouldn't leave me alone. They seemed to think the opportunity lost, if they failed to point the conversation at me, every now and then, and stick the point into me. I might have been an unfortunate little bull in a Spanish arena, I got so smartingly touched up by these moral goads.

Apparently, then, the position of the narrator in psychological time shifts. Usually he remains at some distance from himself-as-Pip, looks *at* Pip rather than out from him, and does not, because he cannot, probe deeply into the mind of the boy. Occasionally, however, and with marked emotion, he comes very close to his past self, even to the point of identification. The normal relation is a kind of dissociation. All in all, Dickens handled his point of view with admirable skill in *Great Expectations*.

SOURCE: *College English*, 23 (1961–62), pp. 122–6, 131.

Martin Meisel 'The Problem of the Novel's Ending' (1965)

Since Forster's *Life of Dickens* and his account of how Bulwer Lytton persuaded Dickens to change the ending of *Great Expectations*, for the worse, the main stream of perceptive comment on the novel has agreed with Forster and regretted the change. The regret, however, has had a peculiarly pharisaical quality, as if it beheld a moral as well as artistic lapse. Tempted by Bulwer, Dickens fell; and in place of an austere ending consistent with the theme of vanished expectations, an ending in which Jack hath not Jill, he concocted an eleventh-hour union to indulge the popular appetite. Until recently even apologists have had to plead as mitigation the primitiveness of the artistic conscience for fiction in pre-George Eliot circles, or Dickens's special and intense relation to his audience. Recently, however, the second ending has found defenders on intrinsic grounds. With its chastened, scarred, no longer youthful couple who join hands and depart from the ruined garden, it is shown to culminate the essential tale of Paradise Lost.[1]

That either ending works very well indeed, once we set aside fashions and prejudices on endings, ought to be enough to vindicate Dickens's artistry. But morality contemplates not just the deed but the intention. And by the puritanical standards of modern artistic morality, there is no defense, even artistic, for Dickens's evident willingness to tinker so casually, not just with any passage, but with the end of his novel, that moment which fixes literary characters in their permanent states of bliss or misery like the Last Judgement itself. There is no defense for his evident willingness to juggle with poetic justice to accommodate an importunate friend and a weak-minded public.

Yet there is a defense, even in such a court, though Dickens seems to have done his best to hang himself. (He wrote to Forster with a coy and philistine smugness, 'I have put in as pretty a little piece of writing as I could, and I have no doubt the story will be more acceptable through the alteration'). The defense is that in the total architecture of the novel neither ending is very important. Each gives a similar graceful coping to a more or less completed structure. Dickens was willing to be accommodating, but only on non-essentials; on a genuine matter of conscience he was like a rock. He begins his confession to Forster, 'You will be surprised to hear that I have changed the end of *Great Expectations* from and after Pip's return to Joe's, and finding his little likeness there'. That scene, the return to Joe's and the finding of little Pip, remains practically unchanged, and it is the true ending of *Great Expectations*.

The effect of the true ending on the narrative line is to bring it full circle, to transform what potentially is infinitely extensible into a closed form. The weight of the scene thematically is to give final definition to issues of redemption and penalty, natural innocence and natural depravity.

'The novel dramatises the loss of innocence', writes Julian Moynahan, 'and does not glibly present the hope of a redemptory second birth for either its guilty hero or the guilty society which shaped him.' [See previous essay—Ed.] That this formulation is true at least where it concerns the hero in his own person is urged upon us by the episode of Pip's illness following hard upon the death of Magwitch. For a while, however, the episode seems to suggest an opposite conclusion. The fever itself with its nightmare crisis recapitulates Pip's life of expectation and the subsequent harrowing of his body and soul, and through it he returns to a physical and spiritual infancy. The crisis of the fever distinctly resembles the crisis of a second birth. Pip's delusions are dreams of imprisonment and desperation to escape, in imagery that suggests the womb of his shaping past and the great social machine in which he had been caught up. That he survives, escapes, and is in some sense reborn is the difference between what he makes of his actual harrowing and what Miss Havisham made of hers. He imagines *her* in the matrix of 'a closed iron furnace in a dark corner of the room, and a voice had called out over and over again that Miss Havisham was consuming within it'.

That Pip has successfully recovered his lost innocence through a redemptory second birth seems to be confirmed as he emerges into awareness and finds himself once more in the care of Joe, 'and I fancied I was little Pip again'. He is 'like a child in [Joe's] hands. He would sit and talk to me in the old confidence and with the old simplicity, and in the old unassertive protecting way, so that I would half believe that all my life since the days of the old kitchen was one of the mental troubles of the fever that was gone.' [ch. 57] Born again, Pip seems to have recovered the lost paradise of Joe's love. Pip's narrative·harps on this return to the perfection of the relationship before Pip's knowledge of guilt began the course of his alienation. Together they look forward to Pip's first venture outdoors 'as we had once looked forward to the day of my apprenticeship'. When the day comes, Joe wraps him up, carries him down in his arms, and puts him in an open carriage 'as if I were still the small helpless creature to whom he had so abundantly given of the wealth of his great nature'. Pip is overwhelmed by the early summer loveliness and its evidence of natural fulfilment, by the 'mere re-membrance' of his fever and the evidence of his salvation; and he lays his head on Joe's shoulder 'as I had laid it long ago when he had taken me to the Fair or where not, and it was too much for my young senses'.

But when they return, and Joe lifts and carries him across the court and up the stairs, Pip thinks 'of that eventful Christmas Day' when the change had begun, 'when he had carried me over the marshes'.

Pip's recovery quickly recapitulates his early growth. He inexorably gets well, and inevitably the formality and protective distance of later days reappears. The return to his childhood is a symbolic event that transcends time; but the return—and this is the culminating point of the episode—must in the nature of things be temporary. The symbolism which transcends time, the symbolism of grace and reprobation, of ultimate spiritual states, gives way in the novel to the symbolism of act and consequence and to the sterner realities of the temporal process. The past is real, and its consequences, regretted and as nearly as possible paid for, must still be lived with.

Throughout Pip's convalescence, he tells us, a second thought has been taking shape, and it emerges on Joe's departure as the 'settled purpose' of marrying Biddy. She loved and comforted him once 'in my first unhappy time'. He wants her to receive him now 'with all my faults and disappointments on my head'; to receive him 'like a forgiven child (and indeed I am as sorry, Biddy, and have as much need of a hushing voice and a soothing hand)'. But chastened and forgiven as he is, Pip is not permitted to go back to Biddy any more than to Joe. He can neither regain nor remake any stage of the past. The perfect mother, teacher, and comforter now marries the at least perfectly loving father, and what has been called Pip's 'second chance'—for indeed there is one—is in the next generation.[2] Bereft of 'this last baffled hope' for himself, Pip yet hopes that Joe and Biddy will have children to love, and in particular 'that some little fellow will sit in this chimney corner of a winter night, who may remind you of another little fellow gone out of it for ever'. [ch. 58] And if Pip is excessively sorry for himself here, he also recognises the finality of his exile, the slimness of his deserts, and his subjection to time.

When Pip returns once more to the blacksmith's cottage after years spent in the East, he finds Joe 'in the old place by the kitchen firelight . . . and there, fenced into the corner with Joe's leg, and sitting on my own little stool looking at the fire, was—I again!' [ch. 59] The child's name is Pip—'we hoped he might grow a little bit like you, and we think he do'—and he and Pip talk the next day 'immensely, understanding one another to perfection'. Everything is the same as in the opening scenes, but in everything there is a difference. Joe's leg is no longer a fence against Joe's wife. Pip the visitor makes a point of *not* rumpling little Pip's hair 'which from my earliest remembrance, as already hinted, I have in my soul denied the right of any fellow-creature to do'. [ch. 12] And when Biddy touches first her little girl (a second chance for Pip requires a second chance for Estella) and then her old friend Pip with 'her good matronly hand', Pip finds something in the action and 'in the light pressure of Biddy's wedding-ring, that had a very pretty eloquence in it'. [ch. 59] It is the eloquence of contrast with 'the ridgy effect of a wedding-ring, passing unsympathetically over the human countenance' [ch. 7], on which Pip, brought up by another kind of hand, was the greatest living authority.

As Biddy and Joe replace the parents who failed the first Pip, first through death, then through harshness and helplessness, so Pip replaces Magwitch as spiritual father to the child christened with his name. 'Biddy,' he announces the second evening of his visit, 'you must give Pip to me, one of these days, or lend him, at all events.' Earlier in the day he has taken young Pip to the churchyard on the marshes. The older Pip had been in his seventh year, at the dawn of responsibility and self knowledge, the point at which the infant becomes the catechumen, when he had found himself in the marsh church on Christmas Eve, and there met his demon godfather. He had been in the very act of discovering 'for certain' who he was and where he was, when Magwitch turned him upside down and sat him 'on a high tombstone' from which Pip showed him the grave of his parents and on which he bent Pip to his will. The younger Pip is also about seven (the years of Pip's absence from England are in no version less than eight); the visit also takes place in December; and in the churchyard Pip sets young Pip 'on a certain tombstone there, and he showed me from that elevation which stone was sacred to the memory of Philip Pirrip, late of this Parish, and Also Georgiana, Wife of the Above'.

There is a deliberate ceremony in Pip's return to his own beginnings in the company of little Pip. By this act he confirms himself as godfather, in place of Magwitch, and commits himself, by sameness, to the difference in the world of little Pip. By it he also accepts his declension from the centre of the stage—something Pip in his hopes of Biddy had not yet been ready to do. For the first time Pip casts himself in an adult if subsidiary role. The ceremony is a formal installation of the young Pip, as the focus of promise and expectation, and a formal abdication of the old.

The novel has come full circle, and the end is a new beginning. The end is an acceptance of irredeemable loss, but it establishes a continuing and perhaps inexhaustible possibility of individual and social redemption, in the children. The seed continues good, despite the losses of earlier generations, despite the blighting legacy of their crimes and follies, despite the universal subjection to time which makes renewal possible as well as loss inevitable. The end in a new beginning does not mean the vanity of an eternal return for Dickens. The continuing possibility of redemption lies precisely in that the future need not be the same as the past. Second Pip need not go the way of first Pip, for as the first declares in wishing Joe and Biddy a child that reminds them of himself, 'only tell him . . . that, as your child, I said it would be natural to him to grow up a much better man than I did'. [ch. 58] And such indeed is the case in a world no longer governed by the captious tyranny of Mrs Joe, a world where Joe's love is effectual, where Pumblechook has his mouth stuffed, and Pip's benevolence has replaced Magwitch's terror.

The last two paragraphs of the novel as originally written are a reinforcing postscript to the conclusion proper. While walking along Piccadilly with little Pip, Pip meets Estella, and the encounter allows the novelist to carry out his obligation of tying up loose ends. Pip learns that Estella too has been harrowed and taught by suffering. She has been widowed, and has remarried. She takes little Pip to be Pip's own child. Pip's possibilities are concluded, his sufferings are confirmed as past, and his future is acknowledged as the little boy.

The substituted passage is longer, more elaborate; but it remains a tidying postscript to the ending proper. Pip's ceremonial visit to the site of the old house complements his visit to the churchyard as a return to his beginnings. He meets Estella in the old garden, and points the structural moral: 'After so many years, it is strange that we should thus meet again, Estella, here where our first meeting was!' They meet in sadness, and in moonlit ruin, like pale ghosts of themselves, full of the knowledge of their loss and the knowledge that comes through suffering. Their departure at nightfall from the ruined garden is no new joint venture in possibility, but a departure whose rising evening mists, in pointed contrast to 'the morning mists [that] had risen long ago when I first left the forge', and whose revealed 'expanse of tranquil light' without a shadow suggest an afterworld without colour, sound, or warmth, a world of pale companionship, sad serenity, and of disembodied contemplation of life by those who have left it for ever.

Source: 'The Ending of *Great Expectations*', *Essays in Criticism*, 15 (1965), pp. 326–31.

NOTES

1. See J. Hillis Miller, *Charles Dickens: The World of His Novels* (Cambridge, Mass., 1958), p. 278, and Monroe Engel, *The Maturity of Charles Dickens* (Cambridge, Mass., 1959), pp. 157–8, 167–8.

2. Engel's term, pp. 166–7.

Barbara Hardy   'The Dickensian Feast'
(1970)

. . . We all know that food has a special place in the novels of Dickens.
He loves feasts and scorns fasts. His celebration of the feast is not that of
the glutton or the gourmet: eating and drinking are valued by him as
proofs of sociability and gusto, but more important still, as ceremonies
of love. The conversion of Scrooge is marked by his present of a goose to
Bob Cratchit and his reunion at his nephew's table: both the giving and
the participation show his newly found ability to love. The Christmas
dinner and the geniality of the English pub are not sentimentalised as
isolated institutions of goodwill, conveniently cut off from the poverty
and hunger outside the window. Good housekeeping is proved by
nourishing and well-ordered meals, and Mrs Jellyby [in *Bleak House*]
cannot feed her family properly; but the same is true of the bleak
housekeeping of England, which cannot feed Jo [the crossing-sweeper]
or the brickmasters. Chadband's superfluous feasts are put beside Jo's
hunger and Guster's loving crust to qualify the approval of good
appetite. The social emphasis in *Great Expectations* is rather different
from that of *Bleak House*, but in both novels, and elsewhere, the same
moral values are attached to meals—to the giving, receiving, eating,
and serving of food. These values might be summed up as good appetite
without greed, hospitality without show, and ceremony without pride
or condescension. Pip's deterioration and change of heart are shown in
terms of these values.

All these values are shown, positively and negatively, in the meals in
Great Expectations. Food is used to define various aspects of love, pride,
social ambition, and gratitude, and the meals are often carefully placed
in order to underline and explain motivation and development.
Dickens's attitude to food has no doubt considerable biographical
interest. Dickens—deprived child, food-lover, great talker, oral type—
juxtaposes Mrs Joe's pincushion breast and her dispensation of bread,
and this may well be his grimmest attack on the maternal image. But in
spite of this grotesque instance, I believe that the generalised association
of food and love in Dickens strikes us less by its neurotic fantasy than by
its use of what we all feel to be the natural appropriateness of the
metaphor 'hunger' when it is used of love. I do not call the meals in *Great
Expectations* symbols: their affirmation of value seems to involve no
conceptual transference and little heightening. It is our awareness of the
Last Supper which often tempts us to describe this kind of significant
meal as symbolic—the meal shared by Bartle Massey and Adam Bede

in the upper room [in George Eliot's novel] is a good example—but the Last Supper (like the Passover and other ritual feasts) became an effective symbol, in part at least, because it tapped the significance of ordinary communion: the eating, giving, and receiving, in public, amongst friends and associates. The meals in Dickens convey no more, I suggest, than the elementary implications of natural domestic and social order, given particularity by the context of the novel. The generalisations which the meals in *Great Expectations* carry involve none of the transference associated with symbolism, nothing of the movement from a first term to a second which is involved in our reading of the symbol of the wild waves, the fog, or the prison. There is certainly an accumulation of significance in *Great Expectations*, and we may come to expect that when characters sit down to eat there will be more than a furtherance of action, local colour, or comic play. We come to expect some extension or qualification of the moral significance already correlated with the meals. This is an extension of the particular definition of character, a way of emphasising the connections and distances between different characters or different events, showing the irony and necessity of the internal moral pattern. The meals themselves are charged with no more than the moral significances of everyday life, where good mothers feed their children lovingly but not excessively or demandingly; where meals are sociable occasions; where good manners are desirable but not all that important; where theft may be condoned if the thief is starving; where there is something distasteful about the host or mother or cook whose meals are merely boasts; where there is something meretricious in the splendid feast which is strikingly different from the routine meals of the same household; where abstinence may be either unhealthy or unselfish.

The first meal in *Great Expectations* is *demanded* in the first chapter. Magwitch in.desperate hunger terrifies Pip into stealing food: 'You know what wittles is . . . you get me wittles.' In the third chapter Pip brings the food, and Magwitch makes the first response of gratitude which begins the long chain of obligation, illusion, pride, and love. It is necessary to see what moves his gratitude: it is not the mere provision of food, important though this is. Pip is doing more than satisfy the physical need, he is allowing nature more than nature needs. Magwitch is eating like a beast but Pip treats him as a guest and makes him respond as a guest:

> He was already handing mincemeat down his throat in the most curious manner—more like a man who was putting it away somewhere in a violent hurry, than a man who was eating it— but he left off to take some of the liquor. He shivered all the while so violently, that it was quite as much as he could do to keep the

neck of the bottle between his teeth, without biting it off . . .

He was gobbling mincemeat, meat bone, bread, cheese, and pork pie, all at once: staring distrustfully while he did so at the mist all round us, and often stopping—even stopping his jaws—to listen.

This is a grotesque table, spread in the wilderness of mist and marshes for a man who is wolfing down the food out of fear. Pip is no more in the conventional position of host than Magwitch is in the conventional position of guest, but the very lack of ceremony moves Pip to do more than steal and give in terror and in minimal satisfaction of need. Pity moves him to sauce the meat with ceremony and turn it into something more than Lady Macbeth's 'bare meeting'. Just as Lady Macbeth's rebuke has special point because it is made at a great feast to the host who is a guest-murderer, so Pip's ceremony has special point in this bare rough meeting where the guest is desperate and the host terrorised:

> Pitying his desolation . . . I made bold to say, 'I am glad you enjoy it'.
> 'Did you speak?'
> 'I said, I am glad you enjoyed it.'
> 'Thankee, my boy. I do.'

The child's civility and pity take no offence from his guest's table-manners. These are carefully observed, without revulsion:

> I had often watched a large dog of ours eating his food; and now I noticed a decided similarity between the dog's way of eating, and the man's. The man took strong sharp sudden bites, just like the dog. He swallowed, or rather snapped up, every mouthful, too soon and too fast; and he looked sideways here and there while he ate, as if he thought there was danger in every direction of somebody's coming to take the pie away. He was altogether too unsettled in his mind over it, to appreciate it comfortably, I thought, or to have anybody to dine with him, without making a chop with his jaws at the visitor. In all of which particulars he was very like the dog.

The detached account makes the politeness more marked. It is apparent that Pip's naïve comparisons, to the dog and to more comfortable meals, imply no sense of social superiority, though the social implications are plain to the reader. Pip is not repelled by the resemblance to the dog, but is sorry for it, and instead of treating the man like a dog, gives with love. The 'I am glad you enjoy it' and the

'Thankee' turn the rudest meal in the novel into an introductory model of ceremony. What makes the ceremony is love, generosity, and gratitude. I need not labour the attachment of this scene to the main themes of the novel.

This meal acts as a model of ceremony, and controls our response to the many related descriptions of meals which succeed it. The gratitude and compassionate love are both present in chapter 5, when Magwitch lies about stealing the food, to protect Pip, and is answered by Joe: 'God knows you're welcome to it—so far as it was ever mine. . . . We don't know what you have done, but we wouldn't have you starved to death for it, poor miserable fellow-creatur.—Would us, Pip?'

This in its turn evokes another response of gratitude—an inarticulate working of the throat—from Magwitch. The first small links are forged in Pip's chain 'of iron or gold, of thorns or flowers'.

It is not until much later, in chapter 38, that Pip sees that this is where his chain really begins, 'before I knew that the world held Estella'. The actual image is narrowed down, in the next chapter, to the 'wretched gold and silver chains' with which Magwitch has loaded him. When the image of the chain first appears (in the singular) it has no connection with the convict for Pip sees its beginning in his encounter with Miss Havisham and Estella, in Satis House. The beginning of his illusory great expectations, like the beginning of the real ones, is marked by a significant meal. Estella is the hostess, Pip the guest. The meal is less grotesque than the meal with Magwitch but it too lacks the ceremonious cover of a roof, for Estella tells Pip to wait in the yard:

> She came back, with some bread and meat and a little mug of beer, she put the mug down on the stones of the yard, and gave me the bread and meat without looking at me, as insolently as if I were a dog in disgrace. I was so humiliated, hurt, spurned, offended, angry, sorry—I cannot hit upon the right name for the smart—God knows what its name was—that tears started to my eyes. [ch. 8]

The contrast is clinched by the comparison with the dog. Pip's full wants are not satisfied, even though this is the hospitality of Satis House, but in terms of physical need he is given enough. He is treated like a dog, given no more than nature needs, but he does not lose his appetite, any more than Magwitch, treated with courtesy, stops eating like a dog. Dickens makes this distinction unsentimentally and truthfully, merely allowing Pip to observe that 'the bread and food were acceptable, and the beer was warming and tingling, and I was soon in spirits to look about me'. Like Magwitch, and for similar reasons of protective love, Pip lies about this meal. His sense of humiliation and his desire to protect Estella from 'the contemplation of Mrs Joe' makes him elaborate the marvellous childish fantasy about the 'cake and wine on gold plates', which Pumblechook and Joe and Mrs Joe, in their social innocence, accept. Pip invents a meal appropriate to Satis House, and hides his shame, but he preserves both the hierarchy and the bizarre quality of his encounter by placing the meal in a coach, and saying that he 'got up behind the coach to eat mine, because she told me to'. Even the dog comes back, magnified into 'four immense dogs' who come off rather better than Pip did since they fight 'for veal-cutlets out of a silver basket'. On his next visit to Satis House we return briefly to the dog: 'I was taken into the yard to be fed in the former dog-like manner.' The two meals respond in perfect antithesis.

The first ceremony of love finds another responsive scene when Magwitch discloses his responsibility and motivation to Pip. We are carefully reminded of the first meal on the marshes: 'I drops my knife many a time in that hut when I was a eating my dinner or my supper, and I says, "Here's the boy again, a looking at me whiles I eats and drinks!" '. [ch. 39]

It is to this actual memory of the meal that he attaches his plan to 'make that boy a gentleman' but when the gentleman serves him with a meal he does not look at him as the boy did:

> He ate in a ravenous manner that was very disagreeable, and all his actions were uncouth, noisy, and greedy. Some of his teeth had failed him since I saw him eat on the marshes, and as he turned his food in his mouth, and turned his head sideways to bring his strongest fangs to bear upon it, he looked terribly like a hungry old dog.
>
> If I had begun with any appetite, he would have taken it away, and I should have sat much as I did—repelled from him by an insurmountable aversion, and gloomily looking at the cloth. [ch. 40]

The uncouth eating, the hunger, the sideways movement, and the comparison with the dog are repetitions from the early scene which emphasise the distance between the child and the man. This time the observation is full of revulsion, the food is not sauced with ceremony. But if the host has changed, the guest has not, and he apologises for his doglike eating with undoglike courtesy:

> 'I'm a heavy grubber, dear boy,' he said, as a polite kind of apology when he had made an end of his meal, 'but I always was. If it had been in my constitution to be a lighter grubber, I might ha' got into lighter trouble.'

The apology is made without shame or self-pity on the part of Magwitch, and provokes no sympathy on the part of Pip. In the early scene the child's pity was impulsive and provoked simply by the desperate eating and panic. In the later scenes, Pip is in a position to see the connection between the heavy grubbing and the heavy trouble, but describes without pity the roughness and greed: 'there was Prisoner, Felon, Bondsman, plain as plain could be'.

The next meal is described without emphasis. We are told that Magwitch wipes his knife on his leg, but by now Pip is too concerned to hear the convict's history to have room for shame and revulsion. The very last meal described—supper on the night before the attempted escape—contains no comment on manners or response: 'It was a dirty place enough . . . but there was a good fire in the kitchen, and there were eggs and bacon to eat, and various liquors to drink.' [ch. 54]

By now Pip's pride has been entirely subdued to the need for action. The quiet disappearance of comment testifies to the naturalness and literalness of the scenes of eating and drinking: a series of related scenes has been established, bringing out the moral significance of needs and hospitality and good manners, but it is brought to no formal climax. There is no explicit comment on the irrelevance of good manners in the crisis of need, no reminiscence of the fellowship of the first meal and the first occasion when Pip helped Magwitch to escape his pursuers, nothing of the climactic recognition of symbolism which we find in James's dove, or Lawrence's rainbow, or Dickens's own wild waves. The meals are only tapped for their moral significance on occasions when men need food desperately or when there is scope for hospitality: towards the end of the story the meals are inartificially subordinated to other features of the action. I do not make this distinction in order to decry the more contrived symbolism in other novels, but merely in order to bring out Dickens's unheightened and sober reliance on everyday moral and social facts. There is, I think, no question of an unconscious moral pattern, for the repetition of details makes the control quite plain, but Dickens is content to subdue this significant series of meals to the proportions and emphases of his story.

With the same almost unobtrusive reflection of ordinary moral fact, the meals with Estella are also described without schematic arrangement. They scarcely develop into a pattern, and Dickens can allow himself to describe a meal without relating it to earlier significances. When Estella and Pip have tea together in the hotel, or when Pip does eventually dine with some ceremony inside Satis House, no moral emphasis is present: on the first occasion Dickens is concerned to develop aspects of the relationship to which need and ceremony are irrelevant; on the second he is concerned with the tense understatement of Jaggers's observation of Estella. But although some of the meals in this novel make no moral definition, it is true that nearly all the characters and families are given, at some point, their significant ceremony of food. Magwitch tells Pip and Herbert how his heavy grubbing explains his troubled career and begins his life-story with the little boy who stole turnips and who was always driven by the need 'to put something into his stomach'. Pip as a child is not physically deprived in this way, but although he is given enough to eat, he is not given his food with love. In chapter 2, between Magwitch's demand for food and Pip's generous response, we are given a glimpse of Mrs Joe's 'bringing up by hand'. She is an unloving mother-surrogate who feeds her family unceremoniously:

> My sister had a trenchant way of cutting our bread-and-butter for us, that never varied. First, with her left hand she jammed the loaf hard and fast against her bib—where it sometimes got a pin into it, and sometimes a needle, which we afterwards got into our mouths. Then she took some butter (not too much) on a knife and spread it on the loaf, in an apothecary kind of way, as if she were making a plaister—using both sides of the knife with a slapping dexterity, and trimming and moulding the butter off round the crust. Then, she gave the knife a final smart wipe on the edge of the plaister . . .

The pins and needles have already been mentioned as characteristic of this unmotherly breast: 'She was tall and bony, and almost always wore a coarse apron, fastened over her figure behind with two loops, and having a square impregnable bib in front, that was stuck full of pins and needles.'

Some of the implications of this juxtaposition are terrifying, but the Gargery household is treated with comedy rather than with the harsh violence which is the medium for the Murdstones. But both the comic mode and the grim seem at times to draw freely on Dickens's fantasy. The moral implications within the novel are plain: Mrs Joe gives unlovingly, to put it mildly, taking most pleasure in the administration of Tar-Water and fasts, while Joe shares the wedges of bread in love and play, and tries to make up for Pip's sufferings at the Christmas dinner with spoonfulls of gravy.

The cold comfort of Mrs Joe's meals, like her uncomfortable cleanliness, makes her an ancestress of Mrs Ogmore-Pritchard, though Dickens inflicts a terrible revenge on her in the action. She has the front-parlour mentality, and the only ceremony in the Gargery household, apart from the rough meals shared by Pip and Joe, is the false ceremony of hospitality. Her showing-off at the dinner-party contrasts rudely with her earlier words to Joe and Pip: 'I ain't a going to have no formal cramming and busting and washing-up now', and they have their slices served out as if they 'were two thousand troops on a forced march instead of a man and boy at home'. I need not dwell on the Christmas dinner, with Mr Wopsle's theatrical declamation of grace, with the adjurations to Pip to be grateful 'to them which brought you up by hand', with Pumblechook's immodest generosity and gluttony and the comic nemesis when he chokes on the Tar-Water. The contrast between the ceremony of love and the false ceremony is there, together with the rebuke of starvation. For Magwitch has eaten the pie and drunk the brandy. This is underlined when Pip observes Pumblechook's possessive appropriation of the wine he has given to Mrs Joe and his generous treating of the flattering sergeant. The false giving and receiving are put in the context of the first meal with Magwitch when Pip comments, 'I thought what terrible good sauce for a dinner my fugitive friend on the marshes was.'

Pip's humiliation by Estella is also put into a larger context when he explains that his susceptibility to injustice and shame was attributable to the unloving home. Joe makes even the hacked bread and superfluous gravy the food of love, but Estella sharpens the sense of false ceremony, in part by denying ceremony, and Pip becomes less conscious of love's seasoning than of good manners. He continues in fantasy, and eventually moves from the back of the coach. The actual social significance of eating habits becomes emphatic in a novel about snobbery and aspiration, and there are other meals which raise the question of love and ceremony. When Pip has his first meal with Herbert Pocket, a difficult social situation is eased by Herbert's friendly delicacy, and he gives both the strawberries and the lessons in etiquette with true ceremony. This is a scene which establishes both the importance of good manners and the importance of love. It contrasts strongly with the second meal with Magwitch, where Pip is the bad host, and is paralleled by the first, when Pip is the true host. It is closest of all to another scene, where Herbert and Pip are entertaining Joe to breakfast. Joe is 'stiff from head to foot', cannot say outright that he prefers tea to coffee, and is as selfconscious in his politeness as Magwitch is unselfconscious in his roughness:

> Then he fell into such unaccountable fits of mediation, with his fork midway between his plate and his mouth; had his eyes attracted in such strange directions; was afflicted with such remarkable coughs; sat so far from the table, and dropped so much more than he ate, and pretended he hadn't dropped it; that I was heartily glad when Herbert left us for the city. [ch. 27]

This failure in hospitality—'I had neither the good sense nor the good

feeling to know that this was all my fault'—prepares us for the greater
failure, the greater social gulf, and the greater shame, when Magwitch
returns and Pip makes a first false, but healthy, comparison between his
shame for Joe and his shame before the convict, for whom he had
deserted Joe.

There are other scenes, more or less emphatic, in which the social
values of eating are defined. There is the false show, lightly touched on,
in the last celebratory supper at the forge before Pip leaves home, when
he sits ashamed in his splendour for their delight and they are all 'very
low' despite roast fowl and flip. This contrasts with another kind of false
show, in the same chapter, when Mr Pumblechook flatters and
celebrates in a travesty of the love-feast. He toasts Pip in extravagant
mock-abasement when he toasts Pip—'May I?—*may* I?'—and elaborately deprecates the chicken and tongue—'one or two little things
had round from the Boar, that I hope you may not despise'—and
apostrophises   the   fowl—'Ah!   poultry,   poultry!   You   little
thought . . . when you was a young fledgling, what was in store for
you.' [ch. 19] At the other social extreme from this exhibition of
hospitable abasement, but close to it morally, is Pip's little fantasy, at
the beginning of the same chapter, of feasting the villagers, 'bestowing a
dinner of roast-beef and plum-pudding, a pint of ale, and a gallon of
condescension'. There are many other details which might be mentioned: the funeral repast after Mrs Joe's death, Jaggers's good food and
ruthless hospitality, the geniality of the pub, Pip's susceptibility to wine
on one or two occasions, the lavishness of his housekeeping with
Herbert, and the ordered, warm, and unpretentious hospitality of
Wemmick.

Almost all characters and groups are given moral and social
definition by their attitudes to food and hospitality. Old Barley keeps
the provisions in his room, and provides Clara with bread and cheese
while he has mutton-chops, potatoes, and split pease stewed up in
butter; he roars and bangs for his grog and growls in pain while trying to
cut through a Double Gloucester with his gouty hand. The ill-fed
children are the unloved children. The baby Pocket, like Pip, is
endangered by being fed on pins, though in his case the inappropriate
food is the result of neglect and disorder not of an aggressive display of
good housekeeping. The disorder, bad economy, and inadequate meals
of the Pocket family are another version of the neglected Jellybys in
Bleak House, and just as Mrs Jellyby is ironically exposed as a model of
displaced charity, so Mrs Pocket is shown in her disorder as another
qualification of class-distinction and great expectations. Her delusions
of grandeur lead to the disregard of proper ceremony. Although each
bad mother is attached to the special theme of each novel, the basic
moral failure is the same. It is a failure in love.

I have not yet mentioned one of the most prominent failures in love in *Great Expectations*. This is Miss Havisham's failure. Her love-feast is preserved in its decay to make the most conspicuous contribution to the themes of love and nature. Nothing remains of the expectations of Satis House but a gruesome parody of ceremony:

> The most prominent object was a long table with a tablecloth spread on it, as if a feast had been in preparation when the house and the clocks all stopped together. An *épergne* or centre-piece of some kind was in the middle of this cloth; it was so heavily overhung with cobwebs that its form was quite undistinguishable; and as I looked along the yellow expanse out of which I remember its seeming to grow, like a black fungus, I saw speckled-legged spiders with blotchy bodies running home to it . . . [ch. 11]

Miss Havisham makes a symbolic correlation between the mouldering wedding-breakfast and her own life. She has been gnawed by pain as the food has been gnawed by mice, she has worn away with the meal, and when she is dead she too will be laid out on that table, where she has allocated the places for her predatory family to sit and 'feast upon' her. The betrayal of love and the hypocritical greedy show of love are both bracketed as false ceremony in this grisly image of transubstantiation. The ghastly conceit stands out from Dickens's other significant correlations of love and food as a product of a diseased fancy and an impossible attempt to pervert nature. Jaggers makes explicit the other implications of the stasis and decay which relate this meal to the pattern of normal routine and relationship:

> He asked me how often I had seen Miss Havisham eat and drink . . .
> I considered, and said, 'Never'. 'And never will, Pip', he retorted, with a frowning smile. 'She has never allowed herself to be seen doing either, since she lived this present life of hers. She wanders about in the night, and then lays hands on such food as she takes.' [ch. 29]

Miss Havisham's rejection of ordinary public meals is like her attempt to shut out the daylight. Food in *Great Expectations*, as in *Macbeth*, is part of the public order, and the meals testify to human need and dependence, and distinguish false ceremony from the ceremony of love. They are not literary symbols but natural demonstrations. Pip's change of heart is a change from the unconditioned act of love to this contaminated false ceremony and back again to the Dickensian natural

man. Like Scrooge, he demonstrates the vulnerable virtue by loss and
gain.

SOURCE: extract from *The Moral Art of Dickens* (1970), pp. 139–
55.

PART THREE

Our Mutual Friend

Our Mutual Friend

Published in monthly parts, from May 1864 to November 1865, with illustrations by Marcus Stone; issued in book form in 1865, in two volumes (with 'Postscript in lieu of Preface').

1. BACKGROUND

R. H. Horne (1850)

The Dust-heap

About a quarter of a mile distant, having a long ditch and a broken-down fence as a foreground, there rose against the muddled-grey sky, a huge Dust-heap of a dirty black colour—being, in fact, one of those immense mounds of cinders, ashes, and other emptyings from dust-holes and bins, which have conferred celebrity on certain suburban neighbourhoods of a great city. . . .

A Dust-heap of this kind is often worth thousands of pounds. The present one was very large and very valuable. It was in fact a large hill, and being in the vicinity of small suburb cottages, it rose above them like a great black mountain. . . .

These Dust-heaps are a wonderful compound of things. A banker's cheque for a considerable sum was found in one of them. . . . But banker's cheques, or gold and silver articles, are the least valuable of their ingredients. Among other things, a variety of useful chemicals are extracted. Their chief value, however, is for the making of bricks. . . .

'Why, if there isn't a man's head in the canal!' suddenly cried little Jem. 'Looky there!—isn't that a man's head?—Yes, it's a drowndedd man!'

'A drowndedd man, as I live!' ejaculated old Doubleyear.

'Let's get him out, and see!' cried Peggy. 'Perhaps the poor soul's not quite gone.' . . . [The body is removed and revived by being buried in the warm ashes of the dust-heap. The rescued man eventually marries the daughter of 'the great Dust-Contractor' who owns the mound.]

'Well, Sir', said the latter, 'you wish to marry my daughter, and she wishes to marry you. . . . I'll make you both an offer. I will give my daughter twenty thousand pounds,—or you shall have the Dust-heap. Choose!' [They choose the money.]

This was the identical Dust-heap, as we know from authentic information, which was subsequently sold for forty thousand pounds, and was exported to Russia to rebuild Moscow. . . .

SOURCE: extract from 'Dust: or Ugliness Redeemed', *Household Words* (13 July 1850).

Dickens (1858, 1861, 1865)

1 Speech in Aid of the Hospital for Sick Children (1858)

. . . Some years ago, being in Scotland, I went with one of the most
humane members of the humane medical profession, on a morning tour
among some of the worst-lodged inhabitants of the old town of
Edinburgh. In the closes and wynds of that picturesque place—I am
sorry to remind you what fast friends picturesqueness and typhus often
are—we saw more poverty and sickness in an hour than many people
would believe in a life. Our way lay from one to another of the most
wretched dwellings—reeking with horrible odours—shut out from the
sky—shut out from the air—mere pits and dens. In a room in one of
these places, where there was an empty porridge-pot on the cold hearth,
with a ragged woman and some ragged children crouching on the bare
ground near it—where, I remember as I speak, that very light, reflected
from a high damp-stained and time-stained house wall, came trembling
in, as if the fever which had shaken everything else there had shaken
even it—there lay, in an old egg-box which the mother had begged from
a shop, a little feeble, wasted, wan, sick child. With his little wasted face,
and his little hot worn hands folded over his breast, and his little bright
attentive eyes, I can see him now, as I have seen him for several years,
looking steadily at us. There he lay in his little frail box, which was not
at all a bad emblem of the little body from which he was slowly
parting—there he lay, quite quiet, quite patient, saying never a word.
He seldom cried, the mother said; he seldom complained; 'he lay there,
seeming to wonder what it was a' aboot'. God knows I thought, as I
stood looking at him, he had his reasons for wondering—reasons for
wondering how it could possibly come to be that he lay there, left alone,
feeble and full of pain, when he ought to have been as bright and as brisk
as the birds that never got near him—reasons for wondering how he
came to be left there, a little decrepit old man, pining to death, quite a
thing of course, as if there were no crowds of healthy and happy children
playing on the grass under the summer's sun within a stone's throw of
him, as if there were no bright moving sea on the other side of the great
hill overhanging the city; as if there were no great clouds rushing over it;
as if there were no life, and movement, and vigour anywhere in the
world—nothing but stoppage and decay. There he lay looking at us,
saying in his silence, more pathetically than I have ever heard anything
said by any orator in my life, 'Will you please to tell us what this means,
strange man? and if you can give me any good reason why I should be so

soon, so far advanced on my way to Him who said that children were to come into His presence, and were not to be forbidden, but who scarcely meant, that they should come by this hard road by which I am travelling—pray give that reason to me, for I seek it very earnestly and wonder about it very much'; and to my mind he has been wondering about it ever since. Many a poor child, sick and neglected, I have seen since that time in this London; many a poor sick child have I seen most affectionately and kindly tended by poor people, in an unwholesome house and under untoward circumstances, wherein its recovery was quite impossible; but at all such times I have seen my poor little drooping friend in his egg-box, and he has always addressed his dumb speech to me, and I have always found him wondering what it meant, and why, in the name of a gracious God, such things should be!

Now, ladies and gentlemen, such things need not be, and will not be, if this company, which is a drop of the life-blood of the great compassionate public heart, will only accept the means of rescue and prevention which is mine to offer. Within a quarter of a mile of this place where I speak, stands a courtly old house, where once, no doubt, blooming children were born, and grew up to be men and women, and married, and brought their own blooming children back to patter up the old oak staircase which stood but the other day, and to wonder at the old oak carvings on the chimney-pieces. In the airy wards into which the old state drawing-rooms and family bedchambers of that house are now converted are such little patients that the attendant nurses look like reclaimed giantesses, and the kind medical practitioner like an amiable Christian ogre. Grouped about the little low tables in the centre of the rooms are such tiny convalescents that they seem to be playing at having been ill. On the dolls' beds are such diminutive creatures, that each poor sufferer is supplied with its tray of toys; and, looking around, you may see how the little tired, flushed cheek has toppled over half the brute creation on its way into the ark; or how one little dimpled arm has mowed down (as I saw myself) the whole tin soldiery of Europe. On the walls of these rooms are graceful, pleasant, bright, childish pictures. At the beds' heads, are pictures of the figure which is the universal embodiment of all mercy and compassion, the figure of Him who was once a child himself, and a poor one.

Besides these little creatures on the beds, you may learn in that place that the number of small Out-patients brought to that house for relief is no fewer than ten thousand in the compass of a single year. In the room in which these are received, you may see against the wall a box, on which it is written, that it has been calculated, that if every grateful mother who brings a child there will drop a penny into it, the Hospital funds may possibly be increased in a year by so large a sum as forty pounds. And you may read in the Hospital report, with a glow of pleasure, that these poor women are so respondent as to have made, even in a toiling year of difficulty and high prices, this estimated forty, fifty pounds. [*Cheers.*] In the printed papers of this same Hospital, you may read with what a generous earnestness the highest and wisest members of the medical profession testify to the great need of it; to the immense difficulty of treating children in the same hospitals with grown-up people, by reason of their different ailments and requirements; to the vast amount of pain that will be assuaged, and of the life that will be saved, through this Hospital—not only among the poor, observe, but among the prosperous too, by reason of the increased knowledge of children's illnesses, which cannot fail to arise from a more systematic mode of studying them. Lastly, gentlemen, and I am sorry to say, worst of all—(for I must present no rose-coloured picture of this place to you—I must not deceive you); lastly—the visitor to this Children's Hospital, reckoning up the number of its beds, will find himself perforce obliged to stop at very little over thirty; and will learn, with sorrow and surprise, that even that small number, so forlornly, so miserably diminutive, compared with this vast London, cannot possibly be maintained unless the Hospital be made better known; I limit myself to saying better known, because I will not believe that in a Christian community of fathers and mothers, and brothers and sisters, it can fail, being better known, to be well and richly endowed. [*Cheers.*]

Now, ladies and gentlemen, this, without a word of adornment—which I resolved when I got up not to allow myself—this is the simple case. This is the pathetic case which I have to put to you: not only on behalf of the thousands of children who annually die in this great city, but also on behalf of the thousands of children who live half-developed, racked with preventable pain, shorn of their natural capacity for health and enjoyment. If these innocent creatures cannot move you for themselves, how can I possibly hope to move you in their name?

SOURCE: extract from K. J. Fielding (ed.), *The Speeches of Charles Dickens* (London, 1960), pp. 250–2.

II Extracts from Letters (1861, 1865)

To John Forster, 1861
. . . I think a man, young and perhaps eccentric, feigning to be dead, and *being* dead to all intents and purposes external to himself, and for a few years retaining the singular view of life and character so imparted, would be a good leading incident for a story. . . . A poor impostor of a man marrying a woman for her money; she marrying *him* for *his* money;

after marriage both finding out their mistake, and entering into a league and covenant against folk in general: with whom I propose to connect some Perfectly New people. Everything new about them. If they presented a father and mother, it seemed as if THEY must be bran new, like the furniture and the carriages—shining with varnish, and just home from the manufacturers. . . . I must use somehow the un-educated father in fustian and the educated boy in spectacles whom Leech and I saw at Chatham. . . .

To the Rev. William Harness, 23 May 1865
. . . I am, and have been, hard at work at your conversion—to the opinion that the story of Our Mutual Friend is very interesting and was from the first tending to a purpose which you couldn't see until I chose to take you into my confidence. Modest this—but true. . . .

SOURCE: W. Dexter (ed.), *The Letters of Charles Dickens* (London, 1938), III, pp. 271, 422.

Henry Mayhew (1862)

Dredgers and Dust-Yards

I

. . . The dredgerman and his boat may be immediately distinguished from all others; there is nothing similar to them on the river. The sharp cutwater fore and aft, and short rounded appearance of the vessel, mark it out at once from the skiff or wherry of the waterman. There is, too, always the appearance of labour about the boat, like a ship returning after a long voyage, daubed and filthy, and looking sadly in need of a thorough cleansing. The grappling irons are over the bow, resting on a coil of rope; while the other end of the boat is filled with coals, bones, and old rope, mixed with the mud of the river. The ropes of the dredging-net hang over the side. A short stout figure, with a face soiled and blackened with perspiration, and surmounted by a tarred sou'-wester, the body habited in a soiled check shirt with the sleeves turned up above the elbows, and exhibiting a pair of sunburnt brawny arms, is pulling at the sculls, not with the ease and lightness of the waterman, but toiling and tugging away like a galley slave, as he scours the bed of the river with his dredging-net in search of some hoped-for prize.

The dredgers . . . are the men who find almost all the bodies of persons drowned. If there be a reward offered for the recovery of a body, numbers of the dredgers will at once endeavour to obtain it, while if there be no reward, there is at least the inquest money to be had—beside other chances. What these chances are may be inferred from the well-known fact that no body recovered by a dredgerman ever happens to have any money about it, when brought to shore. There may, indeed, be a watch in the fob or waistcost pocket, for that article would be likely to be traced. There may, too, be a purse or pocket-book forthcoming, but somehow it is invariably empty. The dredgers cannot by any reasoning or argument be made to comprehend that there is anything like dishonesty in emptying the pockets of a dead man. They consider them as their just perquisite. They say that any one who finds a body does precisely the same, and that if they did not do so the police would. After having had all the trouble and labour, they allege that they have a much better right to whatever is to be got, than the police who have had nothing whatever to do with it. There are also people who shrewdly suspect that some of the coals from the barges lying in the river very often find their way into the dredgers' boats, especially when the dredgers are engaged in night-work; and there are some who do not hold them guiltless of, now and then, when opportunity offers, smuggling things ashore from many of the steamers coming from foreign parts. But such things, I repeat, the dredgers consider in the fair way of their business.

One of the most industrious, and I believe one of the most skilful and successful of this peculiar class, gave me the following epitome of his history.

'Father was a dredger, and grandfather afore him; grandfather was a dredger and a fisherman too. A'most as soon as I was able to crawl, father took me with him in the boat to help him pick the coals, and bones, and other things out of the net, and to use me to the water. When I got bigger and stronger, I was sent to the parish school, but I didn't like it half as well as the boat, and couldn't be got to stay two days together. At last I went above the bridge, and went along with a fisherman, and used to sleep in the boat every night. I liked to sleep in the boat; I used to be as comfortable as could be. Lor bless you! there's a tilt to them boats, and no rain can't git at you. I used to lie awake at night and listen to the water slapping in the boat, and think it fine fun. I might a got bound 'prentice, but I got aboard a smack, where I stayed three or four years, and if I'd a stayed there, I'd a liked it much better. But I heerd as how father was ill, so I com'd home, and took to the dredging, and am at it off and on ever since. I got no larnin'; how could I? Ther's on'y one or two of us dredgers as knows anything of larnin', and they're no better off than the rest. Larnin's no use to a dredger, he hasn't got no time to read; and if he had, why, it wouldn't tell him where the holes and furrows is at the bottom of the river, and where things is to be found.' . . .

II

Dust and rubbish accumulate in houses from a variety of causes, but principally from the residuum of fires, the white ash and cinders, or small fragments of unconsumed coke, giving rise to by far the greater quantity. Some notion of the vast amount of refuse annually produced in London may be formed from the fact that the consumption of coal in the metropolis is, according to the official returns, 3,500,000 tons per annum, which is at the rate of a little more than 11 tons per house; the poorer families, it is true, do not burn more than 2 tons in the course of the year, but then many such families reside in the same house, and hence the average will appear in no way excessive. Now the ashes and cinders arising from this enormous consumption of coal would, it is evident, if allowed to lie scattered about in such a place as London, render, ere long, not only the back streets, but even the important thoroughfares, filthy and impassable. Upon the Officers of the various parishes, therefore, has devolved the duty of seeing that the refuse of the fuel consumed throughout London is removed almost as fast as it is produced; this they do by entering into an agreement for the clearance of the 'dust-bins' of the parishioners as often as required, with some person who possesses all necessary appliances for the purpose—such as horses, carts, baskets, and shovels, together with a plot of waste ground whereon to deposit the refuse. The persons with whom this agreement is made are called 'dust-contractors', and are generally men of considerable wealth. . . .

The dust-yards, or places where the dust is collected and sifted, are generally situated in the suburbs, and they may be found all round London, sometimes occupying open spaces adjoining back streets and lanes, surrounded by the low mean houses of the poor; frequently, however, they cover a large extent of ground in the fields, and there the dust is piled up to a great height in a conical heap, and having much the appearance of a volcanic mountain. . . .

Source: extracts from *London Labour and the London Poor* (London, 1861–62), II, pp. 149, 166, 171.

2. CONTEMPORARY OPINIONS

H. F. Chorley (1865)

A Carefully-Wrought Novel

A new novel by the greatest novelist living is not to be dismissed with a few jaunty phrases of rapture, or of qualification; for a simple yet serious reason. Those who, with understanding, as distinct from that wonderment which belongs to the foolish face of praise, have followed Mr Dickens throughout his career of authorship cannot fail to have perceived that time and success have not made him careless—whether as concerns his art, his public, or himself. . . .

None of the series [of his novels] is so intricate in plot as this tale . . . . The closest attention is required to hold certain of its connecting links. . . . The complications of the story may have necessitated sharp turns and surprises, which bear unfavourably on some of the characters. . . .

Thus much by way of qualification . . . concerning a novel which gains immensely by being perused without 'stop, let, or hindrance'. . . . *Our Mutual Friend* is one of Mr Dickens's richest and most carefully-wrought books . . . [and] must be signalised for an accumulation of fine, exact, characteristic detail, such as would suffice to set up in trade for life a score of the novel-spinners who give us situations without motives, scenes without characters, words without thoughts, and the dialogue, not of real life, but of melodrama. . . .

SOURCE: extract from review in the *Athenaeum* (28 Oct. 1865).

E. S. Dallas (1865)

An Astonishing Fertility

. . . We say deliberately that we have read nothing of Mr Dickens's which has given us a higher idea of his power than this last tale. It would not be wonderful if so voluminous an author should now show some signs of exhaustion. On the contrary, here he is in greater force than ever, astonishing us with a fertility in which we can trace no signs of repetition. We hear people say, 'He has never surpassed *Pickwick.*' They talk of *Pickwick* as if it were his masterpiece. We do not yield to any one in our enjoyment of that extraordinary work. We never tire of it. We are of those who can read it again and again, and can take it up at any page with the certainty of finding in it the most merry-making humour. But we refuse to measure a work of art by the amount of visible effect which it produces; and we are not going to quarrel with tragedy because it is less mirthful than comedy. What if we allow that *Our Mutual Friend* is not nearly so funny as *Pickwick*? It is infinitely better than *Pickwick* in all the higher qualities of a novel, and, in spite of the dead weight of 'The Social Chorus,' we class it with Mr Dickens's best works.

One thing is very remarkable about it—the immense amount of thought which it contains. We scarcely like to speak of the labour bestowed upon it, lest a careless reader should carry away a notion that the work is laboured. What labour Mr Dickens has given to it is a labour of love, and the point which strikes us is that he, who of all our living novelists has the most extraordinary genius, is also of all our living novelists the most careful and painstaking in his work. In all these 600 pages there is not a careless line. There are lines and pages we object to as wrong in execution, or not quite happy in idea; but there is not a page nor a line which is not the product of a full mind bursting with what it has to say, and determined to say it well. Right or wrong, the work is always thoroughgoing and conscientious. There is nothing slurred over—no negligence, no working up to what are called in stage language 'points'—to the detriment of the more level passages. And then see what a mass of matter he lays before his readers. There is a gallery of portraits in the present novel which might set up half a dozen novelists for life: Bella Wilfer, the most charming of all, her father, her mother, her sister; then Boffin and Mrs Boffin, and Silas Wegg, and Venus, the practical anatomist; then, again, Riderhood, and Lizzie Hexam, and Bradley Headstone; once more, Mortimer Lightwood, Wrayburn, the dolls' dressmaker, and her father. There are many more,

and among these we must not forget poor old Betty Higden, because
without such a character as hers Mr Dickens's tales would be unlike
themselves. Mr Dickens cannot write a tale without in some way
bringing it to bear upon a social grievance, with regard to which he has
a strong feeling. He has a strong feeling as to the manner in which the
Poor Law is administered in this country, and he devotes one of his most
powerful chapters to showing with what horror poor Betty Higden
shrinks from parochial charity. . . .

SOURCE: extract from review in *The Times* (29 Nov. 1865).

Henry James (1865)

Dickens Exhausted

Our Mutual Friend is, to our perception, the poorest of Mr Dickens's
works. And it is poor with the poverty not of momentary embarrassment, but of permanent exhaustion. It is wanting in inspiration. For the
last ten years it has seemed to us that Mr Dickens has been unmistakably
forcing himself. *Bleak House* was forced; *Little Dorrit* was labored; the
present work is dug out as with a spade and pickaxe. Of course—to
anticipate the usual argument—who but Dickens could have written it?
Who, indeed? Who else would have established a lady in business in a
novel on the admirably solid basis of her always putting on gloves and
tieing a handkerchief round her head in moments of grief, and of her
habitually addressing her family with 'Peace! hold!' It is needless to say
that Mrs Reginald Wilfer is first and last the occasion of considerable
true humor. When, after conducting her daughter to Mrs Boffin's
carriage, in sight of all the envious neighbors, she is described as
enjoying her triumph during the next quarter of an hour by airing
herself on the door-step 'in a kind of splendidly serene trance,' we laugh
with as uncritical a laugh as could be desired of us. We pay the same
tribute to her assertions, as she narrates the glories of the society she
enjoyed at her father's table, that she has known as many as three
copper-plate engravers exchanging the most exquisite sallies and retorts
there at one time. But when to these we have added a dozen more happy
examples of the humor which was exhaled from every line of Mr
Dickens's earlier writings, we shall have closed the list of the merits of

the work before us. To say that the conduct of the story, with all its
complications, betrays a long-practised hand, is to pay no compliment
worthy the author. If this were, indeed, a compliment, we should be
inclined to carry it further, and congratulate him on his success in what
we should call the manufacture of fiction; for in so doing we should
express a feeling that has attended us throughout the book. Seldom, we
reflected, had we read a book so intensely *written*, so little seen, known,
or felt.

In all Mr Dickens's works the fantastic has been his great resource;
and while his fancy was lively and vigorous it accomplished great
things. But the fantastic, when the fancy is dead, is a very poor business.
The movement of Mr Dickens's fancy in Mrs Wilfer and Mr Boffin and
Lady Tippins, and the Lammles and Miss Wren, and even in Eugene
Wrayburn, is, to our mind, a movement lifeless, forced, mechanical. It
is the letter of his old humor without the spirit. It is hardly too much to
say that every character here put before us is a mere bundle of
eccentricities, animated by no principle of nature whatever. In former
days there reigned in Mr Dickens's extravagances a comparative
consistency; they were exaggerated statements of types that really
existed. We had, perhaps, never known a Newman Noggs, nor a
Pecksniff, nor a Micawber; but we had known persons of whom these
figures were but the strictly logical consummation. But among the
grotesque creatures who occupy the pages before us, there is not one
whom we can refer to as an existing type. In all Mr Dickens's stories,
indeed, the reader has been called upon, and has willingly consented, to
accept a certain number of figures or creatures of pure fancy, for this
was the author's poetry. He was, moreover, always repaid for his
concession by a peculiar beauty or power in these exceptional
characters. But he is now expected to make the same concession with a
very inadequate reward. What do we get in return for accepting Miss
Jenny Wren as a possible person? This young lady is the type of a certain
class of characters of which Mr Dickens has made a speciality, and with
which he has been accustomed to draw alternate smiles and tears,
according as he pressed one spring or another. But this is very cheap
merriment and very cheap pathos. Miss Jenny Wren is a poor little
dwarf, afflicted, as she constantly reiterates, with a 'bad back' and
'queer legs,' who makes dolls' dresses, and is for ever pricking at those
with whom she converses, in the air, with her needle, and assuring them
that she knows their 'tricks and their manners.' Like all Mr Dickens's
pathetic characters, she is a little monster; she is deformed, unhealthy,
unnatural; she belongs to the troop of hunchbacks, imbeciles, and
precocious children who have carried on the sentimental business in all
Mr Dickens's novels; the little Nells, the Smikes, the Paul Dombeys.

Mr Dickens goes as far out of the way for his wicked people as he does for his good ones. Rogue Riderhood, indeed, in the present story, is villanous with a sufficiently natural villany; he belongs to that quarter of society in which the author is most at his ease. But was there ever such wickedness as that of the Lammles and Mr Fledgeby? Not that people have not been as mischievous as they; but was any one ever mischievous in that singular fashion? Did a couple of elegant swindlers ever take such particular pains to be aggressively inhuman?—for we can find no other word for the gratuitous distortions to which they are subjected. The word *humanity* strikes us as strangely discordant, in the midst of these pages; for, let us boldly declare it, there is no humanity here. Humanity is nearer home than the Boffins, and the Lammles, and the Wilfers, and the Veneerings. It is in what men have in common with each other, and not in what they have in distinction. The people just named have nothing in common with each other, except the fact that they have nothing in common with mankind at large. What a world were this world if the world of *Our Mutual Friend* were an honest reflection of it! But a community of eccentrics is impossible. Rules alone are consistent with each other; exceptions are inconsistent. Society is maintained by natural sense and natural feeling. We cannot conceive a society in which these principles are not in some manner represented. Where in these pages are the depositaries of that intelligence without which the movement of life would cease? Who represents nature? Accepting half of Mr Dickens's persons as intentionally grotesque, where are those exemplars of sound humanity who should afford us the proper measure of their companions' variations? We ought not, in justice to the author, to seek them among his weaker—that is, his mere conventional—characters; in John Harmon, Lizzie Hexam, or Mortimer Lightwood; but we assuredly cannot find them among his stronger—that is, his artificial creations. Suppose we take Eugene Wrayburn and Bradley Headstone. They occupy a half-way position between the habitual probable of nature and the habitual impossible of Mr Dickens. A large portion of the story rests upon the enmity borne by Headstone to Wrayburn, both being in love with the same woman. Wrayburn is a gentleman, and Headstone is one of the people. Wrayburn is well-bred, careless, elegant, sceptical, and idle: Headstone is a high-tempered, hard-working, ambitious young schoolmaster. There lay in the opposition of these two characters a very good story. But the prime requisite was that they should *be* characters: Mr Dickens, according to his usual plan, has made them simply figures, and between them the story that was to be, the story that should have been, has evaporated. Wrayburn lounges about with his hands in his pockets, smoking a cigar, and talking nonsense. Headstone strides about, clenching his fists and biting his lips and grasping his stick. There is one scene in which Wrayburn chaffs the schoolmaster with easy insolence, while the latter writhes

impotently under his well-bred sarcasm. This scene is very clever, but it
is very insufficient. If the majority of readers were not so very timid in
the use of words we should call it vulgar. By this we do not mean to
indicate the conventional impropriety of two gentlemen exchanging
lively personalities; we mean to emphasise the essentially small
character of these personalities. In other words, the moment, dramatically, is great, while the author's conception is weak. The friction of two
men, of two characters, of two passions, produces stronger sparks than
Wrayburn's boyish repartees and Headstone's melodramatic commonplaces. Such scenes as this are useful in fixing the limits of Mr
Dickens's insight. Insight is, perhaps, too strong a word; for we are
convinced that it is one of the chief conditions of his genius not to see
beneath the surface of things. If we might hazard a definition of his
literary character, we should, accordingly, call him the greatest of
superficial novelists. We are aware that this definition confines him to
an inferior rank in the department of letters which he adorns; but we
accept this consequence of our proposition. It were, in our opinion, an
offence against humanity to place Mr Dickens among the greatest
novelists. For, to repeat what we have already intimated, he has created
nothing but figure. He has added nothing to our understanding of
human character. He is master of but two alternatives: he reconciles us
to what is commonplace, and he reconciles us to what is odd. The value
of the former service is questionable; and the manner in which Mr
Dickens performs it sometimes conveys a certain impression of charla-
tanism. The value of the latter service is incontestable, and here Mr
Dickens is an honest, an admirable artist. But what is the condition of
the truly great novelist? For him there are no alternatives, for him there
are no oddities, for him there is nothing outside of humanity. He cannot
shirk it; it imposes itself upon him. For him alone, therefore, there is a
true and a false; for him alone it is possible to be right, because it is
possible to be wrong. Mr Dickens is a great observer and a great
humorist, but he is nothing of a philosopher. Some people may
hereupon say, so much the better; we say, so much the worse. For a
novelist very soon has need of a little philosophy. In treating of
Micawber, and Boffin, and Pickwick, *et hoc genus omne*, he can, indeed,
dispense with it, for this—we say it with all deference—is not serious
writing. But when he comes to tell the story of a passion, a story like that
of Headstone and Wrayburn, he becomes a moralist as well as an artist.
He must know *man* as well as *men*, and to know man is to be a
philosopher. The writer who knows men alone, if he have Mr Dickens's
humor and fancy, will give us figures and pictures for which we cannot
be too grateful, for he will enlarge our knowledge of the world. But
when he introduces men and women whose interest is preconceived to
lie not in the poverty, the weakness, the drollery of their natures, but in

their complete and unconscious subjection to ordinary and healthy
human emotions, all his humor, all his fancy, will avail him nothing, if,
out of the fulness of his sympathy, he is unable to prosecute those
generalisations in which alone consists the real greatness of a work of art.
This may sound like very subtle talk about a very simple matter; it is
rather very simple talk about a very subtle matter. A story based upon
those elementary passions in which alone we seek the true and final
manifestation of character must be told in a spirit of intellectual
superiority to those passions. That is, the author must understand what
he is talking about. The perusal of a story so told is one of the most
elevating experiences within the reach of the human mind. The perusal
of a story which is not so told is infinitely depressing and unprofitable.

SOURCE: review in the *Nation* (21 Dec. 1865); reproduced in L.
Edel (ed.), *The House of Fiction* (New York, 1957).

John Forster (1874)

A Lack of Freshness

. . . The book thus begun and continued under adverse influences,
though with fancy in it, descriptive power, and characters well
designed, will never rank with his higher efforts. It has some pictures of a
rare veracity of soul amid the lowest forms of social degradation,
placed beside others of sheer falsehood and pretence amid unimpeach-
able social correctness, which lifted the writer to his old place; but the
judgement of it on the whole must be, that it wants freshness and natural
development. This indeed will be most freely admitted by those who
feel most strongly that all the old cunning of the master hand is yet in the
wayward, loving Bella Wilfer, in the vulgar, canting Podsnap, and in
the dolls' dressmaker Jenny Wren, whose keen little quaint weird ways,
and precocious wit sharpened by trouble, are fitted into a character as
original and delightfully conceived as it is vividly carried through to the
last. A dull coarse web her small life seems made of; but even from its
taskwork, which is undertaken for childhood itself, there are glittering
threads cast across its woof and warp of care. The unconscious
philosophy of her tricks and manners has in it more of the subtler vein of

the satire aimed at in the book, than even the voices of society which the tale begins and ends with. In her very kindliness there is the touch of malice that shows a childish playfulness familiar with unnatural privations; this gives a depth as well as tenderness to her humours which entitles them to rank with the writer's happiest things; and though the odd little creature's talk is incessant when she is on the scene, it has the individuality that so seldom tires. It is veritably her own small 'trick' and 'manner', and is never mistakable for anyone else's. 'I have been reading', Dickens wrote to me from France while he was writing the book, 'a capital little story by Edmond About—*The Notary's Nose*. I have been trying other books; but so infernally conversational, that I forget who the people are before they have done talking, and don't in the least remember what they talked about before when they begin talking again!' The extreme contrast to his own art could not be defined more exactly; and other examples from this tale will be found in the differing members of the Wilfer family, in the riverside people at the Fellowship Porters, in such marvellous serio-comic scenes as that of Rogue Riderhood's restoration from drowning, and in those short and simple annals of Betty Higden's life and death which might have given saving virtue to a book more likely than this to perish prematurely. It has not the creative power which crowded his earlier page, and transformed into popular realities the shadows of his fancy; but the observation and humour he excelled in are not wanting to it, nor had there been, in his first completed work, more eloquent or generous pleading for the poor and neglected, than this last completed work contains. Betty Higden finishes what Oliver Twist began.

SOURCE: extract from the *Life of Charles Dickens* (London, 1872– 74).

3. LATER CRITICISM

Jack Lindsay   'The Symbolic Dust-
Heap' (1950)

. . . *Our Mutual Friend*, to which Dickens at last nerved himself, is in
many ways his supreme work. It lacks the concision and dramatic close
texture of *Great Expectations*; but instead it owns a spacious breadth of
definition. Even the elements of turbid confusion contribute to the total
effect, in which a complete judgement on the life of Dickens's world is
delivered. Nothing less than the conjuring up of the whole of society, its
tangled cross-currents and involved patterning, will suffice for such a
definitive vision. At moments he seems tiring; but always he pulls
himself together in time. The result is one of the greatest works of prose
ever written. A work which finally vindicates Dickens's right to stand,
as no other English writer can stand, at the side of Shakespeare.

Dombey, Bleak House, and *Little Dorrit* had been mature works before
this, in which he attempted a broadly based picture of the human
condition and Victorian society. The first had shown the withering
effects of the money-ethic on human values; the second, taking the law
as the symbol of the State and all its powers, had uttered a basic
rejection of the existing State form; the third had dealt with the lie, the
rottenness of guilt and fear, at the social core. In *Our Mutual Friend*
Dickens resumes all these judgements in a huge involved novel, in
which he carries his forms, artistically and emotionally, to their limit of
significant expansion. The fundamental contrast in all his writings,
between the vileness of all existing forms of State organisation and the
indomitable powers of renewal in man, is here carried to breaking
point.

The central idea of *Our Mutual Friend* is the struggle for a dust-heap.
Rubbish in the mid-Victorian period was a valuable product for
contractors, but a curse for Londoners. Such removals as went on were
the work of private agents who collected the dust and rubbish in dumps
in North London (roughly in the area now filled by King's Cross and St.
Pancras stations). These dumps were sifted for rags, cinders and fine
dust—for paper-making, for fuel to smelters, for concrete-making. No

doubt the idea for the novel came through a paragraph in the newspapers which told of a very large fortune left by one of the dust contractors. But the reason why a chance jest was felt by Dickens to provide the main theme for his most serious novel was because the notion of wealth as a foul dust-heap, over which men spent their time struggling, stirred his deepest ironies. The equation of money and filth or dung goes far down in the psyche, as dream-analysis has shown. In using the dust-heap as the emblem of the great prize for which men were fighting, Dickens starts off with a fantasy-image which fitly utters his contempt and hatred. (At the same time his own increasing obsession with the readings as a money source means an element of self-contempt driving him on into the attack.)

But there is a further point in the choice. Since the early days of his reporting, Dickens had used the term 'dust-heap' to express his contempt and hatred of Parliament, of the whole State system. And indeed, William Morris, who was soaked in Dickens's imagery, carries on the image; in his lecture *Communism* he speaks of England as 'a counting-house on the top of a cinder-heap, with Podsnap's drawing-room in the offing'. The citation of Podsnap shows how definitely he was drawing on the Dickensian myth. In *Hard Times* it appears in a variation: 'He [Gradgrind] then returned with promptitude to the national cinder-heap, and resumed his sifting for the odds and ends he wanted, and his throwing dust into the eyes of other people who wanted other odds and other ends—in fact, resumed his parliamentary duties.'

The fight for the dust-heap, the intrigue over the inheritance of the dust-heap, is thus in one sense an allegory of the struggle for control of the State. Clearly, this is a point which must not be pressed too far. There is no carefully worked out allegorical scheme; but at the same time there can be no doubt that much of the originating dynamic of the theme comes from these hidden significances of the dust-heap for Dickens. It draws its sources from a deep imagery-cluster from which come also the '*merde*' of Merdle and the rags and bones of Krook, the symbolic Lord Chancellor of *Bleak House*, on the one hand, and, on the other, the paternal grave of *Copperfield*—'. . . and the light upon the window of our room shone out upon the earthly bourne of all such travellers, and the mound above the ashes and the dust that once was he, without whom I had never been.'

Source: extract from *Charles Dickens* (London, 1950), pp. 380–1.

Arnold Kettle   'Dickens and Class'
(1962)

MOST PEOPLE today who take Dickens seriously as a writer would probably agree with what was, in 1937, the minority view expressed by T. A. Jackson when he wrote, referring to the later novels:

Dickens sought, by means of the incident-plot of his novels, to achieve a moral-plot indicative of and symbolising a politico-ethical criticism of the social life of his time.[1]

There may be, perhaps, from the metaphysicians and myth-critics a certain jibbing at 'politico-ethical' and even 'social', but even from such quarters there will be agreement that Dickens's plots are 'more than' plots and that the later novels, especially, embody a more complex and profound level of organisation and significance than most early literary criticism of Dickens, however enthusiastic, recognised.

This is not to suggest that there is anything abstract or even allegorical about the conception of a novel like *Our Mutual Friend*. About *Hard Times* and even *Great Expectations* there is indeed a certain recognisable background of abstract thinking which emerges, interestingly, in their very titles; but by and large the images around and through which Dickens worked are not conceived at all in an abstract way. What he mostly thought about was, indeed, his plots and characters; but to get these plots and characters 'right', to satisfy the essential, not necessarily fully formulated, end he was after, required, as he went on, their more and more careful subordination to a whole, and in that whole a moral view and purpose is predominant.

More critical notice has been taken of the grammar of the title of *Our Mutual Friend* than of its significance. This is not altogether surprising, for a consideration of Dickens's titles is not always rewarding. It is hard to make much of *Martin Chuzzlewit* as a title and *Little Dorrit* is a good deal less interesting than its rejected alternative *Nobody's Fault*. Yet it is perhaps significant that in this big, ambitious, eminently serious novel Dickens should have underlined in his title the rôle of John Harmon. It is of course obvious that in the incident-plot (hereinafter referred to simply as 'plot') John Harmon, alias Handford, alias Rokesmith, is the king-pin. It is his inheritance and his supposed murder that sets the whole thing going; he is indeed the Beginning of the story, 'the man from nowhere'. But, without overdoing Harmon/Rokesmith's significance (he doesn't really bear too much loading with that commodity) I think it is worth noticing that his part in the moral-plot (hereinafter termed 'the pattern') is also important. For his function within the novel is to link not only diverse characters but diverse areas. Not least important is the actual topographical link he supplies, for it is he who brings the mounds or dust-heaps into relation with the river and this, as we shall see, is fundamental to the imagery of *Our Mutual Friend*. But there is another respect, thematic rather than concrete, in which Harmon/Rokesmith forms a vital link. He connects the area of wealth with the area of poverty. And this is fundamental to the conception of the novel. T. A. Jackson puts it quite correctly: 'Class-contrast and class-antagonism, class-hatred and class-contempt are woven into the innermost texture of *Our Mutual Friend*.'[2]

The idea of mutuality as involving more than the isolable *personal* relationships of individual characters is, of course, very deep in Dickens. There is a deeply-felt moment in *Bleak House*, more important in the pattern of that book than is generally recognised, when Esther Summerson tries to sum up her feelings and Ada's about their first ghastly visit, with Mrs Pardiggle, to the brickmakers' cottage:

> We both felt painfully sensible that between us and these people there was an iron barrier, which could not be removed by our new friend (Mrs Pardiggle). By whom, or how, it could be removed we did not know; but we knew that. [*Bleak House*, ch. 8]

All Dickens's novels might be described on one level as explorations into the human effects of this iron barrier and the ways of removing it, and *Our Mutual Friend* is perhaps the most profound and consistent of these explorations. What underlies Mr Boffin's description of Harmon/Rokesmith as 'our mutual friend' (he is talking to Mrs Wilfer) is that character's part in bridging and, in a sense, loosening up the class-relationships of the whole world of the novel. For not merely does Harmon/Rokesmith connect the Boffins with the Wilfers but he is also the unwitting means of introducing Eugene Wrayburn to Lizzie Hexam, a connection just as important to the pattern of *Our Mutual Friend*.

In the Boffin–Wilfer relationship class-antagonism as such does not arise, though there is a great deal of caste-antagonism and caste-contempt. Mrs Wilfer is every bit as snobbish as Lady Tippins, but the joke is, of course, that her snobbery has no real social basis: she is a tragedy-queen out of a tenth-rate repertory company. And Bella's mercenariness, though almost fatal, is in an important sense unlike the mercenariness of Podsnappery, based on shares and exploitation; hers is a working-class mercenariness, not much different in essence from that of Richardson's Pamela, based simply on the bitter experience of what not having money involves. What is fought out in the Boffin–

Rokesmith–Wilfer area of the novel is a moral battle which is a class-battle in the quite fundamental sense that it hinges on class-values. Is the way out of poverty the way of Podsnappian acquisitiveness? Bella at first thinks it is. She learns better through the example of the apparent corruption of Mr Boffin.

This episode, which has often been objected to as improbable or clumsy, seems to me one of Dickens's happiest inspirations. It serves a double purpose, not in the facile sense of getting two effects for the price of one but in the rarer way of revealing simultaneously two sides of the same coin. Bella is tested and changed by her experiences, graduating in the school of nineteenth-century heroines from the status of a Dora (in *David Copperfield*) to somewhere approaching that of a Nora (in *The Doll's House*); and at the same time the possibilities of corruption inherent in the Boffin-situation are triumphantly revealed. Dickens gets it both ways: the alternative possibilities before Boffin are both dramatised, and the degrading horror of the one throws into relief the humane excellence of the other. These alternative possibilities of corruption and human decency are underlined meanwhile within the Boffin area of the book by the respective paths of Messrs Wegg and Venus. The relationship between Boffin and Wegg seems to me extraordinarily well done. Not only Wegg's meanness but Boffin's own vulnerability emerge in episodes as psychologically subtle as they are funny. There is more than a touch of the nastier kind of unease in Boffin's naïve dealings with his literary man. Because he is in the position of patron he begins behaving like a patron—he who so hates patronage (it is a recurring theme of consideration throughout the book). One understands Wegg's irritation, even though his basic reactions are of course unforgivable. And it must also be said that Dickens's plot, towards the end of the Boffin–Wegg strand, gets him into one of those rare situations in which he is not quite on top of things. Boffin's dissimulation is fair enough in relation to Bella, but when the golden dustman has simultaneously to unravel the complicated machinations of Wegg and Venus it is not always clear in which persona he is performing or who is leading whom up the dust-heap or why.

The question that both Bella and the Boffins have to face is whether, given the opportunity, they want to 'rise', i.e. emerge morally from the working-class world into the world of Podsnap the bourgeois. This, it is worth stressing, is the real issue, an issue not of money as such but of values. The corrupting force in *Our Mutual Friend* is not money but bourgeois attitudes to it. That is why critics who take the superficial view that class is simply a matter of birth or level of income can make little of the pattern of *Our Mutual Friend* and are likely to end by presenting an image of Dickens as a comfortable middle-class do-gooder with vulgar tastes and a soft spot for the deserving poor.

The question that both Bella and the Boffins have to face is the Hexams' and the Veneerings' problem as well as the Wilfers' and the Boffins'. One of the central aspects of the problem is—as in so much Victorian literature and thinking—that of education. Almost the first thing Mr Boffin does when he gets his money is to employ Wegg to improve his education. Again, one recalls the importance of books in preserving David Copperfield's integrity and the wonderful moment in *Bleak House* when old Krook is found teaching *himself* to read and write because he cannot trust anyone else to teach him right. To insist that Dickens was keen on education is to miss half the point. What he also recognised was that in a class-divided society education itself has a double tendency, to corrupt as well as to liberate. At the school where Charley Hexam learns and Bradley Headstone teaches—a 'temple of good intentions' Dickens calls it—'an exceptionally sharp boy exceptionally determined to learn, could learn something' and the worth of that something is not underestimated. But the *values* which Charley Hexam imbibes are also part of his education and they, of course, are not merely snobbish in the more superficial sense, making him socially contemptuous of Lizzie and her friends, but infected at the core with anti-working-class attitudes, especially the idea of 'getting up in the world'. The imagery used to describe Bradley Headstone's mind is extraordinarily telling:

> From his early childhood up, his mind had been a place of mechanical stowage. The arrangement of his wholesale warehouse, so that it might be always ready to meet the demands of retail dealers—history here, geography there, astronomy to the right, political economy to the left . . . this care had imparted to his countenance a look of care. [Bk II, ch. 1]

Not only is the educational system as such here linked with the processes of capitalist economy, but Headstone's own personal neuroses connected organically with the socio-intellectual system of which he is a cog, a system which is revealed as inhuman not only in its underlying values—commercial and mechanical—but in its division of knowledge and experience into isolated compartments. In a single sentence Dickens is indeed, in terms entirely relevant to the personal situation he is depicting, producing a profound humanist critique of the modern British educational system.

'Rising' is a desperate danger in the world of *Our Mutual Friend*, for to 'rise' is to enter the sphere of the Podsnaps and the Veneerings. Charley Hexam does not enter that sphere financially but spiritually he does, and his spiritual corruption is inseparable from his social ambitions, his undeviating, fanatical determination to make himself 'respectable in

the scale of society'. And when, in his nauseating complacency, he
finally turns on the wretched Headstone, his tone and language are
those of Mr Podsnap. Charley's final judgement on his sister [Bk IV, ch.
7] and Podsnap's [Bk IV, last chapter], though made from socially
different positions, are interchangeable. For level of income is not the
determining feature of Podsnappery and an increase in income is not
the same as 'rising'. Lizzie Hexam will not be corrupted by becoming
Mrs Eugene Wrayburn any more than Mrs Boffin is spoiled by her
innocent enthusiasm for Fashion and her frank enjoyment of the
pleasures of wealth.

Does this mean that Dickens makes a simple division between 'good'
and 'bad' characters and that the 'good', irrespective of social status or
class position, resist corruption while the 'bad' are drawn under, like
Rogue Riderhood drawn under the treacherous waters of the Thames?
I do not think such an assessment stands up to a thorough-going
examination. Obviously Dickens is not, in a crude sense, a social
determinist; he does not imply that the social 'background' of a
character is inescapable. Lizzie and Charley Hexam grow up in the
same house, subjected to the same general social influences, but turn out
quite differently. Lizzie, so to speak, moves upstream, Charley down.
But Charley's deterioration is bound up, not just with 'character' in an
isolated, unchanging sense, but with specific social choices, including
Lizzie's own ambitions for him as opposed to her lack of ambition for
herself. We understand why Lizzie wants to get Charley away from the
riverside and we respect her for it, but we are forced to recognise, as she
herself never quite does, that she has, in all innocence, made a frightful
error in judgement, an error which, faced with a temptation of her own,
she manages to avoid. Lizzie refuses to be drawn into corruption, just as
Jenny Wren and Mr Riah and Mr Venus do, and though the refusal
costs each of them something, what is maintained is moral independence. These people, despite their poverty, decline to 'rise' by
grasping 'opportunities' that will undermine their humanity.

This is the significance of the Betty Higden episode which is all too
easily seen as merely a bit of doubtless well-intentioned propaganda
against the workhouses and their 'honourable boards', a not very
relevant return to the preoccupations of *Oliver Twist*. In naturalistic
terms old Betty is no doubt overdone (rather in the way Firs, the old
servant in *The Cherry Orchard*, can be felt to be overdone), yet her
uncompromising and obsessional determination to be beholden to no
one, even the undemanding Mrs Boffin, is an important, and I think
necessary, strand in the pattern of Dickens's presentation of the
problems of poverty and working-class morality. To accept patronage is
to lose independence, to drift into the arms of the 'honourable boards' is
to accept human degradation. It is notable that in *Our Mutual Friend* it is

not the idea of social services that is attacked: Dickens goes out of his way to praise the children's hospital and to show that old Betty's suspicions of it are groundless. He is not holding up Mrs Higden's sturdy independence as something preferable to the acceptance of a decently conceived system of planned social welfare. What he is underlining is a moral embedded deep in this novel: that a genuine emancipation or even amelioration involves the maintenance of their moral independence by working-class people and that such independence is incompatible either with 'rising' or with the acceptance of the sort of charity which has bourgeois strings attached.

For of all of Dickens's novels this is the one most deeply and consistently impregnated with a consciousness of the power of the bourgeoisie. How essential the 'society' chapters—set in the homes of the Podsnaps and Veneerings—are to the basic conception of the novel is emphasised by the nature and positioning of Chapter the Last, which is very different from the usual final chapter of a Victorian novel, tying up loose ends and adding more or less irrelevant information about the future careers of the characters. 'The Voice of Society' it is called and it is clear that Dickens is using the word 'society' with deliberate and effective ambiguity; for though the voice referred to is in fact 'society' in the narrower sense of those who people the 'society columns' of the newspapers, it is the implication of the whole novel that their voice is the one which dominates society as a whole and that their values are in a precise sense the ruling values of the world of *Our Mutual Friend*. These values get their fullest and most insistent symbolic expression in the novel in the recurring emphases on dust and shares. The dust-heaps are the dominant visual image of the accumulation of wealth and power; but it is a feature of that power that it operates not openly but mysteriously, through bits of paper: wills, promissory notes, the offer of reward which Rogue Riderhood clutches, above all, through shares.

> As is well known to the wise in their generation, traffic in Shares is the one thing to have to do with in this world. Have no antecedents, no established character, no cultivation, no ideas, no manners; have Shares. Have Shares enough to be on Boards of Direction in capital letters, oscillate on mysterious business between London and Paris, and be great. Where does he come from? Shares. Where is he going to? Shares. What are his tastes? Shares. Has he any principles? Shares. What squeezes him into Parliament? Shares. Perhaps he never of himself achieved success in anything, never originated anything, never produced anything? Sufficient answer to all; Shares, O mighty Shares! [Bk 1, ch. 10]

Such a passage, quoted out of context, may give the impression of an aside, a perhaps not quite legitimate intrusion of one of Dickens's hobby-horses. In fact it is fully integrated into the structure of the novel. The immediate occasion of it is the approaching marriage of the Lammles, one of the minor triumphs of the book and a brilliant advance on Thackeray's treatment of a similar theme in the 'how to live on nothing a year' part of *Vanity Fair*, because the emotional nature of the Lammles's impasse is suggested in a way Thackeray cannot reach. But it is not simply the Lammles's career that the passage touches: it is the whole operation of Podsnappery, from the honourable boards that terrify Betty Higden and the honourable debt that almost ruins Mr Twemlow to the whole marvellously funny career of the Veneerings who emerge from nothing and disappear into nothing, but take in a seat in Parliament on their way, people from nowhere, spreading a sort of doom.[3]

It is, I suppose, the uncompromising nature of this insight, so fundamental to *Our Mutual Friend* of the null and friendless nature of the Podsnap world, that has led, as much as anything, to the underestimating of this novel. Henry James's unfavourable contemporary review in *The Nation*, though it does Dickens less than justice (the later James would have been more generous, though whether he would have been as frank is perhaps more doubtful), centres on this very question. [Kettle quotes the passage beginning 'What a world were this if the world of *Our Mutual Friend* were an honest reflection of it!' . . . See James's review reproduced in the preceding section—Ed.] . . . The tone of sophisticated outrage is arresting and straightway illuminates the gap between the worlds of, say, George Eliot, Matthew Arnold, and Henry James on the one side and Dickens on the other. Who represents nature indeed? One recalls Mr Squeers's rich philosophical aside to the effect that nature is a rum'n. Or perhaps the simplest reply is to ask: whose nature? It is of the very essence of *Our Mutual Friend* that Podsnappery does represent a significant area of nature—bourgeois nature—and that for 'natural sense and natural feeling' this particular area of aspiration, to use an expressive phrase of the Artful Dodger's, 'ain't the shop'.

The Jamesian shift [noted here], from 'natural sense and natural feeling' to 'depositories of intelligence', is in itself interesting. Clearly, . . . because he is unable to see the Boffins as the depositories of the kind of intelligence which he, Arnold-like, associates with those whose destiny it is to set standards for society and spread sweetness and light, . . . Henry James cannot even recognise their natural sense and natural feeling. James sees the Boffins as eccentrics, whereas to Dickens it is they, above all, who are the representatives of the sort of nature he was most interested in—popular nature in the true nineteenth-century sense of popular, expressive of the worth and potentiality of the People as opposed to those who rule and exploit them.[4]

The two most important concrete visual images in *Our Mutual Friend*, as everyone recognises, are the mounds and the river. It is worth emphasising that they are not, in any abstract or schematic sense, symbols, but straightforward poetic images, embodying in the richness of their relevant qualities and the manifold 'rightness' of their relationship to one another, the central content and meaning of the novel. Several critics, especially perhaps Humphry House, have helped us to see the full importance of the dust-heaps, not merely as historical phenomena, actual outcrops on the face of Victorian London and specific examples of capital accumulation and speculation, but in the nature of their content of waste and even excrement.[5] The mounds get their effect in the novel in a number of ways working simultaneously. Visually they are huge, ugly, barren, man-made, yet in their operation there is a kind of perverse fertility about them, the fertility of manure and—the connection is not arbitrary—dividends. They keep the system going. To own them is not merely to be rich but to control the processes of social continuity. And the poor live within their shadow and their stench.

The mounds are connected with the river in several ways. Visually or geographically they rear up as a sort of artificial Primrose Hill, overlooking North London. In terms of the plot it is, as I have already suggested, Harmon/Rokesmith who links the two areas and a subsidiary link is provided by the ludicrous romance of Mr Venus and Pleasant Riderhood. An interesting associative connection has been suggested in the form of the Houses of Parliament ('the national cinder-heap') which stand by the river.[6] But though this may be a trifle far-fetched, the main relationship is clear. It is the filth of London, itself one vast fog-infested dust-heap, that pollutes the river and turns it from a pleasing and refreshing stream into a flowing sewer of filth and refuse. There is indeed a grim and significant parallel between the image of old Harmon (and Silas Wegg) fishing his wealth out of the dust of commercial London and Gaffer Hexam fishing his sordid living out of the polluted waters of the chartered Thames.

Rivers nowadays always seem to tempt the Jungians to their most absurd excesses and no one familiar with the ways of twentieth-century American criticism especially will be surprised to find the Thames of *Our Mutual Friend* saddled with every conceivable kind of ritual significance. Unfortunately for these interpretations, on the only occasion really conducive to such an emphasis—the rescue and revival of Rogue Riderhood—Dickens goes out of his way to laugh at any such idea as the restorative power of drowning. Pleasant Riderhood is visited by some vague idea that the old evil is drowned out of him, and that if he should happily come back to resume his occupation of the empty form that lies upon his bed, his spirit will be altered. In which state of mind she kisses the stony lips, and quite believes that the impassive hand she chafes will revive a tender hand, if it revive ever.

Sweet delusion for Pleasant Riderhood. . . . [Bk III ch. 3]

It is quite true of course that Eugene's conversion follows his immersion in the river; but here the point is no more 'mythic' than in the case of the unconverted Riderhood. The reason that Eugene has to be rescued in that particular way is simply that this is the sphere in which Lizzie, the female waterman, is uniquely capable of achieving such a rescue.

Not that one would wish to under-emphasise the importance of the Thames in *Our Mutual Friend*. It is, in the early reaches of the book and the lower ones of the river, the very mainstream of corruption and wretchedness. This is a persistent image in Dickens's work. The prostitute Martha in *David Copperfield* is drawn towards the river:

'I know it's like me!' she exclaimed. 'I know that I belong to it. I know that it's the natural company of such as I am! It comes from country places, where there was once no harm in it—and it creeps through the dismal streets, defiled and miserable—and it goes away, like my life, to a great sea that is always troubled—and I feel that I must go with it.' [*Copperfield*, ch. 47]

Even here, though, the corruption and wretchedness are not in the least mysterious, let alone metaphysical. The filth is the actual filth of London, the wretchedness is poverty. Almost all the poor characters of *Our Mutual Friend* live around the river, and when Charley Hexam is trying to persuade Lizzie to marry Headstone and get away from the house in Smith Square he argues that she 'would at last get quit of the river-side and the old disagreeables belonging to it.' [Bk II, ch. 15]

Even the upper reach of the river, the idyllic Berkshire valley, takes on a sinister colour when the inhabitants of the corrupted lower river, Riderhood and Headstone, invade it. But by and large it is a place of sweet contrast and it is obviously not fortuitous that the model factory should be placed here or that Betty Higden should escape westwards in her flight from the honourable boards. It is to Chertsey, Walton, Kingston, and Staines that Betty goes.

In those pleasant little towns on Thames, you may hear the fall of the water over the weirs, or even, in still weather, the rustle of the rushes; and from the bridge you may see the young river, dimpled like a young child, playfully gliding away among the trees, unpolluted by the defilements that lie in wait for it on its course . . . [Bk III, ch. 8]

If one is to talk of 'waste-land' imagery in connection with this novel it must be in a very naturalistic and precise sense.

Between the mounds and the river the complex, cunningly interwoven dramas of *Our Mutual Friend* are worked out, merging into a single drama in which the values of humanity struggle against those of Podsnappery. That it is in the profoundest sense a class struggle would be clear even if the 'moral' were not underlined in the final chapter where, with the greatest analytical candour, the personal relationships involved in the plot are examined and judged in the light of the moral preoccupations which control the novel's pattern. The bourgeois class delivers its judgement on the marriage of Lizzie and Eugene; and Mr Twemlow, the dim little aristocrat, who has learned at any rate something from his dealings with the Lammles and Fascination Fledgeby, dissociates himself from it, standing up even to the veiled threat of Podsnap to tell Lord Snigsworth of his class-apostasy. Perhaps the most significant moment of the whole scene is the judgement of 'the Contractor, of five hundred thousand power':

> It appears to this potentate[7] that what the man in question should have done, would have been to buy the young woman a boat and a small annuity, and set her up for herself. These things are a question of beefsteaks and porter. You buy the young woman a boat. Very good. You buy her, at the same time, a small annuity. You speak of that annuity in pounds sterling, but it is in reality so many pounds of beefsteaks and so many pints of porter. On the one hand, the young woman has the boat. On the other hand, she consumes so many pounds of beefsteaks and so many pints of porter. Those beefsteaks and that porter are the fuel to that young woman's engine. She derives therefrom a certain amount of power to row the boat; that power will produce so much money; you add that to the small annuity; and thus you get at the young woman's income. That (it seems to the Contractor) is the way of looking at it. [Bk IV, Chapter the Last.]

It is particularly telling, not only because of the brutal connections it reveals between the Contractor's morals and his social position, but because it echoes Eugene's own cynical morality of his unregenerate days. Then he was able to say to Jenny Wren:

> 'I think of setting up a doll, Miss Jenny.'

'You had better not', replied the dressmaker.

'Why not?'

'You are sure to break it. All you children do.'

'But that makes good for trade, you know, Miss Wren', returned Eugene. 'Much as people's breaking promises and contracts and bargains of all sorts, makes good for *my* trade.'

'I don't know about that', Miss Wren retorted; 'but you had better by half set up a penwiper, and turn industrious and use it.'

'Why, if we were all as industrious as you, little Busy-Body, we should begin to work as soon as we could crawl, and there would be a bad thing!'

'Do you mean', returned the little creature, with a flush suffusing her face, 'bad for your backs and your legs?'

'No, no, no,' said Eugene; shocked—to do him justice—at the thought of trifling with her infirmity. 'Bad for business, bad for business. If we all set to work as soon as we could use our hands, it would be all over with the dolls' dressmakers.'

'There's something in that', replied Miss Wren; 'you have a sort of an idea in your noddle sometimes.' Then, in a changed tone: 'Talking of ideas, my Lizzie', they were sitting side by side as they had sat at first, 'I wonder how it happens that when I am work, work, working here, all alone in the summer-time, I smell flowers.' [Bk II, ch. 2]

I think this is a most interesting and subtle passage, revealing very strikingly the profundity of Dickens's moral control of his plot. Here the essential conflict of values at the heart of *Our Mutual Friend* is expressed simply, yet in the most richly complex terms. Eugene's attitudes emerge in all their crudity. The doll is obviously Lizzie, though its 'setting up' can also imply the bribing of Jenny, and Eugene has no hesitation in discussing the whole affair in terms of the morality of trade. But even he is shocked when Jenny puts the working-class case in equally crude and personal terms, associating her own infirmities with her class position. And Jenny herself is forced to acknowledge that, in the competitive world she lives in, 'there's something in' Eugene's cynical morality. But she is unconvinced and turns to Lizzie (who seems, incidentally, to understand nothing of the implications of the conversation) with her thought about smelling flowers, a theme that is then developed at sufficient length to associate Jenny's dreams and her morality with the nature-imagery of the upper-Thames sections of the book. What Jenny is granting in this passage is the short-term expediency of the Wrayburn/Contractor morality, while clinging to a scale of values and aspiration not only more humane but altogether more 'natural'. And it is only when Eugene himself comes to accept those values—the popular values of those who work with their hands, as opposed to the ruling-class values of Podsnappery—that the conflict within the novel can be resolved and Mortimer Lightwood can fare to the Temple, gaily.

It is only those who, like George Orwell, wear blinkers which prevent a recognition of what Dickens is saying and of what class-conflict really is, who fail to see the profundity and consistency of the artistic structure of *Our Mutual Friend*. I think Jack Lindsay is doing the novel no more than justice when he describes it as one of the greatest works of prose ever written, a work which finally vindicates Dickens's right to stand, as no other English writer can stand, at the side of Shakespeare.[8]

SOURCE: *'Our Mutual Friend'*, in John Gross and Gabriel Pearson (eds), *Dickens and the Twentieth Century* (London, 1962), pp. 213–25.

NOTES

1. T. A. Jackson, *Charles Dickens: The Progress of a Radical* (London, 1962), p. 203.

2. Ibid, p. 204.

3. Mr Hillis Miller, in an interpretation of *Our Mutual Friend* which strikes me as being, by and large , of almost ludicrous irrelevance, makes an excellent point when he refers to the 'nullity' of the Veneerings (*Charles Dickens: The World of His Novels*(1958), p. 297.)

4. Dickens's clearest expression of his conscious commitment to the 'popular' side in precisely this sense is to be found in the famous speech at Birmingham, 27 Sept. 1869: see K. J. Fielding (ed.), *The Speeches of Charles Dickens* (London, 1960), p. 407.

5. Humphry House, *The Dickens World* (London, 1941), pp. 166ff.

6. Edgar Johnson, *Charles Dickens: His Tragedy and Triumph* (Boston, Mass., 1952), p. 1030.

7. Cf. Mr Venus's early description of Pleasant Riderhood: 'She is worthy to be loved by a Potentate.'

8. Jack Lindsay, *Charles Dickens* (London, 1950), p. 380. [See preceding excerpt—Ed.]

Philip Collins   'The Trained Teacher and Social Mobility' (1963)

... *Our Mutual Friend*, written ten years after *Hard Times*, contains much less about the aims and methods of teaching, though its schoolmaster character, instead of disappearing after two chapters, has a leading part in the story. Most of Dickens's comments on education in this novel have already been quoted: his accounts of the Ragged School and of Bradley Headstone's 'acquiring mechanically a great store of teacher's knowledge', his complaint that needlework was insufficiently regarded in girls' schools, his jokes about children holding up their hands and learning to write an essay one slate long. Like M'Choakumchild, Headstone and his colleague Miss Peecher are competent and conscientious, if in a narrow mechanical way. Their schools—'for they were twofold, as the sexes'—were like a thousand other schools all over the country; the school-buildings, like the teachers, were 'all according to pattern and engendered in the light of the latest Gospel according to Monotony'. It was a favourite theme, but Dickens does not pursue it further here. His main educational interest in this novel is the sociology of the new race of trained teachers.

Dickens has chosen to depict two very unfavourable specimens of the new profession, in Bradley Headstone and Charley Hexam: unfavourable not for intellectual but for moral reasons. In making this choice, he was following his natural preference for the negative approach, at least towards groups who were by common consent funny or disagreeable. The college-trained teacher of Dickens's later years could not be regarded as a subject for pathos; unlike Mr Marton a quarter of a century earlier, he was relatively well paid. Usually he had risen, like Headstone and Hexam, from a humble origin; his success in doing so might be regarded as admirable, and his decent salary a well-earned reward for hard work. At least as often, however, it touched off lower-class prejudices against the man who deserts his kind, and middle-class prejudices against the *parvenu*. Such prejudices help to form the material, and the attitude, of *Our Mutual Friend*. George Gissing, defining the limits of Dickens's radicalism, reminds us that he was decidedly middle-class and far from preaching equality. 'He would not have used the phrase, but he thought the thought, that humble folk must know "their station".' The 'good' poor in his novels do so; as Gissing asserts, the only notable working-class malcontent is Charley Hexam—'He, indeed, makes a very good exception, for he is precisely the one member of his class whom Dickens shows as tolerably educated.'[1]

He had campaigned for universal education, but he showed his middle-class instincts when he depicted Headstone and Hexam as specimens of the best education available to a boy from a poor home. The emphasis is wholly on the dangers, not the benefits, of the system, and any sympathy for these young men, faced with formidable social and intellectual difficulties, is annulled by their viciousness of temperament. Charley Hexam, it has been said, is 'surely the most detestable boy on record', while Bradley Headstone attempts two murders. An actual schoolmaster, describing two years later the stream of inquisitive callers at his school, says that among them were 'those who have read Mr Dickens's delineation of a national schoolmaster, and are anxious to inspect the curiosity (and who, after all, will probably be disappointed)'.[2] One would hope so. Nevertheless, Dickens's presentation of these teachers, though unsympathetic and incomplete, is a notable piece of social analysis, shrewd and original in its study of that part of the truth on which he has chosen to concentrate.

In 1853, a teacher began his book on *A Schoolmaster's Difficulties* by discussing the worst difficulty of all, one which had only arisen recently, as teachers were becoming more competent and education a burning question of the day. 'What then is his calling? Whereabouts in the sliding scale of society is his position? . . . The labourer, the mechanic, the tradesman, the professional man, the clergy, all have their place and calling in the great hive: whereabouts is the schoolmaster's, and what is it?'[3] How difficult it was to answer these questions, and how deeply they bothered teachers in the next few decades, has been shown in detail in Dr Asher Tropp's book *The School Teachers* (1957). Of course they had other grievances, about salaries, security, and professional conditions, but all of these, says Dr Tropp, were subordinated to their demand for a higher social position. This, they felt, was their right, as men of superior education engaged in an important and respectable job, and they were the more bitterly insistent on this because generally they had risen from poor families, and wanted reassurance that they were accepted into middle-class society; and they had risen by their own wits and by the long grind as pupil-teacher and training college student, and they were jealous of their self-styled 'betters' who held an assured position without having had to prove themselves so strenuously. Dickens, says Dr Tropp, 'summed the complex of emotions around the claim in a few lines'—and he refers to Bradley Headstone's indignant speeches to Eugene Wrayburn, a young gentleman of public-school background.

> 'You think me of no more value than the dirt under your feet', said Bradley to Eugene, speaking in a carefully weighed

and measured tone, or he could not have spoken at all.

'I assure you, Schoolmaster', replied Eugene, 'I don't think about you.' . . .

'Mr Wrayburn, at least I know very well that it would be idle to set myself against you in insolent words or overbearing manners. That lad who has just gone out [Charley Hexam] could put you to shame in half-a-dozen branches of knowledge in half an hour, but you can throw him aside like an inferior. You can do as much by me, I have no doubt. . . . You reproach me with my origin; you cast insinuations at my bringing-up. But I tell you, sir, I have worked my way onward, out of both and in spite of both, and have a right to be considered a better man than you, with better reasons for being proud.'[4]

This scene between Eugene and Headstone is crucial both in the plot and in Dickens's presentation of the educational issue, and we shall return to it. But, first, the situation of the characters involved should be explained.

Charley Hexam is the son of a rough Thames waterside man, who refuses to let his children have an education which would make him feel inferior. When he discovers that Charley has surreptitiously attended the Ragged School and wants to become a teacher, he says, in words echoed by generations of baffled parents, 'His own father ain't good enough for him. He's disowned his own father.' (Dickens had noted the possibilities of this theme several years before, when he wrote—'I must use somehow the uneducated father in fustian and the educated boy in spectacles whom . . . I saw at Chatham.') [See Extracts from Letters, above—Ed.] Charley has been helped by his sister Lizzie, who has covered up his absences from home, and who for his sake has sacrificed her own chances of going to school. (This situation, of selfless sister caught between ungrateful brother and unsympathetic father, is a favourite with Dickens, other examples being Louisa Gradgrind and Little Dorrit.)

After attending the Ragged School, Charley becomes a pupil-teacher under Bradley Headstone, and the first words Headstone speaks in the novel are concerned with the schoolmaster's problem of respectability.

'So you want to go and see your sister, Hexam? . . . Look here, Hexam. . . . I hope your sister may be good company for you? . . . You see, Hexam, you will be one of us. In good time you are sure to pass a creditable examination and become one of us. Then the question is— . . . . Whether you had not better leave well alone.'

'Is it well to leave my sister alone, Mr Headstone?'

'I do not say so, because I do not know. I put it to you. I ask
you to think of it. I want you to consider. You know how well
you are doing here.'
                'After all, she got me here', said the boy, with a struggle.

Charley invites his master to meet Lizzie, and judge for himself;
Headstone does so, and falls passionately in love with her, though he
tries to overcome this imprudent desire for a girl who is 'not on his level'.
The sensible thing to do, he knows, is to marry another teacher, and he
knows that his professional standing is such that he could capture any of
the 'best qualified, and most distinguished' young ladies engaged in his
calling. Lizzie is grateful to him for helping Charley, but finds him
personally obnoxious. His anger at being rejected is increased when he
discovers that Eugene Wrayburn is paying her attentions; moreover,
she is taking lessons, which Eugene pays for (she can allow herself an
education, Gaffer Hexam now being dead). Lizzie is embarrassed by
Eugene's attentions, for though they are not dishonourable she cannot
aspire to marry him (and Eugene cannot decide how seriously he feels
about her). So she is in a difficult position: besieged by Bradley
Headstone, whose passion is terrible in its violence—ill-at-ease over
Eugene's gentler approaches—and bitterly reproached by her brother
Charley, who is outraged that she rejects his master and is cheapening
herself by allowing Eugene to visit her. 'And so', says Charley, 'all my
endeavours to cancel the past and to raise myself in the world, and to
raise you with me, are to be beaten down by *your* low whims; are
they? . . . But you shall not disgrace me. I am determined that after I
have climbed up out of the mire, you shall not pull me down. You can't
disgrace me if I have nothing to do with you, and I *will* have nothing to
do with you for the future.'
    Both master and pupil are terribly vulnerable in their precarious
respectability. Both want to forget and conceal their inglorious origins.
Dickens has taken extreme examples—few teachers came from so low in
the social scale (Headstone had been a pauper lad), and few could have
been so ruthlessly selfish as Charley Hexam, or have resorted to murder,
as Headstone did, when—'a man of rapid passions and sluggish
intelligence'—he lost control of 'what was animal, and what was fiery
(though smouldering)' in him, qualities still visible beneath his stiffly
decent exterior. This phrase, from the opening description of
Headstone, echoes the opening description of Charley, many chapters
earlier. Charley is first seen in the library at the Veneerings' house,
where Mortimer Lightwood, a young lawyer, is questioning him about
a corpse which Gaffer Hexam has fished out of the river. It is a sharp
passage, which neatly introduces many themes of the plot—Charley's
proud ostentation of learning, his father's jealous ignorance, and the

boy's feelings for his sister, half grateful and half contemptuous.

There was a curious mixture in the boy, of uncompleted savagery, and uncompleted civilisation. His voice was hoarse and coarse, and his face was coarse, and his stunted figure was coarse; but he was cleaner than other boys of his type; and his writing, though large and round, was good; and he glanced at the backs of the books, with an awakened curiosity that went below the binding. No one who can read, ever looks at a book, even unopened on a shelf, like one who cannot.

'Were any means taken, do you know, boy, to ascertain if it was possible to restore life?' Mortimer inquired. . . .

'You wouldn't ask, sir, if you knew his state. Pharaoh's multitude, that were drowned in the Red Sea, ain't more beyond restoring to life. If Lazarus was only half as far gone, that was the greatest of all the miracles.'

'Halloa!' cried Mortimer, . . . 'you seem to be at home in the Red Sea, my young friend?'

'Read of it with teacher at the school', said the boy. . . . 'But don't you tell my father! We should have no peace in our place, if that got touched upon. It's my sister's contriving.'

'You seem to have a good sister.'

'She ain't half bad', said the boy; 'but if she knows her letters it's the most she does—and them I learned her.'

From the beginning, both Charley and his master are seen as the prey of strain and conflict—domestic, intellectual, social, and psychological. Charley ruthlessly suppresses or abandons whatever, within him or without, seems to threaten his gaining that coveted place in society. During most of the novel he is still a pupil-teacher (Dickens ignores his training college period), but he ends up as a qualified teacher with good prospects. He hopes soon to succeed his present headmaster, and might even marry the schoolmistress, 'though some years older than I': such are his plans for keeping himself 'strictly respectable in the scale of society'.

Headstone is less successful in living up to the respectability of his calling. He is ruined by the conflict suggested when first we see him:

Bradley Headstone, in his decent black coat and waistcoat, and decent white shirt, and decent formal black tie, and decent pantaloons of pepper and salt, with his decent silver watch in his pocket and its decent hair-guard round his neck, looked a thoroughly decent young man of six-and-twenty. He was never seen in any other dress, and yet there was a certain stiffness in his

manner of wearing this, as if there were a want of adaptation
between him and it, recalling some mechanics in their holiday
clothes.

His wild jealousy of Eugene Wrayburn is, of course, his undoing and the
jealousy normal to an unsuccessful rival is exacerbated by Headstone's
bitter feeling of injustice that he, as a schoolmaster, should lose to this
indolent young briefless barrister. It is interesting to see how Dickens
handles this variant on the familiar situation of a low-born maiden
loved by two men, one a gentleman and the other a member of her own
class. There are two conventional solutions in Victorian fiction: either
the girl is seduced and abandoned by the glamorous gentleman, and
ends the novel dead or a penitent spinster (Emily in *David Copperfield* and
Hetty in *Adam Bede* are examples), or she comes to realise the vanity of
her ambition to marry the young squire or master, and returns to her
faithful humble lover (as happens in *Mary Barton*). It is rare for the girl
to marry the gentleman, happily and with the author's approval, but
this is Dickens's solution here, and it is the more striking because this is
the only time he marries a low-born heroine to an upper-class man.[5]
Lizzie is, certainly, shown as 'worthy' of Eugene's rather belated
proposal, and Eugene is more attractive than Headstone. Maybe he is
insolent and idle, and culpably off-hand in indulging so long in his
indecisive pursuit of Lizzie, but at least he makes no squirearchal move
to seduce her, and he has none of the terrible propensities of his rival.

It is significant, however, that Dickens chose to distribute the virtues
and vices in this way. Even when he is inviting us to disapprove of
Eugene's peccadilloes, he insists on his charm, and he consistently takes
Eugene's side in the rivalry over Lizzie Hexam. This is clear, not only
when eventually Lizzie is given to Eugene, but even in his quarrel with
Headstone. Much of Headstone's indignation seems justified. Eugene is
insolent, taunting his rival as 'Schoolmaster'; moreover, a young
gentleman's paying such marked attentions to a riverside girl would
have a nasty look even to an observer more disinterested than
Headstone can be. Headstone speaks up for his profession, but Dickens
had loaded the dice against him: Eugene, as we know, is innocent of any
evil intent, and Headstone makes a fool of himself by losing his temper
and acting uncouthly. The result is that the profession, and not only its
representative in this scene, stands convicted—an impression which is
confirmed rather than qualified by the behaviour of Charley Hexam
here and elsewhere in the book.

The scene begins with both parties morally condemned. Headstone
has accompanied Charley to this interview, the purpose of which is to
warn Eugene off, and to protest against his appointing and paying a
teacher for Lizzie. Eugene had seen Headstone once before, while out

walking with her, and when she told him it was the schoolmaster he had
replied, 'To be sure. Looked like it.' But now he pretends not to know
who 'this person' is. 'Composedly smoking, he leaned an elbow on the
chimney-piece, at the side of the fire, and looked at the schoolmaster. It
was a cruel look, in its cold disdain of him, as a creature of no worth.'
Headstone's look is cruel, too, with 'raging jealousy and fiery wrath'.
Both Headstone and his pupil betray their ignorance of social
conventions by addressing him as 'Mr Eugene Wrayburn', and
Headstone is so inflammable over any remark that might be construed
as reflecting on his origins that Eugene can justly comment, on his
departure, 'A curious monomaniac. The man seems to believe that
everybody was acquainted with his mother!' Charley makes a gauche
speech protesting against Eugene's educating Lizzie when she has
already rejected a similar offer from Headstone, 'the most competent
authority, as his certificates would easily prove, that could be
produced'. Eugene is taking a liberty, continues Charley, by doing this
'without my consent, when I am raising myself in the scale of
society . . . and have no right to have any darkness cast upon my
prospects, or any imputation upon my respectability, through my
sister'. Dickens's comment at this point is interesting: 'The boyish
weakness of this speech, combined with its great selfishness, made it a
poor one indeed. And yet Bradley Headstone, used to the little audience
of a school, and unused to the larger ways of men, showed a kind of
exultation in it.'

Certainly it was a nasty little speech, and Headstone's approval of it
shows his lack of wisdom and sensitivity, but Dickens's comment shows
no compassion for the inexperience and indignation which betray them
into expressing themselves like this. Instead, we are invited to identify
ourselves with 'the larger ways of men', the world which includes the
self-possessed Eugene Wrayburn and his friend Mortimer Lightwood,
who is also present. The interview ends with Headstone departing 'with
a consciously bad grace and stiff manner, as Wrayburn looked so easily
and calmly on'. It has been a walkover for Eugene, and the two young
gentlemen are left in possession of the scene; it is their reactions, not
those of Headstone and Hexam, that Dickens chooses to explore.
Mortimer comments, 'Eugene, Eugene, Eugene, I am sorry for this'—
but he is not registering any protest against Eugene's insufferable
behaviour towards his social inferiors; he is grieved and worried to
discover that Eugene is carrying on some sort of an affair with Lizzie
Hexam—'What is to come of it? What are you doing? Where are you
going?' Eugene has no answer to these questions, but he puts himself in
the right with the reader by speaking up loyally for the girl ('There is no
better girl in all this London than Lizzie Hexam. There is no better
among my people at home; no better among your people'). Lightwood

speaks to him 'affectionately', and Eugene's 'frankness of face and manner' is stressed. Eugene is let down lightly on a similar occasion, when he is flippant and insolent towards the venerable Jew, Mr Riah. At the end of that episode, Dickens comments: 'But now that his part was played out for the evening, and when in turning his back upon the Jew he came off the stage, he was thoughtful himself'—a suggestion, not adequately pursued elsewhere, that Eugene's insolence as well as his flippancy was a pose and not the real man.[6] Much is forgiven to Eugene, for his charm of manner (to the people he likes) and for his final decision to scout Society by marrying beneath him (though not before Lizzie has saved his life at the risk of her own). His rival is never treated with such indulgence.

When *Our Mutual Friend* appeared, Henry James reviewed it very unfavourably. [See the review in the preceding section—Ed.] The episode he chose, to justify his judgement that it was 'the poorest of Mr Dickens's works', was this scene between Headstone and Eugene—'very clever, but very insufficient.' In the opposition between these two characters, he admitted, there lay a very good story, and this moment of their collision is dramatically great; but 'the author's conception is weak'. Realised *characters* are needed, but

Mr Dickens, according to his usual plan, has made them simply figures, and between them the story that was to be, the story that should have been, has evaporated. . . . The friction of two *men*, of two characters, of two passions, produces stronger sparks than Wrayburn's boyish repartees and Headstone's melodramatic commonplaces. Such scenes as this are useful in fixing the limits of Mr Dickens's insight. Insight is, perhaps, too strong a word; for we are convinced that it is one of the chief conditions of his genius not to see beneath the surface of things. If we might hazard a definition of his literary character, we should, accordingly, call him the greatest of superficial novelists.

Some of James's criticisms must be accepted. Eugene is not presented with sufficient clarity: the interesting case of a young man uncertain about himself is so handled that the reader suspects that it is Dickens who is uncertain (about his character's psychology and social tone). Mortimer keeps saying, through his laughter, 'What an absurd fellow you are, Eugene!' and suchlike, but Eugene's line in sophisticated badinage is rarely as convincing or as delightful as Dickens intends it to be. James is right: Eugene is not fully adequate to the situation Dickens has devised. The walking-gentleman type, in which Dickens had never shown great felicity, is here required to be and do more than usual.[7] 'The limits of Mr Dickens's insight' are more surprisingly apparent in his refusal of sympathy towards Hexam and Headstone. These low-born characters are seen much more from Eugene's point of view than from their own. Dickens's categorical habit of mind allows no qualifications in the adverse judgement impressed upon us from the start. Even the efficiency which, no doubt, they displayed as teachers is never counted to their credit.

Nevertheless, Dickens does display considerable insight in devising this story of the schoolmaster and the gentleman. As James agreed, it was an excellent situation—and original; no other novelist, I think, had dramatised this important aspect of contemporary social and educational developments. In this episode, Dickens's habitual juxtaposition of various social levels becomes direct opposition. The novel had begun (as so many do) with chapters successively exploring disparate groups— the Hexams, fishing in the river for drowned bodies, and then the Veneerings, a family so successfully *arriviste* that they can command, as a dinner-table ornament, Mr Twemlow, first cousin of Lord Snigsworth. (It is Headstone's misfortune that, while his veneer of middle-class culture is thicker than theirs, his profession does not obtain the financial rewards with which the Veneerings can buy themselves a secure place in society.) Through Hexam and Headstone, Dickens presents, as we have seen, the main elements in the social position of the new *déclassé* race of teachers: the strain inside the family, the struggle to achieve the essential Certificate, the conceit caused by their success in doing so, the temptation to cut away from their roots as a safeguard of their newfound respectability, the jealousy of social groups who enjoyed high prestige without having to sweat for it. If Dickens chose extreme examples of the corruption these pressures could cause, he certainly achieved completeness in this, the negative, side of the picture. The certificated teacher was a phenomenon not only interesting in himself and in relation to the schooling of the period, but also the best available example of the social difficulties in rising from the lower to the middle class—for this was then the only way a poor boy could obtain a higher education, and when he had obtained it he must perforce appear impeccably respectable, though he was modestly paid, and was likely to suffer both the jealousy of the class he had left and the disdain of the class he aspired to enter.

It was, then, a crucial example of social mobility, and Dickens deserves praise for examining it and for giving an effective, if a partial, account of his two schoolmasters. For they have much more dramatic life than Eugene. In other passages than the encounter with Eugene, they are characters, not the mere 'figures' that James will allow. Headstone becomes a striking picture of frustrated love. Throughout the latter part of the book, Dickens cleverly exploits the contrast between Headstone's murderous thoughts and his schoolroom decorum. Even the little jokes made against him as schoolmaster have a deeper irony than usual—as when, the day after his attempt to murder Eugene, he kept 'doing the deed and doing it better' as he went through the daily routine of prayers and mental arithmetic and question-and-answer. 'He had half a mind to draw a line or two upon the board, and show himself what he meant.'[8]

Kay-Shuttleworth, to whom more than anyone else England owes her training colleges, realised from the start the social perils the new schoolmasters would face. The student would easily form 'an overweening estimate of his knowledge and ability', comparing himself with his friends and neighbours. 'If his mind were not thoroughly impregnated by a religious principle, or if a presumptuous or mercenary tone had been given to his character, he might go forth to bring discredit upon education by exhibiting a precocious vanity, an insubordinate spirit, or a selfish ambition.' The training college discipline must therefore prepare students for 'a humble and subordinate position' of 'modest respectability.' Thus he argued against allowing 'a period of recreation employed according to the discretion of the students', since it might often be spent 'in listless sauntering, or in violent exertion', or in forming associations inconsistent with the college discipline.[9] It is an attitude which has died hard in training colleges, and students and teachers have long resented it. A few years before *Our Mutual Friend*, an article in *The Times* had touched this persistent source of friction. The leader-writer deplored the fact that the great truths of religion were taught by 'the hard race of schoolmasters and schoolmistresses, generally of so inferior a class that they do not even venture to sit down in the presence of the clergymen. . . . These unfortunates generally take to education because they are not fit for anything else'—and so on. When 'A Poor Schoolmaster' wrote to the editor, protesting Headstone-like against the patronage of this 'gentleman', *The Times*—which rarely displays much alacrity in making the *amende honorable*—declined to print the letter. A teachers' magazine did so. The schoolmaster argued that his colleagues were pious and public-spirited, and had gone through a long and gruelling college course, and he warned the offending 'gentleman' that 'a race of teachers has at length sprung up, who will not quietly submit to misrepresentation and insult'.[10] It was a situation in which legitimate professional pride could easily be confused with, or turn into, prickly conceit. In his later years, Kay-Shuttleworth was more understanding over the problems which he had helped to create. Whenever he heard schoolmasters harshly criticised for such defects as a tendency to conceit, he would reply with a kindly rejoinder that they were the results of a 'hot-house training', and that they should be tenderly judged.[11]

Tenderness and sympathy are notably absent from Dickens's

judgement on his two schoolmasters in *Our Mutual Friend*. Charley
Hexam is just such a creature of selfish ambition as Kay-Shuttleworth
had feared. It was 'his better nature' to be true to his sister, Dickens had
commented early in the story, 'if it were his worse nature to be wholly
selfish. And as yet the better nature had the stronger hold.' His better
nature soon gives way, and by the end of the novel, wholly selfish but
successful in his narrow ambition, he has also cast off his other
benefactor. It is one of the ironies of the novel, and part of the ample
punishment Dickens metes out to Headstone, that Charley pitilessly
turns against the man to whom he owes his start in life. When the news
arrives that Eugene has been killed (news which later proves to be false),
Charley calls upon Headstone, whom he rightly suspects, and for once
Headstone is seen as a figure deserving pity.

> He looked at young Hexam as if he were waiting for a scholar to
> go on with a lesson that he knew by heart and was deadly tired
> of. . . .
>   'If you had any part—I don't say what—in this attack',
> pursued the boy; 'or if you know anything about it—I don't say
> how much—or if you know who did it—I go no closer—you did
> an injury to me that's never to be forgiven. . . . I am going to be
> plain with you, Mr Headstone. . . . What I mean is this: if you
> were a good master, I was a good pupil. I have done you plenty
> of credit, and in improving my own reputation I have improved
> yours quite as much. Very well then. . . . You have compro-
> mised me by being seen about with me, endeavouring to
> counteract this Mr Eugene Wrayburn. . . . If my character and
> my now dropping you help me out of that, Mr Headstone, the
> deliverance is to be attributed to me, and not to you. No thanks
> to you for it!'

Even the attempted murder is seen as another selfish blow against
Charley—'You have justified my sister in being firmly set against you
from first to last, and you have put me in the wrong again!' Bursting into
tears, Charley continues in his egregious self-pity: 'It is an extraordinary
circumstance attendant on my life, that every effort I make towards
perfect respectability is impeded by somebody else through no fault of
mine! . . . However, I have made up my mind that I will become
respectable in the scale of society, and that I will not be dragged down
by others. I have done with my sister as well as with you.'

When Charley leaves him after this diatribe, Bradley Headstone
shrinks to the ground, where he grovels 'in unutterable misery, and
unrelieved by a single tear'. Perhaps, Dickens comments, he had taken
the boy to heart during the laborious years when he 'found his drudgery

lightened by communication with a brighter and more apprehensive spirit than his own'. A few chapters later, he dies, trying to kill Rogue Riderhood, who has discovered that he is guilty of the attack upon Eugene and is blackmailing him to sell everything he owns. 'Yours is a 'spectable calling. To save your 'spectability, it's worth your while.' Headstone has already lost everything—his girl, his favourite pupil, his peace of mind, his heritage. Loyal neither to his origins nor to the code of his adopted life, he has destroyed himself—'But *Our Mutual Friend* everywhere gives evidence that for Dickens in his last completed novel no one can escape his given place.'[12] Introducing Headstone, Dickens remarked upon that fiery animal quality, constrained by the stiff conventionality of his calling, but still visible enough 'to suggest that if young Bradley Headstone, when a pauper lad, had chanced to be told off for the sea, he would not have been the last man in a ship's crew'. Probably Dickens would have been the first to praise him, had he risen from the ranks in that profession, and become the master of a ship instead of a school.

SOURCE: extract from *Dickens and Education* (London, 1963), pp. 159–71.

NOTES

1. George Gissing, *Charles Dickens* (rev. edn, London, 1903), pp. 256–9. (Gissing apparently forgot Orlick, a very interesting malcontent underdog: see Humphry House, *All in Due Time*, 1955, p. 218). One other character in the later novels, it should be added, becomes a teacher, apparently under the new system, but remains uncorrupted—Biddy. 'You know', she tells Pip, remembering Mr Wopsle's great-aunt's school where she had assisted, 'the new schools are not like the old.' But Dickens is not interested in her career as a teacher; she is absent from the novel between the two references to 'the new school' where she goes to teach, and the second of these occurs on her wedding-day, not an ideal time for educational enquiries.

2. G. M. Young, *Early Victorian England* (London, 1934), II, p. 466; 'The Schoolmaster at Home', *All the Year Round*, 2 Nov. 1867, XVIII, p. 447.

3. *A Schoolmaster's Difficulties Abroad and at Home* (1853), 1–4. Anonymous: published by Longman, Brown, Green and Longmans.

4. Asher Tropp, *The School Teachers* (London, 1957), pp. 35–6.

5. Toots, indeed, marries Florence Dombey's faithful servant Susan Nipper, but there is no working-class rival, and neither of the characters is played 'straight', so Dickens is not here making a serious point about the class-basis of marriage. On these popular conventions governing a heroine's choice of husband, see Margaret Dalziel, *Popular Fiction 100 Years Ago* (London, 1957), pp. 14–16, 86–7, 108–9; and on Dickens's treatment of Eugene's eventual

decision to marry Lizzie, see Humphry House, *The Dickens World* (London, 1941), pp. 162–3, and George Orwell, *Critical Essays* (London, 1946), pp. 31–4.

6. Riah, one might add, is akin to Dickens's 'good' schoolmasters in his failure to come alive as a character. He is Dickens's 'good' Jew, a willed attempt to disprove the allegation that he was anti-Semitic because he had made Fagin a Jew.

7. On Wrayburn and others, see Angus Wilson, 'The Heroes and Heroines of Dickens', *Review of English Literature*, II (1961), pp. 9–18.

8. Cf. Philip Collins, *Dickens and Crime* (1962), chapter XI, on Headstone as lover and murderer.

9. James Kay-Shuttleworth, *Four Periods of Public Education* (London, 1862), pp. 401–3.

10. *The Times*, 11 Dec. 1856; *The School and the Teacher*, IV, March 1857, p. 54.

11. Reminiscences of his son, in Frank Smith, *The Life and Work of Sir James Kay-Shuttleworth* (London, 1923), p. 328.

12. J. Hillis Miller, *Charles Dickens: the World of his Novels* (Cambridge, Mass., 1958), p. 279.

Kenneth Muir   Image and Structure in
Our Mutual Friend (1966)

WHEN the young Henry James reviewed *Our Mutual Friend*, he declared that to his perception it was the poorest of Dickens's works: 'And it is poor with the poverty not of momentary embarrassment but of permanent exhaustion. . . .' [See the review, in the preceding section— Ed.] James allowed that there were a dozen or so examples of humour in the novel, but apart from that he denied that it had any merits at all. 'Seldom, we reflected, had we read a book so intensely *written*, so little seen, known, or felt.' It was completely lacking in humanity:

It were, in our opinion, an offence against humanity to place Mr Dickens among the greatest novelists. For . . . he has created nothing but figures. He has added nothing to our understanding of human character.

In reading this review we must, of course, make allowances for the fact that James himself was to be a totally different kind of novelist, and that both in his qualities and his weaknesses he was the exact antithesis of the subject of his review. It is significant that he should condemn as failures two novels—*Bleak House* and *Little Dorrit*—which some recent critics regard as Dickens's masterpieces.

But critics even today are very much divided in their opinions on *Our Mutual Friend*. On the one hand, Bernard Shaw urged Frank Harris to read *Our Mutual Friend* and other later novels. 'Dickens', he declared, 'made a beginning of his great period with *Hard Times*. But when it came, it was great.' Mr Edgar Johnson regards it as 'one of the supreme works of English fiction' and Mr Jack Lindsay rather absurdly declares that it is 'one of the greatest works of prose ever written'. [See excerpt in this section, above—Ed.] On the other hand, Professor K. J. Fielding, who quotes some of these views in his very judicious book on Dickens, thinks that the novel shows signs of illness, strain and depression, and that there is a lack of coherence in its development: 'This is not to say that there are not fine things in *Our Mutual Friend*, only that it can as well be enjoyed as a loose collection of pieces that might have appeared in the pages of a magazine.'

There are a few loose ends in *Our Mutual Friend*. Nothing is made of the fact that Wilfer works in Veneering's office; Betty Higden and Sloppy are scarcely necessary to the plot; and even the portentous figure of Mr Podsnap, necessary, as we shall see, to the scheme of the book, has little relation to the main plots. It can, nevertheless, be shown that the novel is carefully planned and that we should be missing a great deal if we read it 'as a loose collection of pieces'. It has a series of related plots which are directly connected with Harmon's wills. By the first will he left his money to his son on condition that he marries Bella Wilfer; by the second will he left his money to the Crown, and the discovery of this will by Silas Wegg enables him to blackmail Noddy Boffin; by the third will he left his money to Boffin, thus enabling Boffin to turn the tables on Wegg. The plot stemming from the first will concerns John Harmon's testing of Bella, which the report of his murder facilitates; and subsidiary to this plot is Lizzie Hexam's desire to prove her father's innocence of the Harmon murder. Subsidiary to the sub-plot is the rivalry of Bradley Headstone and Eugene Wrayburn for Lizzie's love which ends with Headstone's attempted murder of Eugene and his actual murder of Riderhood, who is blackmailing him, his own suicide, and Eugene's marriage with Lizzie. The plots are linked in numerous ways: Riderhood accuses Hexam of the Harmon murder and is himself suspected of it; Eugene is a friend of Boffin's lawyer; Headstone is the schoolmaster of Lizzie's brother; Venus, Wegg's fellow-conspirator, and the owner of his amputated leg, is in love with Riderhood's daughter; and Bella and Lizzie become friends.

The book contains a large number of other characters who are on the fringe of the various plots. Lammle, for example, is a friend of Veneering, Wilfer's employer, and he tries to oust Rokesmith as Boffin's

secretary. He had previously tried to arrange a marriage between
Georgiana Podsnap and Fledgeby and he chastises Fledgeby after being
ruined by him. Fledgeby employs Riah, who befriends Lizzie and
Jenny Wren. The Lammles, the Podsnaps, Fledgeby, Eugene and
Mortimer Lightwood all meet at the Veneerings' house. Jenny Wren's
drunken father betrays Lizzie's hiding-place to Eugene. Betty Higden's
death leads to the meeting of Bella and Lizzie, and Sloppy, who is
befriended by the Boffins, provides a husband for Jenny Wren.

The chief advantage of the complex of interrelated plots and of the
numerous characters was that it enabled Dickens to give a comprehensive cross-section of London life from the wealthy to the poverty-
stricken: from the seedy aristocrats, Twemlow and Lady Tippins,
through the *nouveaux riches* Veneerings, Boffins, and Podsnaps, the shady
Lammles and Fledgeby, the shabby genteel Wilfers, the respectable
teachers—Headstone, Charley Hexam, Emma Peecher—down to the
Riderhoods, the Cleavers and Betty Higden. The swift alternation of
scenes—the corpse in the Thames, the Veneering banquet, an inquest,
the home of the Wilfers, Wegg's stall follow each other in quick
succession in the opening chapters—is a powerful means of impressing
the reader with the panoramic sweep of Dickens's picture of London life.

The picture is a grim one: poverty, delirium tremens, two murders,
two cases of blackmail, bankruptcies, chicanery of various kinds; and
these things are the foundations of society, represented by the
Veneerings and their acquaintances. Society is superficial, heartless,
meaningless and self-satisfied. Its chief spokesman and symbol is Mr
Podsnap:

> He never could make out why everybody was not quite satisfied,
> and he felt conscious that he set a brilliant social example in
> being particularly well satisfied with most things, and, above all
> other things, with himself.
>
> Thus happily acquainted with his own merit and impor-
> tance, Mr Podsnap settled that whatever he put behind him he
> put out of existence. There was a dignified conclusiveness—not
> to add a grand convenience—in this way of getting rid of
> disagreeables, which had done much towards establishing Mr
> Podsnap in his lofty place in Mr Podsnap's satisfaction. 'I don't
> want to know about it; I don't choose to discuss it; I don't admit
> it!' Mr Podsnap had even acquired a peculiar flourish of his
> right arm in often clearing the world of its most difficult
> problems, by sweeping them behind him (and consequently
> sheer away) with those words and a flushed face. For they
> affronted him.
>
> A certain institution in Mr Podsnap's mind which he called

'the young person' may be considered to have been embodied in Miss Podsnap, his daughter. It was an inconvenient and exacting institution, as requiring everything in the universe to be filed down and fitted to it. The question about everything was, would it bring a blush into the cheek of the young person? And the inconvenience of the young person was that, according to Mr Podsnap, she seemed always liable to burst into blushes when there was no need at all. There appeared to be no line of demarcation between the young person's excessive innocence, and another person's guiltiest knowledge. Take Mr Podsnap's word for it, and the soberest tints of drab, white, lilac, and grey, were all flaming red to this troublesome Bull of a young person.

This description hits off the insular self-satisfaction of the Victorian Philistine; and its irony is intensified in the context by the fact that there is little in the English scene depicted in the novel to cause a glow of self-satisfaction and nothing at all in the circle in which Mr Podsnap moves.

Dickens himself was compelled, if he wished to retain his popularity, to offer some incense to the Podsnaps. He is noticeably reticent about Nancy in *Oliver Twist*; he softens the horrors of delirium tremens in describing the death of Mr Dolls; and he does not reveal that one of the chief functions of the dust-contractor was to collect the contents of the privies and that (as House mentions) the term 'dust' was used as a euphemism for decaying excrement. But Dickens, particularly in *Bleak House* and *Our Mutual Friend*, was still too outspoken for many of his critics.

The novel is unified not merely by the interrelation of the various plots, but also by Dickens's use of symbolism. Lord Snow has recently declared that

To most English writers, symbolism of almost any kind seems too coarse-meshed an attack on anything as delicate in detail and highly articulated as the novel . . . Dickens's symbols, or 'emblems' as he called them, the fog in *Bleak House*, and so on, seem too often like the inventions of a tired, impatient man.

Lord Snow is perfectly justified in eschewing symbolism in the kind of novel he writes himself; but the emblems of Dickens are far from being the inventions of a tired, impatient man: they were used by him when he was at the height of his powers, and they are an essential part of his method. No one would think of saying that in *King Lear* or *Macbeth*, 'delicate in detail and highly articulated' as they are, Shakespeare's patterns of imagery are the inventions of a tired, impatient man; and in the later novels of Dickens a new dimension was added to his work by his use of emblems.

There are no emblems in Dickens's early masters, Fielding and Smollett; and it seems probable that he got the idea of using them from his reading of Shakespeare, thus forestalling modern imagistic criticism by nearly a century.

The two main symbols of *Our Mutual Friend* are the river and the dust-heaps, as several critics have pointed out. Many of the scenes take place on or near the Thames. From the river both Hexam and Riderhood make a sordid living, and in it both they and Headstone are drowned. Headstone pursues Eugene Wrayburn up the river, and he is himself trailed by Riderhood. Lizzie hides from Eugene in a village by the river and she is able to rescue him by her skill, stressed in the first chapter, of managing a boat. Betty Higden goes up the river to die; Bella takes her father to dine at Greenwich, overlooking the river; she and Rokesmith are married there; and they live during the early months of their marriage in a cottage on Blackheath. John Harmon escapes from death by drowning to live again as Rokesmith; and Eugene, on being rescued, determines to marry his rescuer. As Mr J. Hillis Miller has suggested: 'Their near death permits a transformation of that situation, not an escape from it, or a total rejection of it. It is a liberation from the absurdity, the coerciveness of that situation . . . a liberation which allows their former lives to begin again.'

But the dominant impression of the river is provided by the fine description in the first chapter—one of the best openings in all Dickens's novels—with Lizzie and her father searching for drowned bodies of suicides or victims of murder:

> Allied to the bottom of the river rather than the surface, by reason of the slime and ooze with which it was covered, and its sodden state, this boat and the two figures in it obviously were doing something that they often did, and were seeking what they often sought.

The Thames is filthy with sewage, so that when Hexam leans over the side of the boat to rifle the pockets of the dead man, he dirties his arms. Nor was this an exaggeration. The river was in fact the main sewer of London. Cesspools were abolished in 1847 and the sewers which replaced them flowed into the Thames. By the time Dickens wrote his novel, the stench from the river and the danger to health had reached scandalous proportions.

When Lizzie tells her father that she dislikes the river, Hexam replies:

> 'As if it wasn't your living! As if it wasn't meat and drink to you! . . . How can you be so thankless to your best friend, Lizzie? The very fire that warmed you when you were a baby,

was picked out of the river alongside the coal barges. The very
basket that you slept in, the tide washed ashore. The very
rockers that I put it upon to make a cradle of it, I cut out of a
piece of wood that drifted from some ship or another.'

In most of Hexam's speeches Dickens attempts to suggest his class and
lack of education; but here there is no attempt at naturalism because the
novelist is using the character as his mouthpiece.

The river, therefore, is a symbol of death and rebirth, and of the way,
at the bottom of the social ladder, life and death are inextricably
related. It was part of Dickens's purpose to show that the illiterate
Lizzie, brought up in a foul slum—

where accumulated scum of humanity seemed to be washed
from higher grounds, like so much moral sewage, and to be
pausing until its own weight forced it over the bank and sunk it
in the river—

could display a moral delicacy, heroism and self-sacrifice superior to
that shown by any of the characters drawn from a higher class. Quite
unrealistically, even when talking with Jenny Wren, she apparently
speaks the Queen's English; and when Eugene falls in love with her, he
is very conscious of the difference of class, but not of her speech. Fifty
years later, when Shaw wrote *Pygmalion* he transformed Eliza Doolittle
by training her to speak correct English; and when Lawrence first wrote
Lady Chatterley's Lover he stressed the working-class vulgarity of Mellors's
speech, but in the third version he turned the gamekeeper into an ex-
officer in order to make his marriage with Lady Chatterley more
credible. Dickens makes Lizzie's marriage credible only by ignoring the
question of speech altogether. One of the faults of the book is that
Dickens wants us to think that Eugene is behaving with almost
extravagant virtue in raising Lizzie to his social level by marrying her
when he thinks he is dying, whereas the whole weight of the previous
chapters of the book has demonstrated Lizzie's superiority in all but
birth to the aimless 'gentleman', who has been corrupted by his
environment in a way Lizzie has not been by hers.

The other chief symbol is the Harmon dust mounds. These were a
feature of the London scene, described (as House pointed out) in
Household Words by the poet Horne in 1850, and by George Godwin
seven years later,[1] although there are differences between the sordid
reality of Godwin's account and Dickens's almost genteel description in
the novel. He makes no mention of the danger from disease or of the
stench. The mounds are both the source of the Harmon wealth—and

hence of Boffin's—and the place where the wills are secreted. They symbolise the rotten foundations of riches and their power to corrupt. They corrupt Wegg, they corrupt Venus temporarily, they seem to corrupt both Boffin and Bella.

Most of the characters in the book are tested. Boffin, from being a servant, becomes a man of great wealth, but neither he nor his wife are corrupted by it, and he hands over his fortune to the rightful, though not the legal, heir. Silas Wegg, in contrast, is raised from poverty to comparative comfort through the generosity of Boffin: in return he blackmails his benefactor to try and secure half his fortune. Venus at first falls in with Wegg's plan but afterwards repents. Cleaver betrays his daughter's friend for the drink which is rapidly killing him. Hexam rifles the pockets of the dead, and Riderhood steals, blackmails and possibly murders. The Lammles are tempted by the imaginary wealth of the others and they afterwards betray Georgiana for money. Veneering buys a seat in parliament. Above all, there is the temptation of John Harmon to marry Bella to secure a fortune, and the temptation of Bella herself, who is raised overnight from the horrors and vulgarities of genteel poverty to wealth and luxury. She thinks she will marry for money; she is tempted to forget her family; and she scorns the poor secretary when he confesses his love. She is saved in the end by her love for her poor hen-pecked father, to whom she passes on the £50 given her by Boffin, and by Boffin's treatment of Rokesmith, by which her sense of justice is outraged. Hearing on Boffin's lips the mercenary sentiments which had been her own, she is horrified; and she begins to love the man she had scorned.

Our Mutual Friend might be regarded as a novel on the theme of the danger of wealth—*Radix malorum est cupiditas*—and some of its most moving scenes occur when the human affections triumph over the corruption of the world. When Bella goes home to cook a meal, when she takes her father out to dinner, when she apologises to Rokesmith and offers her friendship to Lizzie, she demonstrates what Wordsworth calls the 'human heart by which we live'. Not that Bella is entirely successful as a portrait. Dickens in several of his later heroines was drawing on his knowledge of Ellen Ternan and we may suppose that Bella's curious relationship with her father as well as her love of Rokesmith reflect two aspects of Ellen's relationship to Dickens, distorted to some extent by sentimentality.

In Karl Marx's early unfinished treatise, *Political Economy and Philosophy*, published long after his death and only recently translated into English, there is a brilliant exposition of a speech in *Timon of Athens* about the power of gold. Money, under capitalism, is the highest good. The unintelligent rich man can 'buy for himself intelligent people to work for him: and is not he who has power over the intelligent more intelligent than they?' We are reminded of Magwitch's remark in *Great Expectations*:

> 'If I ain't a gentleman, nor yet ain't got no learning, I'm the owner of such. All on you owns stock and land; which on you owns a bought-up London gentleman?'

Marx goes on to show that money is the visible divinity because it transforms all natural qualities into their opposites, 'idea into reality, and reality into a mere idea'.

It can just as easily turn the real, natural and essential powers of men into abstract ideas, and so into imperfections, into torturing phantoms of the mind, as it can turn real imperfections and phantoms of the mind into actual essential powers and capacity.

As Timon had declared, money turns

loyalty into disloyalty, love into hate, virtue into vice, vice into virtue, slave into master, master into slave, stupidity into intelligence, intelligence into stupidity.

But in a fully human society these bitter paradoxes on the power of money become falsified. Money no longer has the same power over men's souls, since 'if you regard a man as a human being and his relationship to the world as a human one, you can only exchange love for love, trust for trust, and so on'.

The world of *Our Mutual Friend*, overshadowed by the Harmon dust-heaps, is the world described by Marx. Boffin is known as the Golden Dustman; Hexam and Riderhood rob the dead; Veneering buys a seat in parliament and, though he cannot buy real friends, he buys acquaintances; Bella, before her conversion, declares 'I have money always in my thoughts and my desires'; Harmon's father tries from the grave to bribe him to marry Bella; and Wegg is brought into contact with Venus by his desire to purchase his amputated leg, though it is useful to Venus and useless to Wegg. The book read by Wegg to Boffin [Gibbon], was chosen by Dickens, it has been suggested, because the British, like the Romans, could be described as 'those enervated and corrupted masters of the world'. At the end of the book, it turns out that Boffin has not been corrupted by his wealth and Bella rejects the temptation of making a mercenary marriage and, in choosing a man Mrs Wilfer calls a mendicant, she becomes, we are told, 'true golden gold at heart' and 'all the gold in the world' to her husband.

Professor K. J. Fielding, while admitting that the novel may be interpreted as a study of an acquisitive and possessive society, and that the dust-heaps 'symbolise the dust and ashes of all misdirected human effort in a society in which true values have been distorted by an all-pervading greed for money', nevertheless feels that the symbol is used ambiguously. The ending seems to imply that it is all right to inherit wealth without working for it 'and that it is only wrong for a man like Old Harmon to build it up by providing an honest service for the community'.[2]

It must be admitted that Dickens shares the ambivalent attitude to wealth and work of most of his contemporaries. He had in *Great Expectations* and *Little Dorrit* made it clear that money obtained by honest labour was morally innocent, that wealth obtained by other means was apt to demoralise, and that the gentleman with no duties or responsibilities did not deserve the snobbish respect which he was usually accorded. It is made apparent in *Our Mutual Friend* that Eugene, well-meaning as he is, is spoilt as a person by the fact that his private income enables him to be virtually unemployed. But Professor Fielding and other critics are right to complain of the attitude of Dickens towards the marriage of Eugene and Lizzie, inevitable as that attitude was at the time the book was written.

Yet it may be reasonably maintained that Old Harmon is criticised, not because he makes a fortune by collecting dust, but because he uses the wealth he has amassed in immoral ways. He is a miser; he has no sense of stewardship or of responsibility to society; he treats his children badly; and he tries to control the actions of his son from beyond the grave. Boffin, on the other hand, is generous with the money he has inherited; and he uses it to give happiness to others.

The function of the 'dust' imagery is certainly to suggest the deceitfulness of riches in a society perverted by greed; and this function is supported by the miserliness of Harmon, the pretended miserliness of Boffin, the avarice of Bella in the early part of the book, and the criminal activities of Hexam, Riderhood and Wegg. It is equally supported by the Lammles marriage and by the financial chicanery of Fledgeby and Veneering. It is difficult to see that the dust-mounds symbol is weakened by the fact that dust-collecting in itself is a necessary service to the community, or even by the fact that Boffin acts as a steward of the wealth he has inherited. It is not wealth but cupidity which is said to be the root of evil.

The complaints made against the ambiguity of Dickens's symbolism could be levelled with equal justice against the use of imagery in some of Shakespeare's plays. One has only to think of the different ways in which the sickness imagery of *Hamlet* has been interpreted by reputable critics, or consider the imagery of *Troilus and Cressida*. The iterative image, as Caroline Spurgeon demonstrated, is drawn from cooking, the sexual appetite being compared to the appetite for food. But this does not mean that Shakespeare thought that cooking and sex were bad in themselves.

But, although we may defend Dickens's use of symbols on these lines, it is true, of course, that his perfectly valid social criticism was marred at times by sentimentality. He was always proclaiming that kind hearts were more than coronets; that the illegitimate Esther, the illiterate Joe and Boffin, the hen-pecked Wilfer were better than their betters; and that wealth was a danger to the soul. But such simple truths were sometimes expressed in an embarrassingly emotional way. The rhetorical preaching on the subject of Betty Higden, the scenes in which Jenny Wren appears, the character of Riah—sentimentalised in reparation for the earlier portrait of Fagin—and some aspects of the two heroines are examples of the weaknesses which are apt to flaw even Dickens's best books.

Professor Kathleen Tillotson has pointed out that Dickens was faced with 'his age's problem of vitalising a heroine in a period of limiting ideals for girlhood'. Little Dorrit is clearly limited in this way and so is Esther in *Bleak House*; but Bella is a more realistically drawn character and her conversion is made credible.

In another respect the later novels show an improvement on the early ones. It is difficult for modern readers to endure the wallowing in pathos in which Dickens frequently indulged. The death-bed scenes in *The Old Curiosity Shop* and *Dombey and Son*, however much to the taste of Dickens's public, now seem to be dreadfully mawkish. But the deaths of Magwitch and even of Johnny and Betty Higden are described with reasonable restraint; and the account of Riderhood's resuscitation is masterly.

Most critics allow that the last five or six of Dickens's novels are more carefully constructed than his early ones, but they complain that the deliberate artistry does not compensate for the comparative absence of brilliance, gusto, invention and humour. Certainly the later novels are more sombre in tone and the humorous passages of *Our Mutual Friend* are brought in for the purpose of comic relief. But in themselves they are as good as ever. Wegg's reading of Gibbon's *Decline and Fall of the Roman Empire* to Boffin is uproariously funny, especially when he extricates himself from the difficulty of explaining the difference between the Roman empire and the Russian empire with which Boffin had confused it:

> 'The difference, sir?' Mr Wegg was faltering and in danger of breaking down, when a bright thought flashed upon him. 'The difference, sir? There you place me in a difficulty, Mr Boffin. Suffice it to observe, that the difference is best postponed to some other occasion when Mrs Boffin does not honour us with her

company. In Mrs Boffin's presence, sir, we had better drop it.'

Equally effective is the account of the Boffins' visit to the Wilfers' house:

> Mr and Mrs Boffin became aware of the entrance of Mrs Wilfer, majestically faint, and with a condescending stitch in her side: which was her company manner.
>
> 'Pardon me', said Mrs Wilfer, after the first salutations, and as soon as she had adjusted the handkerchief under her chin, and waved her gloved hands, 'to what am I indebted for this honour?'
>
> 'To make short of it, ma'am', returned Mr Boffin, 'perhaps you may be acquainted with the names of me and Mrs Boffin, as having come into a certain property.'
>
> 'And I dare say, ma'am', pursued Mr Boffin, while Mrs Boffin added confirmatory nods and smiles, 'you are not very much inclined to take kindly to us?'
>
> 'Pardon me', said Mrs Wilfer. ' 'Twere unjust to visit upon Mr and Mrs Boffin a calamity which was doubtless a dispensation.' These words were rendered the more effective by a serenely heroic expression of suffering.

Henry James, in the review we have quoted, declared that Dickens had added nothing to our understanding of human nature. Certainly his characterisation, even in the later novels, makes no pretensions to realism. In some ways his method is nearer to the Jonsonian comedy of humours than it is to that of George Eliot or Trollope. But by isolating and exaggerating a few salient characteristics he reveals human nature in a distorting mirror. No one was ever quite like Mrs Wilfer or Mr Podsnap, but it is surely wrong to pretend that they add nothing to our understanding of human nature.

It is not merely in his method of characterisation that Dickens resembles the poetic dramatist. His interweaving of plots, his fondness for violent action, and his conscious use of symbolism all show that he had as much affinity with Jacobean dramatists as with most Victorian novelists. It is significant that he was a good actor and very successful in his public readings of his own novels.

Compared with those of George Eliot or Henry James, the methods, the criticism of life and the mind of Dickens appear to be naïve and unsophisticated. The moral problems with which he deals are basically simple. He was not concerned with the subtle temptations which assail the extraordinary man or woman. He would probably have found Strether's dilemma unintelligible. But the advantage of dealing with basic moral problems—the fact that we are members one of another, the evil of loveless religion, the danger of riches, the false values of society, even the necessity of reforming the poor law and improving sanitation—is that they are more universal than those with which James deals. Very few children can have been placed in Maisie's position, very few men have been faced with Densher's temptation, and the question of whether a girl who has read a certain French novel is a suitable bride for a man who has also read it is a problem which is now difficult to take seriously, despite the magnificence of James's art.

SOURCE: essay in R. M. Wilson (ed.), *Essays and Studies, 1966* (London, 1966), pp. 92–105.

NOTES

1. Cf. K. J. Fielding's article in *The Dickensian*, No. 346 (May 1965).
2. K. J. Fielding, *Charles Dickens* (London, 1965), pp. 230–2.

Norman Page   'The Problem of Speech'
(1969)

Several recent critics have been a good deal concerned over the apparent disparity between Lizzie Hexam's background and her speech. Professor Hobsbaum finds the transformation of the child of the streets and the waterside into a middle-class heroine unconvincing: he comments that Dickens's decision to take his heroine 'from the lowest and most illiterate classes . . . would have more point if her behaviour and accent were less resolutely that of a middle-class heroine',[1] and quotes from a scene in the last section of the novel to justify his comment. Professor Muir expresses puzzlement at Lizzie's command of Standard English . . . [See preceding essay—Ed.] R. C. Churchill refers to the 'incredible figures of Lizzie Hexam and Eugene Wrayburn', describing the former as 'one of the worst examples of the misplaced heroic', and quoting A. W. Ward as saying that Lizzie 'has to discard the colour of her surroundings and talk the conventional dialect as well as express the conventional sentiments of the heroic world'.[2] And Angus Wilson, while finding considerable interest in the character of Eugene, dismisses Lizzie as a 'nullity'.[3]

One might reflect that such criticisms constitute a somewhat oblique tribute to Dickens for his boldness in creating a heroine of such unconventional social status. Against all this, however, may be set a comment of Professor Kathleen Tillotson, who (though not referring specifically to *Our Mutal Friend*) sees Little Dorrit, like Oliver Twist and Little Nell, as representing the idea of

the strength and indestructibility of natural, innocent virtue . . . her goodness, with such an upbringing, may be thought implausible; but it must be seen as expressing what still survived of Dickens's own indestructible faith—expressing it almost allegorically, with the validity of fairy tale.[4]

In this class, Lizzie may perhaps also claim a place; and just as it is unreasonable to entertain expectations of realistic dialogue in fairy-tale and allegory, so we may to some extent have to reconsider our expectations in approaching Dickens's novel, and ask ourselves whether attitudes derived from a reading of realistic fiction are entirely appropriate.

Although there is fairly obviously a Lizzie Hexam problem, it will be argued here that it is by no means as extreme or as incapable of solution as some of the views already quoted seem to imply. It is perfectly possible that the evidence of the text does not provide full support for the animadversions of such critics as Muir and Churchill, who are conceivably recollecting specific scenes from the middle and later sections of the novel, rather than viewing the total presentation of Lizzie's speech throughout the twelve chapters of the novel in which she makes an appearance. Dickens was in fact at some pains in her early appearances to mark her speech as deviating noticeably from Standard English in some respects. Lizzie's speech is, therefore, not a constant, but develops as her character itself develops, particularly through her relationships with Wrayburn and Headstone, and as she takes her place as heroine—a role which is by no means unambiguously announced at the outset. Speech is presented in the novel—and not only in relation to Lizzie—as one of the facets of social behaviour which are the correlates of social class; and class-consciousness is itself one of the themes of the novel. It may, then, be argued that Dickens is not so much giving his heroine a ready-made idiom that happens to come to hand, as making her speech and the changes it undergoes an index of her development. To justify this view, it will be necessary to look in some detail at her successive appearances. And because one of the themes of the novel is, as already suggested, class-consciousness and class-mobility—a preoccupation manifest not only in the Veneerings and their circle, the Podsnaps, the Boffins and the Wilfers, but (more relevantly to the present instance) in the two rivals for Lizzie's love—it will be necessary to consider her speech, and the kind of status it implies, not as an isolated phenomenon but in the light of these relationships.

An examination of her earliest appearances suggests that there may be some exaggeration in the view of her as speaking only 'the Queen's English' or 'the conventional dialect . . . of the heroic world'. At this stage she is in fact relatively taciturn: in chapter 1 she accompanies her father on the river as a mainly silent witness of his ghastly occupation, uttering only three short speeches—twenty-eight words in all—in the course of the chapter. She talks more freely to her brother in chapter 3, and there are various indications of the homely quality of her speech, which includes such forms as *a'most, a-looking, of an evening, in revenge-like*, and such a sentence as the following:

> 'I was all in a tremble of another sort when you owned to father you could write a little.'

It is in the same chapter that the theme of social mobility through education is first mooted: whereas the father's illiteracy is stressed (' "I can't read, nor I don't want to it . . ." '), the son's case is very different: his 'writing, though large and round, was good', and Charley's prospective rise into another social class is already apparent. This difference is sharply reflected in their speech: that of Gaffer Hexam is abundantly marked with indications of uneducated pronunciation and non-standard grammatical forms, whereas the boy's, though not yet so free from grammatical faults as it will later become, is unmarked by deviant spellings. Two brief quotations will illustrate the contrast between father and son:

> ' 'Taint not to say here, but it's close by. I do everything reg'lar. I've giv' notice of the circumstarnce to the police, and the police have took possession of it. No time ain't been lost, on any hand . . .'

> 'It's a goodish stretch, sir. I come up in a cab, and the cab's waiting to be paid. We could go back in it before you paid it, if you like. I went first to your office, according to the direction of the papers found in the pockets, and there I see nobody but a chap of about my age who sent me on here.'

Lizzie's third appearance shows her addressing the tavern proprietress as 'Miss' (as will emerge shortly, forms of address are employed with some subtlety in the depicting of her changing status), and she again addresses her father in homely idiom:

> 'The meat's ready now, father. Eat it while it's hot and comfortable.'

We then, apart from a single very brief appearance, see no more of Lizzie for another eleven chapters. Book II opens with chapters titled 'Of an Educational Character' and 'Still Educational', and her social and educational progress now becomes one of the main features of her development. Headstone's attraction to her is at this stage somewhat moderated by awareness of the limitations of her background: ' "I suppose—your sister— . . . has received hardly any teaching, Hexam?" ' He realises that, from a careerist's point of view, a match with Lizzie might be very much improved on; and he is hypersensitively conscious of class differences and the gulf between the Hexam family and the level to which, by his own exertions, he has raised himself—a feeling that will later give ironical effectiveness to Wrayburn's gibes at the schoolmaster's status, and his deliberately insulting use of 'Schoolmaster' as a form of address.

Headstone prompts Charley to suggest that he, the schoolmaster, should undertake to have Lizzie taught in order to qualify her for a rise in status: as with Rosa in *Bleak House*, Dickens stresses the power of education as an instrument of social mobility. A few pages later Wrayburn arrives at the same decision, and proposes to pay for her to be given 'certain instruction', of the value of which she must be fully aware:

> 'You know that it's good to have it, or you would never have so devoted yourself to your brother's having it.'

Here, tribute is paid to the power of education by—strikingly enough— a member of the privileged classes; and it is in the context of these questions of educational opportunity and awareness of status that the change in Lizzie's speech must be viewed.

At this stage her relationship to the two men who are taking an interest in her is still that of an inferior to her acknowledged betters: she calls both 'sir', and is ruefully conscious of being at a disadvantage in speaking to the effortlessly eloquent Eugene:

> 'It's not easy for me to talk to you . . . for you see all the consequences of what I say, as soon as I say it.'

In her next major appearance, however [Bk II, ch. 11], she begins to

display both the moral dignity of a heroine and the command of
language that can adequately give verbal expression to this quality.
The scene in question (in his notes for the tenth number, Dickens calls it
the 'Declaration scene between Bradley and Lizzie') contains a
dialogue with Headstone in which he begins to reveal the strength of his
passion for Lizzie and his jealousy of his upper-class rival; and Lizzie
herself shows here a firmness of purpose and a refusal to be intimidated
that reflect a growing self-confidence. Significantly, the form of address
she employs now changes from 'sir', used twice at the beginning of the
scene, to 'Mr Headstone', used five times in the latter part with an effect
of cold dignity and even reproof, after he has revealed his attitude to
Wrayburn: 'she answered him very steadily'. It would be wrong to
suppose, however, that Dickens has abruptly transformed the reticent
Lizzie into a model of self-confident eloquence: she speaks comparatively little in the course of this scene, her total contribution to the
dialogue amounting to almost exactly one-third of that of her
interlocutor, and a good part of it being contained in a single speech.
But the emphasis in the novelist's intention has clearly shifted: there are
no further reminders of her lowly origins in the form of homely
expressions or occasional orthographic indications of uneducated
pronunciation; she now speaks Standard English, though of a plain and
unadorned variety. The contrast in this scene is not between the
schoolmaster and the illiterate, but between two temperaments, and the
need to assert *moral* status has for the novelist assumed priority over
considerations of realism, since the representation of the speech of a girl
whose education is as yet incomplete (though she has clearly made
progress in this direction) would hardly have served the purpose of
making a heroine of Lizzie.

The same considerations are maintained in her next interview with
Headstone [ch. 15], where her simple but fearless declarations contrast
strongly with the growingly obsessive quality of his speech, his
abnormal emotional state being conveyed by extensive use of repetition
and parallelism in his utterances, whilst the expression of his passionate
feelings in coherent and carefully-structured sentences indicates the
tremendous self-control he is exerting. Compare, for instance, her quiet
protestation:

> 'Mr Headstone, I have heard enough. Let me stop you here. It
> will be better for you and better for me. Let us find my brother.'

with the subsequent speech of Headstone which includes such passages
as

> 'You could draw me to fire, you could draw me to water, you

> could draw me to the gallows, you could draw me to any death, you could draw me to anything I have most avoided, you could draw me to any exposure and disgrace . . .'

There is also a minor but interesting piece of manuscript evidence bearing on the form of address used by Lizzie in speaking to Bradley. Her repeated use of his name and title ('Mr Headstone') perhaps points to the distance which, by establishing and maintaining an element of formality in their relationship, she hopes to keep between them. In one place, however, the manuscript shows that at the point where her own strong feelings lead her to abandon restraint and reproach him in forceful terms, the name, though originally written, was cancelled on second thoughts: the relevant sentence reads

> 'You asked me to hear you out [Mr Headstone] and you will not speak.'

The cancellation adds to the dramatic effectiveness by implying, in the final version, that Lizzie momentarily abandons, in the intensity of her indignation, the coldly courteous manner she has prescribed for herself.

Another contrast in personalities in which differences in both social and moral status are also seen to operate is provided by the conversation between Lizzie and Bella in the ninth chapter of Book III. Lizzie's serious and modest manner is emphasised by contrast with its antithesis, Bella's

> wayward, playful, affectionate nature, giddy for want of the weight of some sustaining purpose, and capricious because it was always fluttering among little things.

That the contrast was for Dickens the main point of the scene is shown by his manuscript note in the plan for the thirteenth number: 'Lizzie to work an influence on Bella's character at its wavering point' (under-lined twice), and again in a separate note on this chapter: 'Bella persuaded to contrast herself with Lizzie'. The speeches in which the girls make reference to the men who love them will illustrate that this contrast is exemplified plainly enough by their speech:

> (1) 'Well! Perhaps one', said Bella. 'I am sure I don't know. I *had* one, but what he may think about it at the present time, I can't say. Perhaps I have half a one (of course I don't count that Idiot, George Sampson). However, never mind me. I want to hear about you.'

(2) 'There is a certain man', said Lizzie, 'a passionate and angry man, who says he loves me, and who I must believe does love me. He is the friend of my brother. I shrank from him within myself when my brother first brought him to me; but the last time I saw him, he terrified me more than I can say.'

Bella's impulsive manner of speech is conveyed by short sentences; her idiom is colloquial from the outset, whilst Lizzie's is formal at first but becomes somewhat less so as the relationship between the two girls develops. Again, the difference between them is partly marked by the forms of address employed: from her first words, Bella refers to the other as 'Lizzie', 'dear' and 'my dear', whilst to Lizzie she only becomes 'my dear' in the last part of the scene, after their intimacy has become established. Similarly, in a later dialogue with Wrayburn [Bk IV, ch. 6], though he calls her 'Lizzie' from the start, he is 'Mr Wrayburn' to her throughout, marking the social contrast between them—a contrast at one point made quite explicit:

'It is impossible, Mr Wrayburn. How can I think of you as being on equal terms with me?'

There follows her rescue of Eugene and their subsequent marriage; and it is only *after* the ceremony that she uses his Christian name for the first time—a point whose significance is not intended to be lost upon the reader. Her use of his name is credited with almost supernatural power, calling him back from the unconsciousness that threatens him as he hovers between life and death:

' . . . speak to me by my name, and I think I shall come back.'
'Yes, dear Eugene.'
'There!' he exclaimed, smiling. 'I should have gone then but for that!'

This is the climax of Lizzie's role in the novel, and apart from a brief appearance in the penultimate chapter, her part is concluded. Professor Collins has pointed out that this is the only occasion on which Dickens marries a low-born heroine to a man of the upper classes.[5] [See excerpt reproduced in this section—Ed.]. But Lizzie has fitted herself to be Wrayburn's wife not only by her heroism but by the increase in self-confidence and self-awareness which her moral courage in the face of adversity has nurtured; and this development, extending throughout almost the whole compass of the novel, is at intervals accompanied by markers—unobtrusive but not insignificant—of the corresponding changes in her use of language. In other words, the modifications in her idiom reflect the growth of her character, which is itself plausibly and sensitively rendered in the course of the book.

To return, in the light of these comments, to the observations quoted earlier from critics of *Our Mutual Friend*: a good deal of the uneasiness that Lizzie's speech seems to have caused stems from an approach that not only disregards some of the evidence of the novel, but also misses an important point—that Lizzie (who is certainly not unique in this respect) belongs to the class of fairy-tale heroines whose rags and squalid surroundings conceal only temporarily an innate excellence, and on whose lips realistic speech would be disconcertingly out of place. At the same time, however, Dickens has made the concession to realism of laying the ground in her early appearances for the development of her speech, which is accompanied by a development in moral stature. We are shown the point from which she starts, and in the early chapters she is certainly far from being Professor Hobsbaum's 'middle-class' heroine.

SOURCE: 'A Language Fit for Heroes', *The Dickensian*, 65 (1969), pp. 100–7.

NOTES

1. P. Hobsbaum, 'The Critics and *Our Mutual Friend*', *Essays in Criticism*, XIII (1963), p. 233.

2. R. C. Churchill, 'Dickens, Drama and Tradition', *Scrutiny*, x (1942).

3. Angus Wilson, 'The Heroes and Heroines of Dickens', in J. Gross and G. Pearson (eds), *Dickens and the Twentieth Century* (London, 1962), p. 10.

4. J. Butt and K. Tillotson, *Dickens at Work* (London, 1957), pp. 230–1.

5. P. Collins, 'Dickens and the Trained Schoolmaster', *Researches and Studies*, University of Leeds Institute of Education, XXII (1961), p. 49; subsequently embodied in his book *Dickens and Education* (London, 1963).

SELECT BIBLIOGRAPHY

BIOGRAPHY, BIBLIOGRAPHY AND TEXTS

The standard modern biography is Edgar Johnson's *Charles Dickens: His Tragedy and Triumph* (Boston, Mass., 1952), in two volumes, though John Forster's biography (London, 1872–74) remains essential reading for the serious student of Dickens.

There is a very useful bibliography of texts and criticism by Philip Collins in volume III of *The New Cambridge Bibliography of English Literature* (Cambridge, 1969).

The Penguin English Library editions of Dickens's novels provide sound texts for study purposes.

BOOKS AND ARTICLES

The following books and articles are recommended. Other works suitable for further reading are given in the references in the main body of the Casebook.

(a) *General*

Philip Collins (ed.), *Dickens: The Critical Heritage* (London, 1971).
K. J. Fielding, *Charles Dickens: A Critical Introduction* (London, 1958).
George H. Ford, *Dickens and His Readers* (Princeton, N. J., 1955).
J. Hillis Miller, *Charles Dickens: The World of His Novels* (Cambridge, Mass., 1958).
Sylvère Monod, *Dickens the Novelist* (Norman, Okla., 1968).
Angus Wilson, *The World of Charles Dickens* (London, 1970).

(b) *Hard Times*

K. J. Fielding, 'The Battle for Preston', *The Dickensian*, L (1954); 'Dickens and the Department of Practical Art', *Modern Language Review*, XLVIII (1953).
F. R. Leavis, in his *The Great Tradition* (London, 1948); the essay is reprinted, with an additional note, in F. R. and Q. D. Leavis, *Dickens the Novelist* (London, 1970).

(c) *Great Expectations*

·T. E. Connolly, 'Technique in *Great Expectations*', *Philological Quarterly*, XXXIV (1955).

Q. D. Leavis, 'How we must read *Great Expectations*' in F. R. and Q. D. Leavis, *Dickens the Novelist* (London, 1970).

Martin Meisel, 'Miss Havisham Brought to Book', *PMLA*, LXXXI (1966).

Christopher Ricks, '*Great Expectations*', in J. Gross and G. Pearson (eds), *Dickens and the Twentieth Century* (London, 1962).

Dorothy Van Ghent, 'On *Great Expectations*', in *The English Novel; Form and Function* (New York, 1953).

(d) *Our Mutual Friend*

Robert Barnard, 'The Choral Symphony in *Our Mutual Friend*', *A Review of English Literature*, II (1961).

Ernest Boll, 'The Plotting of *Our Mutual Friend*', *Modern Philology*, XLII (1944–45).

H. S. Nelson, '*Our Mutual Friend* and Mayhew's *London Labour and the London Poor*', *Nineteenth Century Fiction*, XX (1966).

Harry Stone, 'Dickens and the Jews', *Victorian Studies*, II (1959).

NOTES ON CONTRIBUTORS

JOHN BUTT: at the time of his death in 1965 he was Regius Professor of English Literature, University of Edinburgh; his publications include *The Augustan Age* (1950) and editions of Pope's poems and letters.

G. K. CHESTERTON (1874–1936): poet, novelist and critic.

H. F. CHORLEY (1808–72): novelist, dramatist and critic, and friend of Dickens.

PHILIP COLLINS: Professor of English Literature, University of Leicester; his publications include *Dickens and Crime* (1962) and *Dickens and Education* (1963), and the edited volumes *Dickens: The Critical Heritage* (1971) and *Charles Dickens: The Public Readings* (1975).

E. S. DALLAS (1828–79): journalist, author and critic.

JOHN FORSTER (1812–76): friend of Dickens; editor of the *Daily News* (1846) and of the *Examiner* (1847–55) and, in addition to his life of Dickens, biographer of Goldsmith, Landor and Swift.

GEORGE GISSING (1857–1903): realist novelist and critic, much influenced by Dickens.

BARBARA HARDY: Professor of English Literature at Birkbeck College, University of London; her publications include *The Novels of George Eliot* (1959), *The Appropriate Form* (1964), *The Exposure of Luxury: Radical Themes in Thackeray* (1972), *A Reading of Jane Austen* (1975) and *Tellers and Listeners* (1976).

R. H. HORNE (1803–84): poet, critic, journalist and Crown lands commissioner in Australia; collaborated with Elizabeth Barrett Browning in his *A New Spirit of the Age* (1844).

HUMPHRY HOUSE (1908–1955): former Senior Lecturer in English Literature, University of Oxford; his publications include *Coleridge* (1953) and *All in Due Time* (1956) and the edition of *Notebooks and Papers of Gerard Manley Hopkins* (1937).

HENRY JAMES (1843–1916): novelist and critic; his critical studies include *Partial Portraits* (1888) and *Notes on Novelists* (1914), and there is a good selection in Morris Shapira (ed.), *Henry James: Selected Literary Criticism* (1963).

ARNOLD KETTLE: Professor of Literature at The Open University; his publications include *An Introduction to the English Novel*, in two volumes (1951, 1953).

JACK LINDSAY: prolific novelist, poet and translator.

DAVID LODGE: novelist, and Professor of Modern English Literature, University of Birmingham; his critical studies include *The Language of Fiction* (1966) and *The Novelist at the Crossroads* (1971), and the Casebook on Jane Austen's *Emma* (1968).

HENRY MAYHEW (1812–87): journalist and author, and an early contributor to *Punch*.

MARTIN MEISEL: Professor of English, Columbia University; his publications include *Shaw and the Nineteenth-Century Theatre* (1963).

JULIAN MOYNAHAN: Professor of English, Rutgers University; his publications include *Deed of Life: The Novels and Tales of D. H. Lawrence* (1963) and *Vladimir Nabokov* (1970)

KENNETH MUIR: formerly (1951–74) King Alfred Professor of English Literature, University of Liverpool, and now Professor Emeritus. Widely known as a Shakespearean scholar and as the author of many studies and editions of Shakespeare, Wyatt and other poets; editor of the Casebook on *The Winter's Tale*.

MARGARET OLIPHANT (1828–97): novelist and literary critic.

NORMAN PAGE: Professor of English, University of Alberta; his publications include *The Language of Jane Austen* (1972), *Speech in the English Novel* (1973), *Thomas Hardy* (1977), the edited volume *Wilkie Collins: The Critical Heritage* (1974), and an edition of *Bleak House* (1971).

ROBERT PARTLOW Jnr: Professor of English, Southern Illinois University, Carbondale, and editor of *Dickens Studies Annual* and *Dickens Studies Newsletter*; his publications include the edited volume *Dickens the Craftsman* (1970).

JOHN RUSKIN (1819–1900): art-critic and one of the most influential Victorian writers on cultural and social themes.

GEORGE BERNARD SHAW (1856–1950): Irish critic, playwright and political writer.

RICHARD SIMPSON (1820–76): critic, musician and Shakespearean scholar and a leading figure in Liberal Catholic circles.

HIPPOLYTE TAINE (1828–93): French historian and critic; his historical survey of English literature (Paris, 1859) was translated in 1873.

KATHLEEN TILLOTSON: formerly (1958–71) Hildred Carlile Professor of English Literature at Bedford College, University of London, and now Emeritus Professor; her publications include *Novels of the Eighteen-Forties* (1954) and *Mid-Victorian Studies*, with Geoffrey Tillotson (1965); she is General Editor of the Clarendon Dickens, and Associate Editor of the Pilgrim Edition of the Letters of Charles Dickens.

EDWIN WHIPPLE (1819–86): American critic and essayist.

INDEX